Variable Objects

Variable Objects
Shakespeare and Speculative Appropriation

Edited by Valerie M. Fazel
and Louise Geddes

EDINBURGH
University Press

Edinburgh University Press is one of the leading university presses in the UK. We publish academic books and journals in our selected subject areas across the humanities and social sciences, combining cutting-edge scholarship with high editorial and production values to produce academic works of lasting importance. For more information visit our website: edinburghuniversitypress.com

© editorial matter and organisation Valerie M. Fazel and Louise Geddes, 2021, 2022
© the chapters their several authors, 2021, 2022

Edinburgh University Press Ltd
The Tun – Holyrood Road, 12(2f) Jackson's Entry, Edinburgh EH8 8PJ

First published in hardback by Edinburgh University Press 2021

Typeset in 11/13 Bembo by
IDSUK (DataConnection) Ltd

A CIP record for this book is available from the British Library

ISBN 978 1 4744 8139 7 (hardback)
ISBN 978 1 4744 8140 3 (paperback)
ISBN 978 1 4744 8141 0 (webready PDF)
ISBN 978 1 4744 8142 7 (epub)

The right of Valerie M. Fazel and Louise Geddes to be identified as the editor of this work has been asserted in accordance with the Copyright, Designs and Patents Act 1988, and the Copyright and Related Rights Regulations 2003 (SI No. 2498).

Contents

Acknowledgements	vii
Contributors	viii
Introduction: Bound in a Nutshell – Shakespeare's Vibrant Matter *Valerie M. Fazel and Louise Geddes*	1

PART I: DISCIPLINARY OBJECTS

1. Beds, Handkerchiefs and Moving Objects in *Othello*   21
   Sujata Iyengar
2. The Collectible Ofelia: Object-Oriented Feminisms and the Un-Human Corpus of Q1's Dispensaniac   37
   Molly Seremet
3. Bitcoin, Blockchains and the Bard   59
   Robert Sawyer

PART II: MEDIA OBJECTS

4. 'Were I human': Beingness and the Postcolonial Object in *Westworld*'s Appropriation of *The Tempest*   85
   L. Monique Pittman, Vanessa I. Corredera,
   Kristin N. Denslow and Karl G. Bailey
5. Finding Ludonarrative Harmony in the Limited Agency of Ophelia in *Elsinore*   108
   Andrew Darr
6. Sympathise with the Losers: Performing Intellectual Loserdom in Shakespearean Biopic   127
   Anna Blackwell

7. Prosthetic Properties: The Materiality of Race and Gender
   in *The Hollow Crown: The Wars of the Roses* 151
   Emily MacLeod

PART III: HUMAN OBJECTS

8. 'Intermission!': Reading Race in the Objects of *Key &
   Peele*'s 'Othello Tis My Shite' 167
   Shanelle E. Kim

9. Sight Unseen: Visualising Variability through Ontological
   Representations in *Macbeth* 192
   Valerie Clayman Pye and Cara Gargano

10. The Thing Itself: Performance and the Celebrity Text 210
    Louise Geddes

11. 'The Promised End': Shakespeare and Extinction 230
    Michael Lutz

Index 248

Acknowledgements

This collection originated in 2018 as part of the Speculative Shakespeares seminar at the 46th Shakespeare Association of America Annual Conference in Los Angeles. We are thankful to the organisers of the conference for including our seminar in their excellent programme, and to the participants in the seminar, some of whom are included in this book. We are grateful to Michelle Houston, whose guidance has made EUP a welcoming home for this project. Our appreciation extends to include Geoff Way and Vanessa Corredera, who are always available with brilliant advice and generous support, and L. Monique Pittman, whose keen eye and insightful criticism have improved the book beyond the scope of her own extraordinary chapter. We owe thanks to all of our authors for contributing their excellent work to this book, and for enduring our comments with attention and grace. This book is indebted to Christy Desmet and her trailblazing work in Shakespeare adaptation studies. Her brilliant thinking, her generosity of spirit and her unfailing kindness to emerging scholars continues to inspire us.

Finally, we thank our families – Abbas, Michael, Nadia and Jordan, Natasha and Zachary, Aaron and Jillian, Charlotte, and Tessa – for everything.

Contributors

Karl G. Bailey is a Professor of Psychology at Andrews University. Trained as an interdisciplinary cognitive scientist, he works on a wide range of projects: religiosity and well-being, folk conceptions of human nature, critical thinking in the college classroom, and the intersection of language and vision.

Anna Blackwell is a senior lecturer and programme leader in English Literature at De Montfort University and author of *Shakespearean Celebrity in the Digital Age: Fan Cultures and Remediation*. She researches the intersections between Shakespeare, internet culture and celebrity, and her current project examines craft adaptations of literature.

Vanessa I. Corredera is an Associate Professor and Chair of the Department of English at Andrews University. Her work has appeared in *Borrowers and Lenders*, *The Journal of American Studies*, *The Routledge Handbook of Shakespeare and Global Appropriation* and *Shakespeare Quarterly*. Her book on appropriations of *Othello* in post-racial America is forthcoming with Edinburgh University Press.

Andrew Darr is an English teacher at Centralia High School in mid-Missouri. He recently completed his PhD at the University of Missouri focusing on representations of gender in adaptations of *Hamlet*. He most recently contributed a chapter to *Sex, Gender, and Sexualities in Edward Albee's Plays*, published by Brill.

Kristin N. Denslow is an Associate Professor of English and director of the Honors Program at Southwestern Adventist University where she teaches courses in English literature, Shakespeare and adaptation, and literary theory. Her recent work studies the intersections of Shakespeare, adaptation and technology.

Valerie M. Fazel, Instructor at Arizona State University, is, with Louise Geddes, co-editor of *The Shakespeare User: Critical and Creative Appropriation in a Networked Culture* and co-author of *The Shakespeare Multiverse: Fandom as Literary Praxis*. Her essays on Shakespeare, social media and fandom appear in *Borrowers and Lenders* and *Shakespeare's Audiences*.

Cara Gargano is chair of the Department of Theatre, Dance, and Arts Management and Professor of Dance and Theatre at the Post Campus of Long Island University. She has twice been president of the Congress on Research in Dance and recipient of the Dixie Durr Award for Outstanding Service to Dance Research.

Louise Geddes, Associate Professor of English at Adelphi University, is the author of *Shakespeare in Appropriation: A Cultural History of Pyramus and Thisbe*, and, with Valerie Fazel, is co-editor of *The Shakespeare User: Critical and Creative Appropriation in a Networked Culture* and co-author of *The Shakespeare Multiverse: Fandom as Literary Praxis*.

Sujata Iyengar, Professor of English at the University of Georgia, is currently working on two monographs – *Shakespeare and Adaptation Theory* (contracted, Arden Bloomsbury) and *Shakespeare and the Art of the Book*. With Miriam Jacobson and the late Christy Desmet, she recently published the co-edited *Shakespeare and Global Appropriation* with Routledge.

Shanelle E. Kim is currently a PhD student of early modern literature in the Department of English and Comparative Literature at Columbia University. She focuses on race in early modern drama. Her research interests include Shakespeare appropriations, theatricality, early modern embodiment and popular culture studies.

Michael Lutz is a Research Assistant at the Massachusetts Institute of Technology. He studies intersections of early modern drama, historical humanism and new media. He is a co-host of the academic podcast *Game Studies Study Buddies* and is currently at work on a monograph, *Speculative Humanism on the Shakespearean Stage*.

Emily MacLeod is a PhD candidate in English at George Washington University. Her dissertation focuses on the actor and embodiment in the early modern repertory. Her writing can be found online in *The Rambling* and in theatre reviews for *Shakespeare Bulletin*. She also works as a dramaturg for Brave Spirits Theatre.

L. Monique Pittman is Professor of English and director of the J. N. Andrews Honors Program at Andrews University. Her recent articles and previous monograph (2011) examine how constructions of Shakespearean authority shape the portrayal of gender, class and racial identities. Her forthcoming book, *Shakespeare's Contested Nations* (Routledge), explores multicultural Britain and Shakespearean historiography in performance.

Valerie Clayman Pye is an Assistant Professor of Theatre at LIU Post. Her research focuses on actor training pedagogy, Shakespeare's Globe, Shakespeare tourism and practice-as-research. She is the author of *Unearthing Shakespeare: Embodied Performance and the Globe*, and the co-editor of *Objectives, Obstacles, and Tactics in Practice: Perspectives on Activating the Actor*.

Robert Sawyer is Professor of English at East Tennessee State University, where he teaches Shakespeare, Victorian literature and literary criticism. He is the author of *Victorian Appropriations of Shakespeare*, *Marlowe and Shakespeare: The Critical Rivalry* and *Shakespeare Between the World Wars*. His essay on Elisabeth Bergner will appear in Volume 19 of *The Shakespearean International Yearbook* (2020).

Molly Seremet is Assistant Professor of Theatre at Mary Baldwin University, specialising in devised theatremaking and dramaturgy. Her research interests circulate around performing objects, object-oriented feminisms and cyborg theatre. She holds an MFA/MLitt in Shakespeare and Performance from Mary Baldwin University and an MRes with Distinction from Roehampton University.

Introduction: Bound in a Nutshell – Shakespeare's Vibrant Matter

Valerie M. Fazel and Louise Geddes

> Haply the seas, and countries different,
> With variable objects, shall expel
> This something-settled matter in his heart,
> Whereon his brains still beating puts him thus
> From fashion of himself.
> (*Hamlet* III.i.185–9)

In his design to shuffle his troubled and troublesome nephew/stepson off to England and away from the Danish court, Claudius explains to Polonius that sending Hamlet abroad would distract the younger man from his confused thoughts of violence and revenge. The experience with other cultures, Claudius hopes, will return Hamlet to his 'true' self, and the king imagines how the 'variable objects' encountered in other places will work affectively to remind the prince that he is Hamlet the Dane. Although Claudius's motivation is actually far more sinister than his public show of concern for his stepson suggests, his stated assumption, uncontested by Polonius, is that objects exert their own force of affect on other things – in this case, an ambiguous unsettled 'matter' that has already worked on the prince's heart and brain. Claudius's observation is entirely consistent with a play that expands the power of affective objects to include words, spectres and body parts. In the following scene Hamlet rebukes Guildenstern – 'Why, look you now, how unworthy a thing you make of me!' – in his attempt to distinguish himself from an object. Hamlet further asserts his human autonomy when he tells Guildenstern, 'Call me what instrument you will, though you can fret me, yet you cannot play upon me' (III.ii.402). The play, however, repeatedly contradicts Hamlet's claim to anthropomorphic supremacy through the latent power of Hecuba's tears, a patch of land and Ophelia's flowers. Later in the play, Hamlet's unexpected comprehension of Yorick's metamorphosis into a bunghole illustrates *Hamlet*'s willingness to overlap human and object to such an extent that objects confound the eponymous character. The something-settled matter in *Hamlet*, including the text itself, exerts remarkable power, and the play's convoluted humanism has fascinated its audiences for generations.

This book takes Hamlet's recognition of the interchangeability of humans and objects as its starting point, and asks what is to be gained from understanding the extent to which material things work on us. In particular, the chapters in this collection examine how appropriation identifies the fecundity of Shakespeare fragments, disbursing them from, and returning them to, a more flexible, inclusive understanding of what Shakespeare is. Furthermore, the volume's chapters consider the ways in which Christy Desmet's alien networks and Douglas M. Lanier's rhizome do not lead us away from Shakespeare as their theories suggest, but draw us back to him as part of an affective dialogic relationship. This collection proposes a speculative approach to questions of fidelity that dismisses the straightforward study of how Shakespeare's influence is manifest in favour of a more nuanced understanding of how material (and immaterial) things work in various contexts. By positioning Shakespeare as an object in possession of infinite meaning, bounded, as it were, in a nutshell, our contributors reconsider how appropriation might work when an object resists a praxis that insists on the absolute interpretative autonomy of the appropriator. The chapters in this volume recognise Shakespeare as a speculative object that sits outside hegemonic cultural orders and intersects, as an equal participant, with the acts of creative, critical use that manifest as Shakespeare appropriation. As this book demonstrates, approaching Shakespeare as an object imbued with its own latent energy unveils a more speculative appropriative logic, a dialectic that recognises a peculiar unpredictability within Shakespeare that cannot always account for consequences or the effects of others' (human or thingly) interventions with it.

As scholarship recognises the latent power in Shakespearean authority, to some extent it participates in acknowledging Shakespeare's transition from author to object. Even as the cult of authorship continues to venerate Shakespeare, appropriation and performance criticisms push further away from him, overwriting the man with posthuman networks of variable meaning. As Barbara Hodgdon, Douglas M. Lanier and Michael Bristol have noted in their respective criticisms (Hodgdon 1998; Lanier 2002; Bristol 1996), Shakespeare is more than an author: he is a brand, a business, a network of diverse meanings. Michael Bristol's recognition of Shakespeare as celebrity acknowledges the extent to which he is both a person of renown and a posthuman symbol of cultural supremacy: 'Notwithstanding a long history of challenges to his cultural authority, Shakespeare has been a celebrity for just about as long as the social state of being a celebrity has existed' (Bristol 1996: 3). Without quibbling too much about his definition of celebrity, it is noteworthy that Bristol understands celebrity as social capital, which might seem to be an odd barometer of value to apply to a man who died four hundred years ago. If we accept that Shakespeare is a celebrity, and we should, his celebrity is embedded in a culture that celebrates him as an icon of white Western achievement. The emphasis on William Shakespeare enables scholars to dismiss the fact that the ideology-imposed Shakespeare eclipses any intentions that the man himself might have held, no matter how much we want to believe in the idea of his genius. His cultural currency is invested in the idea of the all-knowing author, and the vast networks of knowledge that Shakespeare assembles are subjugated to a belief in the literary intentions of one famously brilliant man. Relying on a linear trajectory between the man Shakespeare and those who would appropriate him restricts users to a particular path of outward spread that is defined by William Shakespeare's social capital, and that limits the scope of what appropriation theory – and Shakespeare – can do.

Four hundred years ago, lamenting the loss of the 'Sweet Swan of Avon', Ben Jonson, like Hamlet, conflated the human with the objects that represented him. Summoning Shakespeare in his famous poem, 'To The Memory of My Beloved the Author, Mr. William Shakespeare', Jonson assures the late dramatist that he is 'alive still while thy book doth live / And we have wits to read and praise to give'. Jonson's words affirm an authorial presence typical of the humanist approach to Shakespeare, suggesting that Shakespeare's immortal soul is present in the thing we think of as Shakespeare's work. More tantalisingly, however, Jonson invites us to think of the book as a living object, implying that the book has its own vitality that affects our wits, elicits our praise and gives continued life to William Shakespeare. That a text is a dynamic, open-ended, interactive site of play is not a new idea – certainly 'From Work to Text' (Barthes 1986) makes this point better than we can – but Barthes separates the text from the object itself, imagining a logocentric place for human experimentation and a text that is subjugated to the semiotic alterations that a human culture imposes on its language. This collection reconnects Shakespeare text with its materiality. As Barthes advocates for text as a new object for study, he draws humanist boundaries around it, placing text 'at the limit of the rules of the speech-act' (1986: 58). Elsewhere, the thing to be held in one's hand which Barthes terms the 'work' is presented as enclosed – an irrelevant historical artefact. Because of the multiple texts in play, many theoretical approaches have used the ludic qualities of text to think about a movement from Shakespeare to its appropriation, raising questions about what appropriation does with, or to, Shakespeare, which, in spite of its fundamentally deconstructionist approach, intertwines Shakespeare with new human contexts. Thirty years after Barthes, Margaret Jane Kidnie's transmedial approach to textual appropriation in *Shakespeare and the Problem of Adaptation* argues for 'the work' as a term that identifies 'non-identical examples of [dramatic] text and performance that are somehow recognised as "the same"' (2009: 7). Kidnie advocates that we turn our critical energy away from troublesome questions of fidelity and towards the 'processes of debate that users continue to define their particular ideological, institutional, or political investment in the work' that are latent in Shakespeare appropriation (2009: 9). Kidnie conflates the Barthesian use of the word with the idea of 'work' as a verb, containing the appropriative process within the larger conceptualisation of the thing itself. As the title of her book suggests, without a clear understanding of how we draw from the text, however, appropriation theories invest in mapping out trajectories from one text to another and can only recognise Shakespearean appropriations as discrete iterations that are 'somehow' connected.

Appropriation theory's necessary dependence on separate, material objects has resulted in a discipline that is conceptually ambivalent towards Shakespeare. It is, on one hand, invested in the materiality of objects and insists that the text, as a site of play, can transform, evolve or reproduce itself. By this same criterion, however, appropriation studies perpetuates a framework that can only imagine Shakespeare as an object that is replicated through transformation, reinforcing a false equivalence between the Shakespeare object and a singular artefact created by the man from Stratford. The result, in practice, is an understandable overinvestment in those who would appropriate him, perpetuating the fallacy that appropriation is a process in which Shakespeare plays no part. In the years after the 1999 publication of Desmet and Sawyer's *Shakespeare and Appropriation*, critics including Stephen O'Neill, Alexa Huang, Daniel Fischlin and ourselves have identified different, yet important elements of appropriation (see O'Neill [ed.] 2018; Huang and Rivlin [eds] 2014; Fischlin [ed.] 2014; Fazel and Geddes [eds] 2017). Nonetheless, the specific challenge of defining what role Shakespeare plays in this process remains. Without a tangible understanding of the Shakespeare object, the solution, thus far, has been to focus on what is done to Shakespeare, resulting in a valuable but incomplete picture. Some scholars, including the contributors to our 2017 book, *The Shakespeare User: Creative and Critical Appropriations in a Networked Culture*, suggest that appropriation is driven by artists and critics who use Shakespeare for their own (conscious or otherwise) ideologically driven agenda. Evaluations of the user's agency are crucial to our understanding of how Shakespeare is appropriated, but we cannot attribute that energy exclusively to the appropriators alone and assume that Shakespeare is usable because he is Jonson's artist 'for all time'. Certainly, as the chapters by Sujata Iyengar, Shanelle E. Kim and L. Monique Pittman, Vanessa Corredera, Kristin Denslow and Karl G. Bailey in this collection demonstrate, the argument for Shakespeare's universality is a fallacy that masks ideological agendas and can be used in service of white supremacy. The uses to which Shakespeare is put matter, and it is important to be aware when and how such cultural capital is wielded politically.

A less overtly ideological approach positions the medium as the determining factor in Shakespearean appropriation. In addition to exploring appropriations manifest as novels, television shows and video games, this volume includes performance stagings as part of the appropriate conversation, as they share the same tension between the Shakespeare object and its reiteration. In *Shakespeare Performance Studies*, for instance, W. B. Worthen evokes Kidnie's awareness of appropriation as a process when he theorises that Shakespeare itself is a medium, a platform through which performance is produced. In this, Worthen identifies Shakespeare as a conduit for meta-critical discourses to manifest in theatrical environments, which mirrors user-driven approaches that uses Shakespeare as a means to talk about culture or genre-specific practices. Thomas Cartelli in *Reenacting Shakespeare in the Shakespeare Aftermath* utilises the idea of iterations to separate Shakespeare from the platforms that use him. Cartelli identifies Shakespearean appropriations as an 'aftermath', disconnected from the original performance and the script itself. He defines the practice of remediating Shakespeare in new performance contexts spatially, suggesting that we imagine Shakespeare

> less as a specifically demarcated zone or moment of time or history than as a discursive and performative space and condition of awareness theoretically shared by the makers, if not the receivers, of the performance or experiences on offer that all things Shakespearian are present and available for redoing and reenactment *differently*. (Cartelli 2019: 13)

Cartelli here articulates the unspoken assumption that appropriation study is about parsing out the difference between Shakespeare and its iteration that is echoed in theatre criticism. Performance theory is dominated by the idea of theatre as an event, because it rightly recognises the unrepeatability of a given performance. Such ephemerality is comparable to the rhizome (and theories of appropriation in a more general sense) because it privileges the idea of discrete objects connected by invisible, tenuous connections. As Pye and Gargano explain, however, a cherished belief of Shakespearean theatre practitioners is that staging Shakespeare is an act of connection, one that puts us in community with Shakepseare's original performers. To frame Shakespeare as a medium, or a closed-off object from the long-distant past, overlooks the affective power located in the Shakespeare object and insists on the primacy of the human interpreter. Such a process carries an ideological burden and evokes questions of gatekeeping, emphasising those who are qualified to identify and explain complex allusions or barely visible connections. These tenuous connections draw from fragments of the whole Shakespeare object, and circulate as (among other things) images, characters, plays, cultural capital or other ephemera that get attributed as Shakespeare. These Shakespeare fragments, like any objects under humanist conditions, as Graham Harman suggests, are 'wrongly conceived as eternal, unchanging, simple, or directly accessible by certain privileged observers' (2012: 188), and user-driven approaches strive to articulate who has access to Shakespeare and why.

New media criticism reflects performance studies in its consideration of how innovative technologies shape the appropriative act. As Stephen O'Neill's excellent book *Broadcast Your Shakespeare* suggests, these ideological impulses are compounded, and to a degree driven, by advances in media that exert their own pressure on the Shakespearean subject. Recognising that 'technology' encompasses most twentieth-century media innovations, O'Neill notes,

> Media objects entail volitional human action but also processes that come to function semi-automatically, acquiring a technological or non-human agency, so that Shakespeare is the seed that is scattered not merely by human hands but by the very processes of media technologies themselves. (2018: 5)

O'Neill's metaphor of Shakespeare as 'seed' invites us to return our gaze towards the medium as a substitute for meaningful dialogic interaction with Shakespeare. While it is historically true that technology has offered new capacities to both appropriate and consume Shakespeare, little beyond Lanier's definition of Shakespeare as a 'transmedial set of objects' (2017: 295) has recently or convincingly rationalised how we categorise an object *as* Shakespeare. What we need is a theory that accounts for *Hamlet* being recognisable, whether manifest as a printed Folger edition, a radio broadcast, a vinyl LP, a web page, a Bollywood movie, a video game or a *Star Wars* meme including Luke Skywalker and Darth Vader. We need a theory that dismisses the certainty of what *Hamlet* may mean in favour of a hope of what it *can* mean.

Separating out Shakespeare from its appropriations requires a theory that interrogates how users maintain connections to the source even when newer iterations intersect with other media, platforms and subjects. These approaches situate appropriation as measuring the limits of Shakespeare adjacency. Drawing on Deleuze and Guattari, Lanier's theory of the rhizome tries to more carefully parse out the materiality of a text by imagining the relationships between interpretations, manifest as they are in appropriations, of the 'original' text itself as part of an organic growth from Shakespeare. Lanier speculates that one might understand the appropriative trajectory as a non-human organism – a rhizomatic growth that moves parallel to its original Shakespearean stem – existing as a seemingly discrete object with hidden, underground connections. The rhizome's posthumanist approach extends the idea of a text's reach to its outermost point, proposing that Shakespeare unfurls its network as roots, and contends that the consequent readings and meanings of a text spread ever outwards, offshoots emerging as distinct material properties tethered by a shared radicle. While the theory is valuable in its recognition of an erratic, posthuman network of connections, the rhizome encourages us to inaccurately imagine that appropriation can only evolve away from Shakespeare.

Underpinning any critical stance for appropriation *as* Shakespeare dredges up anxiety that Shakespeare becomes not-Shakespeare once appropriated and reformulated into a construction that is – and is not – quite identifiable as itself. A rhizomatic theory elides substantive recognition of an appropriation's relationship with Shakespeare, and its connections remain frustratingly buried underground. In these instances, appropriation – and its critical study – becomes a speculative practice. In *Shakespeare/Not Shakespeare*, Christy Desmet, Natalie Loper and Jim Casey suggest that such uncertainty is fruitful by positing the space at the border between Shakespeare and not-Shakespeare as potentiality that exists between two incompatible ideas of Shakespeare. The nature of this uncertainty, they propose, is 'troubling for bardolaters who want to control, delimit, regulate, and memorialize Shakespeare, but for bardoclasts and bardo-creators who want to celebrate Shakespeare's boundlessness, multiplicity, and unlimited potential, it is liberating' (Desmet, Loper and Casey 2017: 6). The implication here by virtue of the etymological root of 'bardoclast' is that to recognise Shakespeare's potentiality is an act of breakage and of subsequent new creation, rather than merely acknowledging that these new creations are more fragments that contribute to an ever-growing Shakespeare whole. By this, Desmet, Loper and Casey seem to suggest that the only way to appropriately engage with Shakespeare is manifest through acts of resistance against the contained object that worshippers would 'control, delimit, and regulate'. What, then, this collection asks, might be gained if we proposed containment rather than expansion as the centralising principle of Shakespearean appropriation, and imagine that all of these interpretative meanings are densely bound up as fragments of a larger Shakespeare object? How might we conceptualise the relationship between the appropriator and the appropriated when agency, depending on situation and circumstances, varies and is itself unpredictable? How might we use Shakespeare's variability to find new, speculative connections that live outside hegemonic cultural orders?

Studies of fidelity have long been dismissed in Shakespeare scholarship because the thing we think of as Shakespeare has historically been subject to the idea of the human, and the texts as indifferent subjects to be manipulated, decoded and encoded by users who imbue them with their own ideological (systems of) meaning. Long dead as he is, humanist logic suggests that Shakespeare cannot change the objects that he created, therefore the agency of appropriation lies only in the platforms and users that employ Shakespearean artefacts to build something entirely new and distinct from the 'original'. Shakespeare objects, this logic implies, are passive objects that only transform in the hands of others. But are they? This collection examines the value of an object-oriented philosophical approach for Shakespeare appropriation as a means of empowering the object as one of the agential elements of its appropriation. The chapters each demonstrate how approaching Shakespeare and his plays as objects with their own internal logic – their own 'thing-power' – can restore Shakespeare to the centre of the appropriative act without the obligation to enter into a comparative study of how 'faithful' an appropriation or performance is. Each contribution determines that Shakespeare is built to accommodate endless networks of potential meaning, and altogether this book registers how a new materialist approach can offer a more nuanced description of what we mean when we refer to 'Shakespeare' as the appropriative subject.

In her most recent critical works, Desmet proposes a rethinking of appropriation as an interactive, participatory act that both feeds into and draws from Shakespearean texts; but without a suitably multifaceted understanding of what is being appropriated, envisioning such a process exceeds our capacities. Current approaches to appropriation, useful as they are for recognising the consumption of Shakespeare as acts of reproduction, fail to fully articulate the constitution of Shakespeare as a multiplicitous object that is both human and not. Likewise, they elide the dialogic potential that appropriation promises. The chapters in this collection challenge the simplicity of a humanist trajectory from source to appropriation, and instead suggest that appropriative acts fold back into Shakespeare in a way that accommodates diverse circuits of knowledge expanding beyond the human. Shakespeare appropriation, they demonstrate, pursues its own erratic, but nonetheless affective logic. In her final essays, Desmet advocated for such a dialogic, for a 'recursive process of give and take' (2014: 43) that recognises Shakespeare's place in energetic networks of meaning. Desmet elsewhere defined online Shakespeare appropriations as maintaining an 'alien' logic that perpetuates a network of knowledge outside human understanding. This phenomenology, she contends, 'continues the theoretical effort to debunk the sovereignty of this liberal humanist subject, not only by placing people on the same ontological level with other objects, but also by discovering in "things" many of the qualities previously seen as the sole property of people' (Desmet 2017: 2).

Our collection picks up at this point to ask how, four hundred years after his death, this 'thing' we call Shakespeare must be reconceptualised as a vital participant in the emergence of new meanings. While Desmet's examples of Shakespearean networks are restricted to the technological algorithms of YouTube Shakespeares, this collection binds these infinite networks within the Shakespeare object itself. The chapters in this book unveil Shakespeare's 'thing-power' and examine the uncanny energy that Shakespeare possesses. In their focus on Shakespeare objects – phenomena resulting from and through the interaction of Shakespeare's thing-power with other things – the chapters' authors draw from new materialist work to theorise the multitudinal energy that exists within Shakespeare and to think about how this energy challenges our understanding of object–human relations – and indeed, how and why the term 'humanity' is prescribed.

In her 2010 philosophical treatise, *Vibrant Matter: A Political Ecology of Things*, Jane Bennett argues for a vitality to things 'which refuses to dissolve completely into the milieu of human knowledge' (2010: 3). For Bennett, whose intellectual concerns are bound up in the politics of sustainable ecology, the human tendency to view non-human things as inert 'feeds human hubris' and is an impediment 'to the emergence of . . . more materially sustainable modes of production and consumption' (2010: ix). Bennett proclaims that physical materials – all things, and she includes the human body in her definition of things – are inherently vibrant, agental matter that act alone or in assemblages with other things to create meaning. A thing, she contends, amounts to a force that 'though quite real and powerful, is intrinsically resistant to representation' (2010: xvi). In spite of its inherent resistance, a thing's force – its vibrancy – is pure affect that shapes, and is shaped by, human and non-human acts of assemblage. Organised into recognisable ecologies, vibrant matter finds itself constrained by the materiality of that which represents it, as Iyengar suggests in her study of diverse agential objects, and we understand this inhabited materiality as objects. Object-oriented ontologists, such as Ian Bogost, maintain that objects sustain their own posthuman logic, but for Bennett – and this collection – the slippage between the human and non-human is both inevitable and ontologically unavoidable. When we participate in this process as subject or user, we are drawn by the vibrancy of Shakespeare things, recognising them as part of a larger ecology of variable objects, reassembling them to create meaning (or being reorganised by them), or in the case of appropriation, more new material objects.

The vibrant ontology of matter that exists just shy of a definitive agency is, we contend, the variable meaning that is contained within the things we think of as Shakespeare. Bennett's 'congregational understanding of agency' (2010: 20) comes into focus as things relate to or are put in context with one another. We argue that these contexts are contained within the Shakespeare object. The appearance of causality and a singular trajectory that appropriation offers our understanding of Shakespeare complicates the absolute freedom that Bennett implies is native to vibrant objects in favour of something that is variable but not entirely alien on its own terms. Unlike other inanimate objects – such as Bennett's discarded bottle top or abandoned boot – that may exist for use but not necessarily comprehension, Shakespeare is an object designed to be 'read' in one capacity or another, as, for example, Iyengar argues in her examination of objects in other-language Shakespeare films. The chapters in this collection argue that agency is then disbursed when we appropriate Shakespeare through acts of critical reading, as Molly Seremet does when she considers Ofelia's appropriation of flowers to define her agency, or through direct and indirect appropriation, as Andrew Darr illustrates through his consideration of Shakespeare games. When Bennett draws and expands from Baruch Spinoza's theory that things 'enhance their power *in* or *as a heterogeneous assemblage*' (2010: 23), she alerts us to the chaotic, unsettled energies that resist our capacity to allocate singular or universal meaning.

Assemblages are things working with and against one another to produce meaning that is resistant to the 'capacity localised in a human body or in a collective produced (only) by human efforts' (Bennett 2010: 23). Unlike Spinoza, however, Bennett understands that things and their thing-power are subject to political and ideological ecologies (both human and not-human), recognising things as existing in an in-between space, and that things demonstrate an 'active, earthly, not quite human capaciousness' (2010: 3) to absorb the meaning we afford them. Tethered as it is to humanism, and the idea of the author, Shakespeare can never quite disperse agency on its own terms without human or technological interaction. We therefore term Bennett's vibrancy as variability, suggesting that Shakespeare is constructed through interminable assemblages that we can speculatively comprehend, but that nonetheless must remain inescapably situated among other material objects. Conceptually, Shakespeare can only exist when put to use, when activated as part of a materialist organisation – even the 1623 Folio is, we argue elsewhere, an appropriative assemblage (Fazel and Geddes 2022). The chapters in this collection suggest that Shakespeare is in possession of a potentiality that makes visible the 'complicated web of dissonant connection between bodies' that, when recognised, 'will enable wiser interventions into that ecology' (Bennett 2010: 4). The meanings that the Shakespeare object generates are varied and variable, and this affective authority has the capacity to dispel preconceived notions that may have settled in our hearts by the affective power of new experience.

An object-oriented reading praxis steps outside textual and cultural genealogies in favour of something more speculative. Graham Harman suggests that an object-oriented literary practice might stand in opposition to a new historicist approach because it looks 'at how works reverse or shape what might have been expected in their time and place, or at how some withstand the earthquakes of the centuries much better than others' (2012: 201). Harman's notions empower critics to understand how appropriative texts respond to, or intersect with, Shakespeare. For him, a speculative practice deliberately decontextualises works in order to contemplate that which is inaccessible and learn about the limitations our human frameworks impose on literature. As

Michael Lutz implies in his essay on *King Lear* and the anthropocene, by virtue of being produced by a human man, Shakespeare is always an object, even when it outlives the human. For Robert Sawyer, however, this vitality moves through culture like cryptocurrency, resistant to the human breakage that would break down Shakespeare (and the humanities) to a commodity that can be subjected to neoliberal educational power structures. This collection, then, follows Bennett's lead in trying to imagine the place where human and non-human intersect without disenfranchising the object, and takes up Harman's disruptive methodology. 'Shakespeare', however, weighted by a 400-year cultural history, is itself a composite object that, in spite of its origins, has emerged as the authorial intention of William Shakepeare (and his collaborators). Shakespeare's formation bears the imprint of theatre's materialist history, an Anglocentric understanding of early and pre-modern history, and the assemblage of material objects that include the First Folio. Shakespeare's very origin, therefore, is one that absorbs and exceeds the autonomy of the human William Shakespeare.

We suggest, therefore, that Shakespeare is an object (or a set of objects) that has been mined, transformed, adapted, appropriated, interpreted and speculated about without exhaustion for four hundred years. It transcends the commodification that would give it determined meaning, continuing to surprise us. Shakespeare, this collection contends, is Bennett's vibrant matter manifest in plays, images, text and other cultural objects. And although it submits to human impulses, to human-centric constructs of meaning, it does not permit itself to be irrevocably reduced to the constrained and circumscribed object of human expectation. In appropriation, performance, reading and other acts of Shakespeare consumption, as Bennett notes, 'what is manifest arrives through humans but not entirely because of them' (2010: 17). This is, perhaps, an unusual claim to make for a community of objects that are so famously the product of one man. Shakespeare appropriations constitute their own ecologies of meaning, their own assemblages that are evidence of how Shakespeare is rendered manifest. For object-oriented critics of appropriation, then, navigating the 'web of dissonant connections' (Bennett 2010: 4) without a clear understanding of what these connections might mean forces a re-evaluation of the central object. Understanding how Shakespeare is marked by its own variable vibrancy empowers us to dismiss the conventional appropriative paradigm that uncritically accepts Shakespeare as the stable core. Instead, appropriation is a speculative practice that exists in an unsettled space, and Shakespeare becomes a locus of experiment, imagination and possibility, which, as Sawyer recognises in his chapter, involves both risk and opportunity.

Shakespeare, then, is the thing itself, and when we consume or use it, we recognise it as one of Bennett's federation of actants, all of which draw from, or appropriate, one another in varying degrees. Being the product of the man from Stratford, Shakespeare is both quintessentially human and non-human, traversing a variety of non-human systems from semiotics to hypertext that move in accordance with capitalist values, impervious to human intention. Humans and non-human actants participate in new assemblages of Shakespeare every time we create or consume a Shakespeare play, performance or appropriation. Even the choices to reference Will Shakespeare or William Shakespeare (or the Bard) are part of an implicit acknowledgement of how 'energies and factions . . . fly out' (Bennett 2010: 25) of Shakespeare and merge with the other technological, cultural and affective actants in play 'to produce distinctive effects' (Bennett 2010: 24) that we call appropriation. This organisation of adjacent objects into meaning is indicative of a political ecology crafted in accordance with both human and non-human logic. The various ways in which meaning is generated by such organisational practices, this book suggests, constitute Desmet's dialogics of Shakespeare use as they continuously define and redefine Shakespeare. The chapters in this collection interrogate and embrace the uncertainty of Shakespeare's vitality, but most of all they contend that Shakespeare is constantly reassembling in accordance with culture, politics, geographies, technologies and other, as-yet-unthought-of ecologies. To apply Bennett's theories is to recognise our own situatedness in the sociopolitical moment and to interrogate the place of Shakespeare in an ever-changing political ecology of things, as Iyengar does when she uses global Shakespeares as a new materialist reading methodology. New materialism and object-oriented ontology urge us to view Shakespeare as a composite of four hundred years of technology, culture, affective fandom and shifting cultural values, as Andrew Darr and Emily MacLeod each note. As a variable object, Shakespeare exists as unsettled and unfettered, ever moving in and out of human control as it intersects with other networks of meaning, and this relies on particular patterns of ideologically driven consumption. That is to say, sometimes we define Shakespeare, and sometimes Shakespeare defines itself. Pye and Gargano exemplify this variability when they ask us to imagine *Macbeth* from the dagger's point of view.

Although a new materialist and/or object-oriented approach allows for variable meanings generated through rationales that may seem illogical to the critical outsider, it also requires us to see how these political ecologies function. The mutual indeterminacy of the object and the human that

Bennett's valuation facilitates encourages us to think more carefully about the humanist project. Harman imagines such a literary practice as one of hope. It offers us the opportunity of 'reassessing our standards of quality, not for dissolving all works equally into social products of their inherently equal eras' (Harman 2012: 201). As the chapters by Lutz and Pye and Gargano illustrate, imagining appropriation from the position of the object empowers us to discard the assumptions that literature and readers are disproportionately subject to their cultural situatedness and embrace a more dialogic flow between the object and its users. An object-oriented appropriative theory dismisses – or at least interrogates – the supremacy of humanism as a defining feature of literature. Shakespeare's vibrancy activates the user, the platform and the appropriated object in varying degrees, and allows us to return the meaning to the text to contribute to its evolving archive of meanings, or, as Louise Geddes would suggest, its celebrity, which, in turn, contributes to future readings.

The book aims to elicit new discussions on how we might employ an object-oriented literary approach, and we have actively sought out chapters that interact with, and occasionally challenge, each other, either through their critical approach or Shakespearean topic. Although the collection is divided into parts, we believe that the chapters consistently reach outside their grouping to speak to one another. For example, Sawyer actively pushes back against the currency that Kim and Geddes see as valuable to Shakespeare study, and Seremet asserts an agency for Ofelia that Darr can only envision in ludic appropriation. Furthermore, the arrangement of the volume's chapters challenges the presumed trajectory of appropriation as it shifts away from the centralised human subject to embrace the speculative uncertainty of a posthuman existence, while retaining Shakespeare as organising principle. The structure makes visible Lutz's premise, through his reading of Jean-Luc Godard's *King Lear* and Emily St John Mandel's *Station Eleven*, that Shakespeare's potentiality is often unknowable and sometimes inconceivable to us even as we bear witness to its own becoming, or as it approaches and exceeds its 'promised end'.

The chapters in this book are organised into three parts – Disciplinary Objects, Media Objects and Human Objects – that each define the affective Shakespearean object differently. Methodologically, we hope to make the presence of the human increasingly unsettled as the reader moves through the collection.

Part I examines the possibilities and pitfalls of an object-oriented methodology. For Sujata Iyengar, the experience of watching Shakespeare films in diverse languages that she does not understand forces her to rely on the assemblages of objects within an adaptation (a Shakespearean object itself) to discern meaning and a richer understanding of *Othello*. The *Othello* that unfolds in each film's telling owes both its familiarity and variability to the agency, and the meaning-making interactions, of both non-human and human objects, and for Iyengar, using the concept of 'global Shakespeares' as an object-oriented methodology yields new critical insight. Also illustrating how new awareness of character or text emerges through object-oriented methodology, Molly Seremet examines one Shakespearean object – Ofelia from *Hamlet* Q1. In her application of object-oriented feminism, Seremet argues that Q1 Ofelia accepts her own objectification and becomes a 'dispensiac' who takes control of the fragmentation of herself by giving out the objects that are conflated with her identity. For Seremet, Ofelia is composed of disparate fragments that can be detached and scattered as easily as they are assembled. Seremet uses new materialism to separate out the composite Ophelias that exist in contemporary editions of *Hamlet* and generates new readings through an examination of these fragments. Finally, Robert Sawyer offers a challenge to the data-driven methodologies that underpin much posthumanist work by outlining the stakes of such disaggregation. Sawyer proposes that Shakespearean cultural capital operates as a cryptocurrency and provocatively considers the implications that framing Shakespeare as a neoliberal object have on contemporary discourses of the humanities. For Sawyer, the something humanist that is potentially lost in these processes is counter-intuitive to the work that we do in academe and the classroom, and is constituent of a larger attack on the humanities that seeks to reduce the work that we do to quantifiable outcomes.

Part II focuses on how agency within the Shakespeare object is negotiated as it traverses media. L. Monique Pittman, Vanessa Corredera, Kristin Denslow and Karl G. Bailey examine *Westworld*'s reimagining of *The Tempest*, drawing on both postcolonial and object-oriented theories in their interrogation of the television show's issues of race and gender and the line between person and thing. As is the case with many other chapters in the book, for Pittman, Corredera, Denslow and Bailey, adaptation activates variable meanings that expose Shakespeare to criticism, particularly in relation to issues of race and gender. Also interrogating gender representation, Andrew Darr's chapter highlights the expanded agency of game designers as appropriators to accommodate the speculative nature of video games and players, manifested through the game's ludic appropriation of Ophelia. Drawing on an object-oriented approach to the video game *Elsinore*, Darr suggests that gameplay empowers Ophelia to assert her thing-power, and for Darr, this recognition demands a re-examination of the sexism that pervades video-game culture. Such critiques create tension within Shakespeare studies, as they challenge Shakespeare's cultural supremacy.

Correspondingly, Anna Blackwell addresses issues of authenticity and identity by implicitly acknowledging the work done to resist posthumanism through biopic. Blackwell is concerned with the intersections of Shakespeare and celebrity, manifest as such intersections are in both cultural capital and the popular trope of the 'intellectual loser' that characterises Shakespearean biographical fiction. Blackwell's chapter imagines both William Shakespeare and the actor who plays him in the television series *Upstart Crow* as celebrity objects who deploy their own agency. For Blackwell, the biopic itself is an affective object that facilitates a myth of unappreciated genius that fails to recognise the disenfranchised voices of those who contributed to the works. Emily MacLeod closes Part II and looks ahead to Part III by recognising the instability of Shakespearean meaning in new modalities and the ways the idea of Shakespeare's humanist triumph is undermined through visual representation. MacLeod challenges the claims made on behalf of 'colour-blind' casting in the BBC series *The Hollow Crown* by examining the ways in which actress Sophie Okonedo is turned into an object and, by extension, an emblem of blackness to demonstrate the way the production allows her race and gender to undermine her subjective value as a human participant in the Wars of the Roses.

The volume concludes with four chapters that explore the limits of what we define as human in Shakespeare. Shanelle E. Kim uses Shakespeare as a methodology to critique the ways in which humanity is constructed by Shakespeare and those who consume him. Through an examination of how comedians Key and Peele reappropriate the Shakespeare object in their comedy sketch, Kim argues that object-oriented ontology's default whiteness might be expanded to accommodate black humanist experience. Her focus is on the subjective experience of Elizabethan playgoers Lashawnia and Martinsia to interrogate Shakespeare's complicity in a culture of white supremacy. Kim questions how object-oriented ontology might facilitate conversations over who is granted access to the right to be seen as human.

Using *Macbeth* as an analogy, Valerie Pye and Cara Gargano draw on the idea of invisible-yet-present stage properties to think about how theatrical time can help imagine connections between contemporary performance and Shakespeare's original stagings, drawing Iyengar's global Shakespeares methodology away from the human viewer and relocating it within the performance text itself. In her chapter, Louise Geddes suggests that the human/object slippage that an object-oriented approach offers expands celebrity studies beyond its human subjects to include objects – in this case, the play *Hamlet*. In affording the play the same affective celebrity as we do movie stars, or Shakespeare himself, Geddes suggests that such fame imposes its vast networks of socially conditioned meaning on to contemporary performance, challenging actors who wish to exploit Hamlet's celebrity and generate fame of their own. The objectification of the play is also a crucial element of performance for Pye and Gargano, who focus on the performance as a vast, expansive object. They define performance as one of Bogost's 'tiny' ontologies, a dense mass of matter spread out across time and space. Their chapter imagines the value of a performance network contained within compacted 'theatrical' time that exemplifies the network of meaning available to theatre practitioners that results, presumably, in the choices that potentially use, exploit or expose Shakespeare to the types of critique we see elsewhere in the book.

Finally, Michael Lutz's chapter obliterates the human entirely to imagine what Shakespeare will mean at the end of human experience. Lutz explores the trope of *King Lear* in the anthropocene in both Jean-Luc Godard's *King Lear* and Emily St John Mandel's post-apocalyptic novel *Station Eleven*, to suggest that Shakespeare's cultural authority (and currency) offers opportunities to connect with humanity – even when human extinction means that such connections are purely speculative – as when androids in an interlude of the video game *Nier: Automata* imagine what it is to play human by performing scenes from *Romeo and Juliet*.

The chapters in this collection each consider how the vibrant agency of objects spurs appropriation regardless of, or indifferent to, human intervention, and consider the extent to which the dialogic of human and technology shapes appropriative use. As such, they work together to present a broader discourse on the opportunities – and challenges – of understanding Shakespeare through an object-oriented approach.

Bibliography

Barthes, R. (1986), 'From Work to Text', in *The Rustle of Language*, trans. R. Howard, New York: Hill and Wang, pp. 49–82.

Bennett, J. (2010), *Vibrant Matter: A Political Ecology of Things*, Durham, NC: Duke University Press.

Bogost, I. (2012), *Alien Phenomenology, or What It's Like to Be a Thing*, Minneapolis: University of Minnesota Press.

Bristol, M. (1996), *Big Time Shakespeare*, New York: Routledge.

Cartelli, T. (2019), *Reenacting Shakespeare in the Shakespeare Aftermath: The Intermedial Turn and Turn to Embodiment*, New York: Palgrave Macmillan.
Desmet, C. (2014), 'Recognising Shakespeare, Rethinking Fidelity: A Rhetoric and Ethics of Appropriation', in A. Huang and E. Rivlin (eds), *Shakespeare and the Ethics of Appropriation*, New York: Palgrave Macmillan, pp. 41–58.
Desmet, C. (2017), 'Alien Shakespeares 2.0', *Actes des congrès de la Société française Shakespeare*, 35, DOI: 10.4000/shakespeare.3877 [accessed 28 April 2020].
Desmet, C., N. Loper and J. Casey (2017), 'Introduction', in C. Desmet, N. Loper and J. Casey (eds), *Shakespeare/Not Shakespeare*, New York: Palgrave Macmillan, pp. 1–24.
Desmet, C., and R. Sawyer (eds) (1999), *Shakespeare and Appropriation*, New York: Routledge.
Fazel, V. M., and L. Geddes (2022), *The Shakespeare Multiverse: Fandom as Literary Praxis*, Abingdon: Routledge.
Fazel, V. M., and L. Geddes (eds) (2017), *The Shakespeare User: Critical and Creative Appropriations in a Networked Culture*, New York: Palgrave.
Fischlin, D. (ed.) (2014), *OuterSpeares: Shakespeare, Intermedia, and the Limits of Adaptation*, Toronto: University of Toronto Press.
Harman, G. (2012), 'The Well-Wrought Broken Hammer: Object-Oriented Literary Criticism', *New Literary History*, 43:2, 183–203.
Hodgdon, B. (1998), *The Shakespeare Trade: Performances and Appropriations*, Philadelphia: University of Pennsylvania Press.
Huang, A., and E. Rivlin (eds) (2014), *Shakespeare and the Ethics of Appropriation*, New York: Palgrave Macmillan.
Kidnie, M. J. (2009), *Shakespeare and the Problem of Adaptation*, New York: Routledge.
Lanier, D. M. (2002), *Shakespeare and Modern Popular Culture*, Oxford: Oxford University Press.
Lanier, D. M. (2014), 'Shakespearian Rhizomatics: Adaptation, Ethics, Value', in A. Huang and E. Rivlin (eds), *Shakespeare and the Ethics of Appropriation*, New York: Palgrave Macmillan, pp. 21–40.
Lanier, D. M. (2017), 'Shakespeare/Not Shakespeare: Afterword', in C. Desmet, N. Loper and J. Casey (eds), *Shakespeare/Not Shakespeare*, New York: Palgrave Macmillian, pp. 293–300.
O'Neill, S. (ed.) (2018), *Broadcast your Shakespeare: Continuity and Change Across Media*, New York: Bloomsbury.
Worthen, W. B. (2014), *Shakespeare Performance Studies*, Cambridge: Cambridge University Press.

PART I
DISCIPLINARY OBJECTS

1

Beds, Handkerchiefs and Moving Objects in *Othello*

Sujata Iyengar

This chapter emerged from a series of challenges that Alexa Alice Joubin issued to Shakespeareans in her edited special issue of the British journal *Shakespeare*, in which her own essay, 'Global Shakespeares as Methodology', asks how global Shakespeares might function as a methodology, and what we might learn about Shakespeare without Shakespeare's language (Joubin 2013). Joubin suggests that imagining global Shakespeare as a methodology might include questioning the orientation of our Shakespearean world maps and enquiring where we do *not* find Shakespeare, and why; commenting upon the failure of the metaphor of the map or the globe, and imagining other ways of organising our knowledge about the world; and seeking out archival silences within the record of globalisation, moving from present to past, even as we might also work from past to future in examining the early modern and modern fascination with 'the globe' and the global.

This chapter offers yet another methodological approach to global Shakespeare studies, one that addresses concerns about how Shakespeare might speak or play in translation and in or through variable objects. The medium of film empowers objects particularly strongly because of film's visual nature; moreover, if we watch a Shakespeare film without listening to the soundtrack, or without understanding the language, objects, characters and actions birth new and strange or alien lives for Shakespearean texts. This chapter therefore analyses the variable lives of *Othello* as it shaped itself around fetishistic or magical objects in three film versions in three different languages that I do not understand.

A viewer watching *Othello* in an unfamiliar language can more narrowly focus upon the life of things in the play and in appropriations surrounding it. Two *things* dominate this play: most obviously, the handkerchief; less obviously, because it is sometimes part of the stage, the bed in which Desdemona is smothered. This chapter specifically considers the ways in which a South Indian art film in the Dravidian language Malayalam, a North Indian 'Bollywood' movie in the Utter Pradesh dialect Khariboli, and an Italian teen movie adaptation of *Othello* permit or prohibit objects from acting expressively. These adaptations (*Kaliyattam*, *Omkara* and *Iago*) indigenise and transform both the handkerchief and the 'tragic loading' of the bed, in the last case turning (or returning) the Shakespearean source from tragedy to comedy.

I am deliberately cultivating in this chapter what Jane Bennett calls in *Vibrant Matter* a new 'anthropomorphism', a renewed 'vibrant materialism' – an emphasis on objects in the world and on attributing agency or actantial ability to them. Bennett adapts the vital materialism of Spinoza and Bergson, Driesch's notion of 'entelechy' and the object-oriented ontology of Bruno Latour in order to argue, paradoxically, *against* a deterministic or mechanistic force in the universe and against what seems to us like an intuitive and immoveable distinction between *life* and *matter* (and here politics overtake theory: given the debates surrounding whether or not the matter of a human body is 'alive' when connected to a life-support machine, or whether or not a cluster of cells sending out a pattern of electrical responses constitutes human life in the womb, clearly we need to continue theorising what we understand as life or activity or agency or, to use Bennett's preferred term, *intensities*).

Using examples of material unpredictability ranging from the unprecedented change in the direction of electrons that caused the eastern seaboard blackout in 2003 to the changing status of stem cells in law, Bennett suggests that we start thinking of agents or movers as 'assemblages' rather than individual humans or even individual objects. '"Objects" appear as such because their becoming proceeds at a speed or a level below the threshold of human discernment' (Bennett 2010: 58). Moreover, '[a]ssemblages are not governed by any central head: no one materiality or type of material has sufficient competence to determine consistently the trajectory or impact of the group' (2010: 24). How then can change or action take place? 'Alongside and inside singular human agents there exists a heterogeneous series of actants with partial, overlapping, and conflicting degrees of power and effectivity' (2010: 33). Actions happen collectively, enabled by multiple actants that function together to form the assemblage. Intensities manifest themselves at different points in the process that is action and at different sites within the assemblage. Action is the end result, but it is futile to attempt, in Bennett's materialism, to trace back a sequence of events in order to isolate a single agent or decision that makes an outcome inevitable.

To a certain extent we can predict how actants, including objects, will act through 'entelechy', a force within objects that contains the potential to shape them yet does not define them nor necessitate the object's or the process's taking form in a specific way. Akin, Bennett suggests, to Kant's 'purposiveness' in art, entelechy offers a plan for the object's or the event's development but without compromising the pluripotentiality also inherent within the object. 'Entelechy coordinates parts on behalf of a whole in response to event and does so without following a rigid plan; it answers events innovatively and perspicuously, deciding on the spot and in real time which of the many possible courses of development will in fact happen' (Bennett 2010: 75). In other words, Bennett argues that we cannot predict what material objects, even elements, will do in every particular instance; while she does not attribute agency or identity to material objects, she does suggest that complex events can be better explained by imagining agency as a cluster of 'intensity' that can be transmitted and distributed among human and non-human agents. In other words, life itself emerges from the interactions between human and non-human matter.

Critiques of Latour's object-oriented ontology and of Bennett's vital materialism have emerged from various points on the political spectrum and offer interesting challenges to Shakespeare studies, which has so often relied on humanism to enshrine or defend Shakespeare's works.[1] Some accuse the new vital materialism of reinscribing a kind of holy mysticism or soul within objects, and of enshrining a quietist neo-humanism. Women, and Black, Indigenous and people of colour, including me, might want to observe that there already exists a pernicious history of treating objects as human and certain kinds of humans as objects. Consider the abomination that was chattel slavery and that turned human beings into 'object[s] in the midst of other objects', in the quotation that begins a germinal chapter in Kim F. Hall's *Things of Darkness* (1996). Think of the multiple derogatory British and North American slang terms that turn women into objects, ranging from dehumanising epithets for women whom the speaker considers to be sexually available (for example, the metonymies 'skirts' or 'petticoats', both dating to the early modern period) to words that have come to connote women whom the speaker deems sexually unattractive or aged (reductively and biologically, 'bags', or, fearfully, 'battleaxes', in usages dating from the early twentieth century). Think also of former US presidential candidate Mitt Romney's notorious gaffe at the Iowa State Fair in 2011, 'Corporations are people, my friend', in response to a request for higher corporate taxes to fund social programmes. At the same time, feminist, Black and of colour, and queer critiques of object-oriented ontologies (OOO) echo critical race, feminist, postcolonial and Marxian evaluations of humanism: if OOO risks objectifying humans, it can also draw attention to the persons for whom humanity has always been contingent, contextual and dependent upon an assemblage of their surroundings (including other humans). For Shakespeare studies, this contingency might require us to imagine and extend a politicised dialogue between Shakespeare's purported humanity or universality and the local conditions of production, reception, appropriation and human experiences.

We might also retort that despite Bennett's critique of anthropocentric mechanism, perhaps one of the reasons we cannot predict (in one of her examples) the direction in which a stream of electrons will flow is that we do not *yet* fully understand the underlying principles or forces; taken to its logical conclusion, Bennett's vital materialism might merely *postpone* the triumph of a mechanistic universe dominated by *homo scientificus*. In an interview with Peter Gratton, Bennett admits to the charge of normative biologism but suggests that complex assemblages will never be fully understood:

> I think that we are in fact constrained by some sort of nature, that we are free to operate but within iterated structures . . . nature or materiality constrains human (and nonhuman) activities but because nature or materiality is not a perfect machine, it and we are never fully analyzable. There is always something that escapes . . . The need to be kind and respectful to other bodies will remain, regardless of whether one understands human individuals and groups as embodied minds/souls or as complex materialities. (Bennett, qtd in Gratton 2010)

Bennett defends herself against the charge of quietism by pointing out her own reliance on what she calls 'strategic anthropomorphism' or a 'Machiavellian . . . indirect' political agency. When pressed to imagine specific political changes that vital materialism could inspire, she suggests:

> there seems to be a resonance between the idea of matter as dull stuff/passive resource and a set of gigantically wasteful production and consumption practices . . . [that] endanger and immiserate workers, children, animals, and plants here and abroad. To the extent that the figure of inert matter sustains this consumptive style, another figure might disrupt it. (Bennett, qtd in Khan 2012: 50)

Counter-intuitively, Bennett's vital materialism is 'pragmatic'. She argues that 'ethics and politics have more traction on material assemblages and the way they reproduce patterns of effects than they can have on that elusive spiritual entity called the "moral subject"' (Bennett, qtd in Khan 2012: 54).

There are some inconsistencies in Bennett's position, notably with regard to what is normative or even what she earlier called 'pragmatic'. She acknowledges in the interview with Khan that she 'support[s] medical – in the sense of biochemical – discourses on schizophrenia', including research into 'brain science and pharmacological agents that might recalibrate the delicate chemistry that makes normal thinking possible'. Her support for such endeavours draws from her own experiences growing up with a brother with schizophrenia (Bennett, qtd in Khan 2012: 50). Yet in her essay 'Powers of the Hoard', she asks us to 'Meet the people, the hoarders, not as bearers of mental illness but as differently-abled bodies that might have special sensory access to the call of things' (Bennett 2012: 244), and suggests that we might consider 'paranoia . . . less as a psychological disorder than as an over-extended receptivity to the activeness of material bodies' (2012: 268). Of course, a medicalised and a vibrant materialist outlook are not necessarily incompatible – we could study hoarding as a phenomenon in which 'thing-power' becomes manifest while simultaneously imagining a therapeutic praxis that would attend to the desires of the assemblage of objects, family members, microbiomes, heavy metals and so on that distribute agency around the body of the so-called hoarder – but Bennett herself does not in this essay offer any solutions, pragmatic or otherwise, to the disabling and unhappy predicament in which this distributed agency finds itself. Diana Coole more overtly makes the case for vital matter and other kinds of 'critical new materialism' or 'new material ontologies' as effective political strategies to alleviate 'normative concerns about social justice'; she suggests that it offers 'a detailed phenomenology of diverse lives as they are actually lived – often in ways that are at odds with abstract normative theories or official ideologies' (Coole and Frost 2010: 27).

'Fairey Napkins'

I will return to the ethical repercussions of vibrant materialism or object-oriented critical ontologies later, but first I want to demonstrate the productive generation of this kind of intensity surrounding the famous handkerchief in *Othello* and particular where OOO can infuse the supernatural, the spiritual or the magical – the non-scientific, the extra-rational – into empowered objects. Jonathan Gil Harris in *Shakespeare and Literary Theory* uses Deleuze and Guattari's rhizomatics and Latour's actor-network theory to argue for the handkerchief as a rhizomatic network connecting multiple actors, meanings and even time periods (Harris 2009: 61). Bennett's vibrant materialism also builds on Deleuze and Guattari's analysis and on Bruno Latour's actor-network theory, but she adds to or inflects her sources with a re-enchantment of the material world. (Remember that Bennett suggests that objects only appear as inert matter to us because we move and perceive too slowly to acknowledge their constant process of becoming and of being-in-the-moment.)

The handkerchief in *Othello* is indeed enchanted: it might or might not have been dyed in mummy made from maidens' hearts, but it operates as if alive. It is helpful to think of the handkerchief as a human/non-human hybrid or assemblage, an actant bearing within it a certain entelechy but one that requires the coordination of human and non-human forces (for example, the gravity that lets the handkerchief fall, Othello's pushing it away, Emilia's taking it up) in order for the tragedy to take place. The handkerchief shrouds its movements, at least early on, in mystery. How does it get from Othello to Desdemona and from Desdemona to Emilia? Folio and Quarto offer no help here.[2] The 1622 Quarto reads:

> *Oth*. Your napkin is too little:
> Let it alone, come I'le goe in with you.
> *Des*. I am very sorry that you are not well.
> *Em*. I am glad I haue found this napkin,   *Ex*. Oth. *and* Desd.
> This was her first remembrance from the Moor.
>   (TLN 1961–65, 3.3, Hv, Internet Shakespeare Editions)

Sometime after Desdemona's sympathetic words and the lovers' exit, Emilia sees and obtains the handkerchief. What happens in the space between those lines? Does Othello angrily push the napkin away from him and leave it on the ground, or on a table? Does he trample it underfoot and leave it stained, as in Orson Welles's 1952 film?

The 1623 Folio reads:

> *Oth*. Your Napkin is too little:
> Let it alone: Come, Ile go in with you.   *Exit*
> *Des*. I am very sorry that you are not well.
> *ÆEmil*. I am glad I haue found this Napkin.
> This was her first remembrance from the Moor;
>   (TLN 1921–25, 3.3, TT5 col.1, p. 325, Internet Shakespeare Editions)

This text leaves (barely) open the possibility that Desdemona and Othello exit separately, although if Desdemona remains on stage after Othello leaves, why doesn't she notice the loss of her handkerchief immediately? Does Desdemona 'let it drop by negligence' as Emilia says (III.iii.356)? Does it fall out of Desdemona's bodice? Does Emilia, as she later says, 'filch' it from Desdemona's hand (III.iii.361)?

Paradoxically, attributing power and a kind of agency to objects in Bennett's 'pragmatic' sense alerts us to the ubiquitous moral malice of sexist and racist practices in the world of the play (and beyond). Such practices work invisibly, seemingly supernaturally, and are enabled by a kind of magical thinking and materialised through enchanted or bewitched objects. The situation makes no common or human sense; the handkerchief is unpredictable, a 'trifle . . . light as air', so light that it threatens to render the tragedy farcical, as Thomas Rymer complained in 1693:

> So much ado, so much stress, so much passion and repetition about an Handkerchief! . . . Had it been *Desdemona*'s Garter, the Sagacious Moor might have smelt a rat, but the Handkerchief is so remote a trifle, no Booby, on this side *Mauritania*, could make any consequence from it . . . *Desdemona* dropt the Handkerchief, and missed it that very day after her Marriage; it might have been rumpl'd up with her Wedding sheets: And this Night that she lay in her wedding sheets, the *Fairey* Napkin (whilst *Othello* was stifling her) might have started up to disarm his fury, and stop his ungracious mouth . . . Then might he . . . touch'd with remorse, have honestly cut his own Throat, by the good leave, and with the applause of all the Spectators. Who might thereupon have gone home with a quiet mind, admiring the beauty of Providence; fairly and truly represented on the Theatre. (Rymer 1970: K6–K7)

I do not endorse Rymer's reading, but he is correct that the magic handkerchief or 'Fairey Napkin' connects to other problems in performing *Othello*, particularly the credibility of Iago's deception and the violence of Othello's response, problems to which film-makers respond in different ways.

The three films that I study here attempt to compensate for the handkerchief's lightness by disenchanting it, by substituting for it an object of more immediately erotic significance to Desdemona and Othello, by adding additional motive to the Emilia character and, in *Kaliyattam*, by distributing agency and blame across supernatural actants (Hindu deities) located outside human or human-made assemblages. Identifying the supernatural as the remotely powerful cause distributing agency across multiple actants enables the birth of a new kind of tragedy and a new kind of catharsis, an existential becoming of brave and radical contingency.

Kaliyattam

Jayaraaj's award-winning film *Kaliyattam* transfers Shakespeare's play to the South Indian state of Kerala and casts Othello as Perumalayan Kannan, the lead dancer in a complex religious dance practice and ritual called *Theyyam*. During *Theyyam* the lead dancer becomes the deity incarnate, acting as a manifestation of the divine rather than as himself. Make-up, costume, gesture, music, voice assemble together to enflesh God. Perumalayan wears his make-up to become the deity, but also, in this film, to murder his wife Thamara, tricked by the duplicity of a jealous player in the troupe, Panniyan, who yearns for a leading role. The handkerchief in this film becomes a red and gold *patta*, a scarf or robe that in this film is also used as a bedspread or as ceremonial wedding sheets.

Poonam Trivedi suggests that 'Jayaraaj even betters Shakespeare here' (2007: 151) in associating the handkerchief with the vibrant colour red, associated with fertility. The childless Emilia character Cheerma, Trivedi suggests, now has another motive for her theft, namely her desire to please her husband by giving him children. On the one hand, human agents in *Kaliyattam* such as Cheerma work more intensively towards the tragic denouement. By forcing Cheerma actively to steal the *patta* from Thamara's hope chest and by making the handkerchief explicitly eroticised, the director has effectively done what Rymer suggested and made Desdemona drop her garter.

On the other hand, Shakespeare's play carefully leaves open the possibility that there is indeed 'magic in the web' of the handkerchief (III.iv.81), that it is to a certain extent the centre of what Bennett might call an intensity that approaches agency. A scene in which Panniyan wraps the *patta* around his head like the *pallu* of a sari, in solitary glee, followed by his wife's entry and her joyfully swathing herself in the *patta* like a shawl turns both Panniyan and Cheerma into traditional Hindu brides clothed in red. The point is precisely that the handkerchief floats, a 'trifle light as air', and that Emilia's actions, as Coleridge said of Iago's, are 'motiveless'. The handkerchief-object can only work its magic as part of an unpredictable human/non-human assemblage.

Kaliyattam does not eradicate non-human agents, however; rather, it brings in supernatural elements and the natural world to relocate the enchantment of the handkerchief within the mythology of *Theyyam*.

Recall that *Theyyam*'s mythology includes the entelechy or immanent power within the *Theyyam* costume and make-up, in which these non-human objects transcend the human and material to become vehicles for the divine (much as enspirited air can function in an early modern body to knit together what Donne called the 'subtile knot' of body and soul). Repeated shots of Perumalayan and Thamara smeared with Perumalayan's make-up after love-making, and of the pots shattering on the floor in the violence of their love, sound potentially farcical, erotic and tragic notes through the entelechy adhering to or inhering in these sacralised performing properties (the make-up itself) rather than through the *patta* or handkerchief.

A shot of Thamara and Perumalayan looking at their own besmeared reflections in a circular mirror turns their post-coital languor suddenly ominous, an image that perhaps recalls a well-known moment in Welles's film in which Othello and Iago are mirrored back to themselves and to the viewer as Othello muses, 'Haply for I am black . . .' (III.iii.304; a still from one of the many shots with the circular mirror is reproduced in Stratford 2015). When the anguished Perumalayan calls out to the deities, they come to him on the mountain in full costume and make-up, only to turn their backs on him ostentatiously, lined up in a mesmerising yet minatory row.

After Perumalayan suffocates Thamara and Cheerma reveals the truth about the *patta*, Perumalayan hunts down Panniyan and beats him almost to death, after which Perumalayan immolates himself on the ritual purification fire of the *Theyyam*, with which the film opened. There is no tragic loading of the bed; the lovers die apart.

Omkara

Bhardwaj's *Omkara* sets Shakespeare's play among rough gangsters in Uttar Pradesh, even down to deploying the distinct Khariboli language common among rural peoples of this area rather than the standard Bollywood Hindustani. Dolly, the beloved daughter of a high-ranking lawyer, falls in love with Omkara or Omi, a thug employed by a local politico to knee-cap his opponents. Omkara kidnaps Dolly from her wedding to Rajju (the Rodrigo character) and, with the intercession of the politician, her father is reconciled to the upcoming wedding of Omi and Dolly. After a major coup, Omkara promotes Kesu (Cassio) over Langda (Iago), who vows revenge and convinces his wife Indu to steal a bejewelled *kamarbandh* or waistband, a piece of wedding jewellery belonging to Dolly, which

Langda will use to convince Omkara that Dolly is having a clandestine affair with Kesu. Convinced by the *kamarbandh* and by an overheard conversation, Omkara kills Dolly on their wedding night, killing himself after Indu reveals Dolly's innocence.

The film disenchants the handkerchief by making the token explicitly erotic – it features in nearly every scene in which Omi and Dolly are intimate, and is itself caressed and beloved by other characters. Moreover, it is valuable in itself – made of precious metals and jewels – and, like the *patta* in *Kaliyattam*, forms part of a trousseau or wedding set. At the same time, the movie leaves it mysterious *how* Indu/Emilia acquires this *kamarbandh*. We see it on Dolly's body as the camera pans up before she and Omkara make love, we see Omkara kissing it on her body (on a standing and fixed bed, not a traditional Indian swing-bed), during a love scene interrupted by the brawl (set up by Langda) in which Kesu disgraces himself. Then we next see it during the love-song 'O Saathi Re', in the context of a montage love scene showing Omi and Dolly's romance.

The montage includes defused threats of violence. Kesu teaches Dolly the Stevie Wonder song 'I Just Called To Say I Love You', and when Dolly sings it to Omkara, he laughs at her attempt. Angered, she play-fights him; they mock arm-wrestle; she pretends to threaten Omkara with a shotgun. Next we see Indu, the Emilia character, holding the *kamarbandh* and turning it over in her hands as if envious, watching the happiness of Omi and Dolly. After this scene, the next time we see the *kamarbandh* is when Indu gives it to Langda, who gloats as he dresses himself up as a mock bride with the *kamarbandh* on his face.

Note the parallels with *Kaliyattam* as both Iago characters use the handkerchief-function to mimic the joy of the new bride. In *Omkara*, the image even recalls a specific piece of bridal jewellery to be worn on the head: the *matta pati*. The trope of Iago-as-bride perhaps displaces homoeroticism (a subtext missing from both these films although it appears prominently in Oliver Parker's US film of *Othello* [1995]). In all these shots the *kamarbandh* is treated as a character – in shot – at the expense of human characters.

The sight of the *kamarbandh* on Langda's face intensifies its eroticism because we have previously seen this piece of jewellery on Dolly's belly, pointing towards her lower body. Later scenes associate the *kamarbandh* with the traditional Indian swing-bed. The swing-bed appears many times in this film both to foreshadow the murder scene and to unsettle the viewer's point of view so that we cannot fix the characters' position, just as Langda makes it impossible for Omkara to contemplate Dolly as steadfast or faithful. Kesu, the Cassio character, seems mesmerised by the hypnotic movement of the *kamarbandh* as Langda swings it from side to side as he offers it to Kesu. In this sense the use of the moving bed and the rocking camera recall what Dan Juan Gil calls the 'asocial sexuality' of Orson Welles's *Othello*, brought out by that film through destabilising camera angles and shot/reverse shots that don't quite match (Gil 2005). Asocial sexuality fits particularly well for this film: gangsters are asocial in every sense, anti-social because they break up the social fabric of human relations. Organised crime disenchants objects and dehumanises people.

Iago

My final example takes us from tragedy to farce. Volfgango de Biasi's *Iago* (2009) transforms Shakespeare's tragedy of love into a teen comedy. Set among architecture students in a prestigious college in a 1980s-inflected twenty-first century, the film presents Iago as a hard-working and intelligent orphan who supports his aged aunt, Desdemona as the privileged princess-daughter of the Rector of the university, and Otello as a former childhood playmate of Desdemona, returned after many years, the spoiled, lazy scion of a rich black donor who is Brabantio's close friend. This Cassio is indeed 'a fellow almost damn'd in a fair wife' (I.i.22): he collects women and their pictures, snapping Polaroids of his lovers that he annotates with their telephone numbers and sexual idiosyncrasies and files away in an index-card box.

Iago is a shallow movie: it depends on a hip soundtrack, shiny costumes and sexual innuendo for its claims to popularity. This is Shakespeare mediated through Baz Luhrmann, complete with *Romeo + Juliet*'s masquerade ball and the extravagantly choreographed group dancing of *Moulin Rouge* (1996 and 2001). Nonetheless I found it helpful in thinking about how we understand agency, or rather what Bennett called 'intensities', surrounding action in this play. *Iago* distributes the handkerchief's function among several items: a Polaroid snapshot of Desdemona and Cassio kissing, taken by Iago in a seemingly more innocent time but later used by him to fuel Otello's jealousy; a lace handkerchief left by Desdemona in the ladies' room, stolen by Emilia and planted by Iago in Cassio's bed; and the compact disc containing the architecture group's work, which Iago replaces with a broken one in order to frame Cassio as a drunkard and a slacker. All these objects share the blame, as it were, for Otello's gulling.

Unlike in Shakespeare (or in the first two films I discussed), in this film the bed is not the only place where one might have sex. We see

Otello and Desdemona embracing in an old library; an implied threesome among Iago, Cassio and Bianca in the architectural studio; and Rodrigo, a flamboyant cross-dresser in fabulous ball gown, wig and make-up, fondling the bare legs of the dancing crowd during the great set-piece masquerade ball at which Desdemona and Otello first kiss. Three scenes, however, feature a bed prominently. Brabantio, summoned profanely by Rodrigo (who is disguised in drag) and by Iago, interrupts a post-coital Desdemona and Otello; Desdemona defends herself with dignity, as in Shakespeare's play. Iago plants the handkerchief in Cassio's bed, under the pillow, where Cassio, upon finding it, cannot imagine which of his many conquests might have left it there.

Just as in Shakespeare's *Othello*, the bed appears prominently in the final scene to connote marital union. In this version, however, Otello is long vanquished and the consummation devoutly to be wished emerges between Desdemona and Iago. The sequence begins with Emilia castigating Desdemona for Iago's behaviour, after which a penitent Desdemona is seen approaching Iago's house, a statue of the Virgin Mary in the background behind her. Iago's aunt at first refuses to let Desdemona in, but ultimately relents; Desdemona sits on Iago's bed, a four-poster with red curtains.

As Iago regards Desdemona in surprise, the film frames the bed as a kind of discovery space between the bed-curtains. Desdemona and Iago exchange glances – viewers can see Iago framed by the curtains with a cross in the background – and Desdemona scolds him, removes her leather jacket to reveal that she is wearing a transparent blouse that displays her breasts, walks over to him by the window, kisses him aggressively, and the screen floods with red light. The film ends with the lovers in a clinch, the bed in the background, after which a pair of red curtains close scene, film and play.

Conclusion

Bennett writes, in discussing the energy traders that the press and many consumers considered responsible for the great Northeastern blackout of 2003,

> Autonomy and strong responsibility seem to me to be empirically false, and thus their invocation seems tinged with injustice. In emphasizing the ensemble nature of action and the interconnections between persons and things, a theory of vibrant matter presents individuals as simply incapable of bearing *full responsibility* for their effects. (Bennett 2010: 37; italics mine)

Critics note, however, that the *victims* of the blackout (like the victims of so-called rogue traders during the financial crisis in 2008) bore the *full responsibility* of the consequences. Bennett acknowledges that there is something satisfying, humanly speaking, in attributing blame to 'deregulation and corporate greed', but suggests that a modified ethical response for individual human beings under such circumstances – in which assemblages, rather than individual human entities, distribute both agency and blame – must be to ask oneself about 'the assemblages in which one finds oneself participating . . . Do I attempt to extricate myself from assemblages whose trajectory is likely to do harm?' (2010: 37). Anticipating accusations of quietism, she makes the case for 'moral outrage' under certain circumstances but suggests that de-emphasising 'material agency' merely in order to condemn particular humans risks 'legitimat[ing] vengeance and elevat[ing] violence' over courses of political action (2010: 38).

Avoiding blame is very counter-intuitive to many who identify themselves as political progressives and to those who see themselves as conservatives in the tradition of populism. All of us on some level would love to find someone to blame for the market crash of 2008 (or for the current COVID-19 pandemic, so badly managed by the United States). Yet even as I resisted Bennett's notion of distributed blame among assemblages rather than humans, I thought of the success of Nelson Mandela's Truth and Reconciliation movement in the free South Africa. Resisting the urge to attribute blame to specific human beings in that instance indeed enabled the reconstruction of a more just and free and more unified polity. And peculiarly enough, a focus on material trappings and gloss and sheen in Volfgango di Biasi's teen-movie is what enables tragedy to become comedy. Instead of watching silently during the eavesdropping scene, Otello interrupts Cassio and Bianca and beats Cassio up in order to take the handkerchief back to Desdemona. Otello slaps Desdemona (this is a version of Shakespeare's IV.i), but then directs his anger against the scale model of the town piazza that his group was designing. He destroys the group project, but expresses no more violence towards Desdemona. Then follow a series of angry but non-violent confrontations: Cassio admonishes Iago, Iago censures Otello for shirking his work on the project, Desdemona reproaches Iago for his trickery, Iago rebukes Desdemona for abandoning him, Brabantio reprimands and expels Otello, Desdemona scolds and breaks up with Otello, Emilia castigates Desdemona for being a tease – in other words, a comic resolution requires that blame be quite thoroughly 'distributed' among various persons, situations and objects and that violence be deflected or diverted. Where Shakespeare's Othello, Desdemona,

Emilia and possibly even Iago end the play a tangled assemblage of bodies dead and partly living, *Iago*'s insouciant teens extricate themselves from assemblages that threaten to harm them, with no apparent ill-effects.³

Shakespeare's *Othello* has from its first performances been associated with the problem of blame and evil. Rymer famously and facetiously expressed his own 'vital materialism' in blaming the handkerchief for the tragedy. Readers as diverse as Samuel Taylor Coleridge (Coleridge 1835–36) and Agatha Christie (in her posthumously published novel *Curtain* [1975]) consider Iago the arch-engineer of the tragic plot. Feminist critics have long pointed out that whatever actions Iago takes do not justify Othello's murdering Desdemona, and that we cannot understand the play's outcome independently of race and sexuality (Loomba 1989). In performance, Othello and Iago vie for the role of tragic hero or anti-hero, to such an extent that in 1956 at the Old Vic John Neville and Richard Burton took turns playing each part.

Scholars have proposed various theories of Shakespearean tragedy over the years – tragedy of character (Bradley 1904); radical or decentred tragedy, in which the subject itself is deconstructed (Belsey 1985); tragedy born out of political struggle and the subordination of various kinds of human (Dollimore 2003); 'festive' or sacrificial tragedy (Liebler 1995). But perhaps Shakespearean tragedies are tragedies of entelechy and matter, vital matter. Tragedies of entelechy are Dionysian, in Nietzsche's sense – tragedies of becoming, of humans' inability to perceive objects becoming meaningful and agentic and of their becoming inert matter ('Desdemona dead!' [V.ii.332) from vibrant life ('Kill me tomorrow' [V.ii.100]) – and of the liminal, electron-cloudy space between the two.

Notes

1. See, for example, the special issue of *the minnesota review* edited by medievalist Andrew Cole, which includes essays that both critique and extend the object-oriented turn in medieval studies.
2. Diplomatic transcriptions of Folio and First Quarto texts of *Othello* come from the Internet Shakespeare Editions' facsimile reprints, available at <http://internetshakespeare.uvic.ca/Library/facsimile/overview/play/Oth.html> [accessed 6 November 2017].
3. Richard Burt points out in a personal communication that Shakespeare's play also concludes with a series of blame-ridden confrontations; notably, the epithet 'devil' is used by Othello of Iago, Iago of Emilia, and Emilia of Othello in V.ii. It is also used of Desdemona by Othello in IV.i, and this is the scene that *Iago* transforms into comedy. Instead of tolerating the

blow that Otello strikes, Desdemona leaves him and asserts her independence; instead of destroying Desdemona and then himself, Otello breaks the assembled city-model and then removes himself from the potentially harmful assemblage of Otello, Desdemona and Iago.

Bibliography

Belsey, Catherine (1985), *The Subject of Tragedy*, London: Methuen.
Bennett, Jane (2010), *Vibrant Matter: A Political Ecology of Things*, Durham, NC: Duke University Press.
Bennett, Jane (2012), 'Powers of the Hoard', in Jeffrey Jerome Cohen (ed.), *Animal, Vegetable, Mineral: Ethics and Objects*, Washington, DC: Oliphaunt Books, pp. 237–69.
Bradley, A. C. (1904), *Shakespearean Tragedy* (repr., 2005), Project Gutenberg, <http://www.gutenberg.org/files/16966/16966-h/16966-h.htm> [accessed 24 August 2017].
Burnett, Mark Thornton (2010), 'All That Remains of the Shakespeare Play in Indian Film', in Yong Li Lan and Dennis Kennedy (eds), *Shakespeare in Asia: Contemporary Performance*, Cambridge: Cambridge University Press, pp. 73–108.
Christie, Agatha (1975), *Curtain*, London: Collins Crime Club.
Cole, Andrew (ed.) (2013), 'The Medieval Turn in Theory', *the minnesota review*, 80:3, 80–2.
Coleridge, Samuel Taylor (1835–36), *Table Talk* (repr., 2010), Google Books [accessed 24 August 2017].
Coole, Diana, and Samantha Frost (2010), 'Introducing the New Materialisms', in Diana Coole (ed.), *New Materialisms: Ontology, Agency, and Politics*, Durham, NC: Duke University Press, pp. 1–46.
Dollimore, Jonathan (2003 [1984]), *Radical Tragedy*, Durham, NC: Duke University Press.
Gil, Dan Juan (2005), 'Avant-garde Technique and the Visual Grammar of Sexuality in Orson Welles's Shakespeare Films', *Borrowers and Lenders: The Journal of Shakespeare and Appropriation*, 1:2, <http://www.borrowers.uga.edu/781447/show> [accessed 16 November 2017].
Gratton, Peter (2010), 'Vibrant Matters: An Interview with Jane Bennett', *Philosophy in a Time of Error*, <http://philosophyinatimeoferror.com/2010/04/22/vibrant-matters-an-interview-with-jane-bennett/> [accessed 3 June 2014].
Harris, Jonathan Gil (2009), *Shakespeare and Literary Theory*, Oxford: Oxford University Press.
Henderson, Diana (2016), 'Magic in the Chains: *Othello*, *Omkara*, and the Materiality of Gender across Time and Media', in Valerie Traub (ed.), *The Oxford Handbook of Shakespeare and Embodiment: Gender, Sexuality, and Race*, Oxford: Oxford University Press, pp. 673–93.

Joubin, Alexa Alice [Alexa Huang] (2013), 'Global Shakespeares as Methodology', *Shakespeare*, 9:3, 273–90, DOI: http://dx.doi.org/10.1080/17450918.2013.8 27236 [accessed 24 August 2017].

Khan, Gulshan Ara (2012), 'Vital Materiality and Non-Human Agency: An Interview with Jane Bennett', in Gary Browning, Raia Prokhovnik and Maria Dimova-Cookson (eds), *Dialogues with Contemporary Political Theorists*, Basingstoke: Palgrave, pp. 42–57.

Liebler, Naomi (1995), *Shakespeare's Festive Tragedy*, London: Routledge.

Loomba, Ania (1989), *Gender, Race, Renaissance Drama*, Manchester: Manchester University Press.

Nietzsche, Friedrich (1994 [1872]), *The Birth of Tragedy: Out of the Spirit of Music*, trans. Shaun Whiteside, London: Penguin.

Rymer, Thomas (1970 [1693]), *A Short View of Tragedy*, Menston: Scolar Press.

Shakespeare, William (2017), *Othello*, ed. Barbara Mowat, Paul Werstine, Michael Poston and Rebecca Niles, Folger Shakespeare Library, <www.folgerdigitaltexts.org> [accessed 2 August 2017].

Stratford, Bruce (2015), 'British Film Institute Programmer Reflects on "Great Disruptor"', WellesNet, British Film Institute, <http://www.wellesnet.com/british-film-institute-programmer-reflects-on-great-disruptor/> [accessed 10 October 2017].

Trivedi, Poonam (2007), '*Filmi* Shakespeare', *Literature Film Quarterly*, 35:2, 148–58.

2

The Collectible Ofelia: Object-Oriented Feminisms and the Un-Human Corpus of Q1's Dispensaniac

Molly Seremet

In Jeff Brown's 1964 picture book *Flat Stanley*, we encounter Stanley Lambchop, a little boy who falls asleep under his bulletin board and wakes up in the morning having been compressed under its weight. Stanley's predicament is further compounded by the heavy press of the pictures, messages and maps that Stanley and his brother had pinned to the board. Fortunately, Stanley survives (this is a children's book after all and not a revenge tragedy), but his compaction by souvenir renders him four feet tall, about a foot wide, and half an inch thick. Instead of mourning Stanley's altered state, his family takes pleasure in his reduced circumstances, as he is now the right size to fold conveniently inside an envelope and mail to friends in far-flung places. Shrinking Stanley's proportions allows him to have a world of adventures for the price of an LBJ-era stamp (a nickel, if you are curious). In the space of Stanley's envelope, our flat friend ceases being brother, son and child and instead emerges as a souvenir of his prior self for both himself and those who encounter him on his postage-paid travels, a real-time archival trace of a formerly real boy. At the risk of stretching Brown's metaphor too far, I believe we can apply this flattened logic to a reading of Ofelia within *Hamlet*'s First Quarto,[1] itself a trash(ed)-compacted variant of a canonical story; and further, we can consider that Ofelia's human presence in that text is tamped down at every turn under the weight of the objects she carries.

Rather than folding herself neatly into an envelope like Stanley, however, Ofelia opts instead to strew traces of herself throughout Q1's landscape, a collectible and tradable *memento vivere* of the life she is actively unmaking. The textual topography of *Hamlet* is littered with a host of objectified references to the human, including sallied/sullied/solid flesh, pieces of work masquerading as men, not to mention a quintessence of dust. In Hamlet's rendering, these images conjure a desiccated or dissected corpse, abandoned by the human who can no longer bear to exist within the body's material weight. Hamlet's grief eats at him and his language performs a kind of auto-cannibalism in turn, unmaking his flesh to free his spirit. In contrast, Ofelia offers a new paradigm through the objects she physically carries throughout the play's terrain, particularly because of their close association with her corporeal body and the tangible residues with which she imbues them. Hamlet wishes to transcend mortality while Ofelia reworks the world in her own image through her influence over the objects she accumulates, repurposes and inhabits. Ofelia's remembrances, flowers, songs and even the liminal space of her grave serve as markers throughout Q1 for where her humanness will no longer be, but, unlike Hamlet's distressed metaphors of disappearance, Ofelia's objects allow for the possibility of magnification through the afterlife of an alternate and self-made prosthetic body that surpasses the bounds of the human.

While the objects affiliated with Ofelia are largely organic in nature, we might think of them as signifying a kind of cyborg turn because of the deliberate way Ofelia transfers her human subjectivity to them before her death. Theorist Jennifer Parker-Starbuck invites a reading of objects like this as subject technologies, noting that 'a subject technology emerges when what has previously been considered solely tool, prosthetic extension of the body, or system begins to claim concepts of agency. Subject technology carries its own weight on stage' (2011: 40–1). In these terms, objects need not be digital or cybernetic in order to figure as cyborgs. Rather, these objects become cyborged by enmeshment with human systems in order to take on life onstage, and in so doing, embody agency through this symbiotic relationship. In the case of Q1, Ofelia marks her objects through intimate association with her body and, by this conflation, the objects themselves transcend their organic origins and become subject technologies. This invites the potential to consider Ofelia in terms of the cyborg as she performs acts of deliberate and defiant metonymy.

Consider, for example, that Ofelia's lute is both a complete object in its own right and a repository for sensorial and tactile memories of Ofelia herself. The instrument bears tangible residues of Ofelia's body through the touch of her fingers and serves as a memorial marker for more ephemeral aspects of her presence such as her voice. Q1's lute, therefore, is both musical instrument and metonymic mnemonic device, encapsulating the memory of the musician within the material reality of the musical machine.

By carrying her lute onstage, then, Ofelia performs a kind of mimetic mitosis, dividing herself before our eyes, collapsing the distance between object and subject inside the frame of the lute and the songs in her voice that it will always carry. In performance, the physical presence of the lute conjures Ofelia as she was in the same frame with Ofelia as she is, allowing an additional aggregate Ofelia to emerge in the margins. Through adopting analogue objects as technological prostheses for her own body, Ofelia allows herself to linger long after she disappears from the play's action in the form she deliberately imagines for herself, performing agency through the residues grafted on to the remembrances she creates.

In this conception of the cyborg, then, Ofelia becomes both Frankenstein and the oft-eponymous monster in the same breath, fragmenting her body in order to continue to live. To carry the Frankenstein metaphor further, it is also worth noting that the drive to become cyborg is a processual act, in which Ofelia engages in stages throughout Q1's terrain. Parker-Starbuck envisions this kind of cyborg becoming as a productive tension between the object and the abject in performance. As she explains:

> Abject and object bodies are both bodies at a distance, bodies outside our 'selves'. These bodies triangulate around the 'subject' as those who are refused, rejected, desired, critiqued, or negotiated with. These are the bodies that reiterate who we think we are and where we fit in the world. The abject and the object are bodies in play with the subject, reliant upon context and usage to differentiate between them. This interplay is purposefully structured as a triangulation to allow for the malleability of bodily contexts within fragmented cyborgean systems. (2011: 95)

Considering Ofelia in these terms asks us to understand that the objects she collects and distributes are not disposable trinkets but deliberate and forceful markers of her presence within a play that wants to unmake her at every turn. While Ofelia winds up on the fringes of Hamlet's territory, the objects she strews become landmines throughout the landscape, usefully threatening to erupt at any moment. I propose, therefore, that we might consider Ofelia the imaginary opposite of a kleptomaniac: a dispensaniac as it were, dispensing technological objects that witness her subjectivity and attempt to heal her trauma through the distribution of markers of embodied suffering. Ofelia's dispensania, then, performs the cyborg triangulation that Parker-Starbuck envisions. Ofelia transfers markers and traces of her material body into tangible physical objects that bear witness to her abjection from the play's narrative. Through this triangulated and purposeful act, Ofelia contours an alternate object-body for herself that both memorialises her life and ensures her permanent presence even after the somatic performance of her death.

This chapter will grapple with the collectible Ofelia in terms of Katherine Behar's conception of object-oriented feminism (OOF), Jennifer Parker-Starbuck's work on cyborg theatre, and Rosi Braidotti's vision of the posthuman subject in object-oriented terms. As Behar queries, 'in this new terrain, what does it mean for feminists to objectify someone who is already an object? What is the transformative potential for a feminist politics that assumes no transformation, when all things are and remain objects?' (2016: 9). To open this chapter, I will first ground the First Quarto of *Hamlet* in the realm of cyborg theatre through a close reading of Ofelia's objects as subject technologies throughout Shakespeare's 1603 text. I will then work from this foundation to define Ofelia as a potential cyborg, focusing particularly on her function as somatic witness throughout the early scenes of Q1, and the curious paradox of Ofelia's presence as both human and object throughout the play's landscape. Finally, I will unpack the self-imposed quality of Ofelia's objectification as an agential act, tracing the souvenirs or markers of her physical presence within the scope of Q1's larger dramaturgy. In doing so, I will argue for the performative potential that lies in a realisation of Ofelia that treats her not as a tragic document in feminine-coded madness but rather as a cyborg construction primed to disrupt, destabilise and dematerialise the body of Q1 through the permanence of the (body) parts that she purposely leaves behind. Thus, this chapter will argue that Ofelia's dispensania and entanglement with objects invites a posthuman and cyborg intervention into *Hamlet*'s landscape through the figure of an agential Ofelia who curates her own afterlife.

The Thingified Good of the Bad Quarto

Ofelia's collection of objects becomes the memorial artefact that other characters must deal with when handling Ofelia before and after her death. Through their intimate association with Ofelia's body and the possessiveness she performs towards her collection, these objects surpass their obvious function as stage properties and instead become synecdoche for Ofelia herself. Andrew Sofer illuminates a prop's potential for this type of double life by noting that 'a prop takes on a life of its own, we might say, when it refuses to act *proppily*. By refusing to prop up the drama, the object capsizes audience expectation' (2008: 28). In Q1, the stage directions dictate that Ofelia carries her remembrances into the gallery, but the text stops short of pinpointing what precise form these tokens must take. This suggests that the physical materiality of the objects Hamlet has given to Ofelia is inconsequential; rather, it is essential that we understand that the objects, in whatever form they might take, are prosthetic representations of Ofelia's heart. In performance terms, this intimacy often emerges through blocking choices that have Ofelia remove a packet of letters from her bodice, for example, so that the artefacts she produces enact an unspoken mingling of Hamlet's handwritten text with traces of her own perfume. To borrow Sofer's term, Q1 actively resists love tokens that perform proppily and instead demands objects on to which Ofelia can project herself. In this way, the collection of objects that Q1 Ofelia curates represents not the inconsequential clutter of a chaotic mind, but rather the deliberate intimacy of a woman determined to be remembered in the aggregate.

Because my work on Ofelia hinges on the objects she carries in literal and figurative terms, the choice of the First Quarto text is especially significant. Here, I draw on Paul Menzer's contention that 'both textual evidence and stage directions show Q1 eliminating wherever possible the explicit need for cumbersome stage properties' (2008: 168). Menzer's logic applies beautifully to every facet of Q1 except for those portions that pertain to Ofelia, however. In point of fact, Ofelia's Q1 variant is more encumbered by physical possessions than her Q2 and Folio sisters, as dictated by the stage directions in the 1603 text. In the Q1 version of the mad scene, for example, Ofelia appears 'playing on a lute, and her hair down' (sc. 13, SD),[2] accompanying herself as she sings dirty songs in front of the King and Gertred. Though she exits the stage briefly after her second song, the stage direction that follows her re-entry indicates that she appears 'as before' (sc. 13, SD). The vagueness of this stage direction affords the opportunity to consider that Ofelia still has her lute in hand while she is also grappling with the flowers and herbs she distributes to the horrified court. Both she and Hamlet have their hands full of books in the nunnery sequence as well. The King observes that Hamlet strolls into the gallery 'poring upon a book' (sc. 7, 110), which causes Corambis to order Ofelia to perform in mirror image and 'read you on this book / and walk aloof' (sc. 7, 113–14). Ofelia also tries to return Hamlet's love tokens in this scene as well, suggesting that she has been carrying them somewhere on her person since the scene's beginning. Thus, Q1 sandwiches Hamlet and Ofelia's emotionally charged fight between the pages of a pair of books and an assortment of other nebulous objects that were at one time close to Ofelia, bearing the traces of her corporeality in addition to their innate materiality. An abundance of tactile objects weighs down this scene and continually calls attention to the prominence of things that stand between

Hamlet and Ofelia. While Q1 may otherwise strive to pare down its object terrain, its manifestation of Ofelia struggles under the added weight of additional objects that augment her body throughout the text.

In tandem with the objects Ofelia selects for herself, she also becomes intertwined with the objects of others. Corambis documents this proclivity of his daughter's when he orders her to 'receive none of [Hamlet's] letters, / For lovers' lines are snares to entrap the heart. / Refuse his tokens: both of them are keys to unlock Chastity unto Desire' (sc. 3, 65–8). In this instance of fatherly caution, Corambis reveals his understanding of Ofelia's tendency to collect trinkets and treasures, signalling a recognition of what such touchstones conjure in his daughter's imagination. Through the collection of mementos that Ofelia acquires and archives, she becomes an amalgamation of memorial traces. This paradigm distinguishes Ofelia's relationship with objects from that of other characters in the play, particularly with regard to Gertred. After all, Hamlet must compel Gertred to look upon the portrait of her deceased husband and to close-read her new husband's flaws in relief, almost as if she is seeing them for the first time. In contrast, Ofelia must be ordered away from her souvenirs and the psychic weight they carry. These tactile objects entwine with her physical body, becoming organs of memory and heightening an audience's awareness of her somatic presence as we try to make meaning out of the discrete parts she dissects and lays bare. Through these archival acts, Ofelia supplements her lived reality with souvenirs of a life she has lost or perhaps never quite managed to grasp. This multiple subjectivity complicates attempts to interpret Ofelia as simply a lost little girl wandering the periphery of Hamlet's story.

We might approach Ofelia's subjectivity, then, in posthuman terms. As theorist Rosi Braidotti suggests, 'another name for subjectivity, according to Guattari, is autopoetic subjectivation, or self-styling and it accounts for both living organisms, humans as self-organising systems, and also for inorganic matter, the machines' (2013: 94). Braidotti indicates that these acts of self-genesis run on parallel tracks within the lived experience of humans and objects and, when considering Ofelia's archive, suggests a reading of the character that considers that her construction of self is so entwined with her inscribed objects that she has no self without her collection. After all, as de Grazia reminds us, 'as Hamlet wipes his tables clean when he wants to forget what he has learned, so Ophelia disperses her nosegay' (2007: 117). In this case, Ofelia gives away her poesies not to forget about the twinned losses of her father and her lover, but rather to afford herself the permission to forget to live, shuffling off the demands of subjectivity through the release of the final objects of her affection.

OOOfelia

What, then, are we to make of the autopoetic drive Ofelia manifests towards and through objects in Shakespeare's First Quarto? Rather than representing a glitch in *Hamlet*'s matrix, what if these object-oriented anomalies afford a deliberate opportunity to generatively change Ofelia's function within the structure of the play and to fashion an Ofelia in performance that leverages the agency this autopoiesis offers? What if Ofelia's presence in the play could be interpreted not as an emblem of leaky femininity but rather as an assemblage, an engineered autopoetic self-styling of the human through the language of the object-machine? Valerie Traub provides a model for this type of thought experiment in her work on the figural body and cartography. She explains that, on early maps, 'human figures were relegated to a framing function whose formal status as "marginalia" belies their importance to the map's totality. From the margins, the body continues to speak to and with the geography depicted within' (Traub 2000: 77). The visual and spatial language of mapmaking is, of course, not identical to the process of tracing the object trail that Ofelia scatters throughout Q1, but the notion of marginalia provides a useful metaphor for thinking through the ways Ofelia archives her subjectivity in real time on the margins of the objects she collects and distributes. To continue Traub's metaphor, marginalia on a map can be ignored or glossed over by a reader hyper-focused only on the map's official content, but the mere survival of the paratextual matter authorises its right to be considered part of the map's body. Within the terrain of Q1 *Hamlet*, then, Ofelia's strategies of self-curation leave markers that re-form her body in the imagination of other characters and the audience even when she is not physically present, allowing her 'document in madness' (sc. 13, 81) to stand even after her bodily death, a tension that reaches its zenith within the objectified space of Ofelia's grave.

To frame Ofelia in terms of the machine, we might envision her as a self-made cyborg. In these terms, Ofelia's dispensania paradoxically figures as an additive process of becoming-machine rather than a reductive dissolution in obedience to Hamlet/*Hamlet*'s narrative. It is important to note that, in this construction, cyborg refers not to hyper-technological or digital mediation; in fact, as Chris Hables Gray defines it, 'cyborgs do not have to be part human, for any organism/system that mixes the evolved and the made, the living and the inanimate, is technically a cyborg' (2001: 2). Just as Sofer troubles the accepted inanimate life of stage properties, Gray problematises an easy distinction between organic and inorganic definitions of agency, using the figuration of the cyborg to encapsulate the life between that emerges in the margins. Ofelia's intimate enmeshment with objects determines the manner in which she experiences the world around her. In reporting her perception of Hamlet's madness to her father, for example, Ofelia reads the markers of his mental distress through the distortion she perceives in Hamlet's relationship with his own garments. She pinpoints 'his garters lagging down, his shoes untied' and then shifts the paradigm to view herself through the dehumanising distance of Hamlet's gaze, as he 'fixed his eyes so steadfast on my face / As if they had vowed this is their latest object' (sc. 6, 47–8). Ofelia offers a reading of Hamlet's human condition that aggregates his present behaviour with the traces his actions have left on his own garments and then renders herself in objectified terms in the same frame. In this moment of crisis, Ofelia collapses the distance between the ineffability of human emotion and the traces it leaves on the material world. This composite act allows Ofelia to process an understanding of human emotion through analysis of non-human component parts, and in so doing, bears traces of the cyborg. As Parker-Starbuck explains, 'the cyborg may be a site through which to test out alternative identities, alternative bodies, and fluid possibilities of mergings' (2011: 37) and, for Ofelia, this alterity offers a threshold to disrupt the world around her.

Ofelia's interconnectedness with objects opens up a further cyborg channel of investigation and provides useful language for understanding how contact with Ofelia changes the valences of her souvenirs and their capacity to disrupt the narrative. In object-oriented language, after all, physical materials gain resonance through the degree of intimate entanglement they experience with humans. For this reason, souvenirs are not just markers of destinations we have seen or events we have attended, but touchstones for the remembrance of sensory details of our human participation in the moments that the souvenir memorialises. In her work on the peculiar subjectivity of souvenirs, Jennifer González notes that:

> One of the more common traps of memory is the object made or chosen specifically for this purpose – the souvenir. As the material site of memory, it creates a bond between the concrete particularity of the present and the seemingly intangible past. It does not, however, *unexpectedly* trigger memories from the depth of the past of the unconscious. Rather, it is intended from its very conception, and in some cases fabrication, to become the token for a particular individual or group. (1995: 140)

To extrapolate from González, we might say that souvenirs have their own inner psychic life, exerting agency over the human who collects them. Just as Ofelia interprets Hamlet's distress through the distortions he makes to his garments, Ofelia manipulates the objects she comes in contact with in order to call attention to her own emotions and experiences of trauma. The flowers Ofelia gathers, distributes and eventually sinks into in death become entwined with the tokens and mementos she uses to remember (and reassemble) the shape of Hamlet's dissipated love.

Ofelia's relationship to souvenirs comes full circle in her last living onstage act. In scene 13, Ofelia enters the court singing a bawdy song, the crux of which rests in recognising a man through his outward appearance, 'by his cockle hat, and his staff, / And his sandal shoon' (17–18). These markers harken back to the close-reading Ofelia has performed on Hamlet's appearance; the clothes may not make the man, as the saying goes, but they do allow Ofelia to understand him. She leaves, only to return a few moments later, and, this time, her work is to distribute flowers and herbs, with instructions for their use: 'here is rue for you – you may call it herb-a-grace o'Sundays. Here's some for me too. You must wear your rue with a difference' (sc. 13, 76–8). When taken together, Ofelia's song about recognising a man by his assorted garments and her prescriptive distribution of various herbs become visual fragments of Ofelia's self-narrative, functioning in González's conception as 'prostheses of the mind' (González 1995: 133). When figured in this manner, Ofelia's props are iterative, carrying the trace of her physical body and serving as souvenirs intended to remember the person they memorialise. In this conception, 'objects are force-full – brimming with affect, productive of difference and generative of power' (Shaw and Meehan 2013: 220), and for Ofelia, the objects she curates are carefully selected to archive her own unmaking.

The multiplication of Ofelia's tangible objects and stage properties throughout Q1 also offers the potential to read Ofelia as deliberately fracturing her subjectivity into objects that she knows Hamlet, Leartes and Gertred will not be able to resist identifying inextricably with her body: the lute that conjures her voice, the flowers that remember the touch of her fingers, and Hamlet's uncertain love tokens carried on her person or perhaps next to her skin.[3] In affecting and transforming the objects she bears, Ofelia transfers her human agency into the bodies of the objects themselves. Braidotti frames this type of morbid transference in posthumanist terms, pointing out that 'self-styling one's death is an act of affirmation because it means cultivating an approach, a "style" of life that progressively and continuously fixes the modalities and the stage for the final act, leaving nothing un-attended' (2013: 135). To apply this reading to Ofelia as a cyborg, we might consider that, after Ofelia passes out her flowers, she commands, 'I pray, love, remember. And there's pansy for thoughts' (sc. 13, 79–80). Immediately, Leartes parrots her, exclaiming, 'A document in madness. Thoughts! Remembrance!' (sc. 13, 81). Ofelia has not died yet, but already Leartes commemorates her loss in the manner she has fashioned for herself, activated through the tangible press of rosemary in the palm of his hand. Though organic, flowers and herbs become memory machines in Ofelia's hands, surpassing their natural origins through deployment as subject technologies. Thus, a cyborg Ofelia performs a desire for object permanence, distributing repurposed talismans that will ensure that she cannot be forgotten and allowing her to live on in the memory of Q1 *Hamlet* even before she physically dies.

Because she imbues the objects she carries with this degree of force-full agency, Ofelia occupies a productive middle ground between the purely human and the purely object in Q1's terrain and, as such, she succeeds in remaking her human self in object or mechanical terms. Ofelia's use of flowers is especially significant as, paradoxically, the plants must die in order to serve her purposes. Though organic in nature, Ofelia's flowers are plucked and therefore in the process of dying from the moment she carries them into the court. This allows these organic objects to function more like man-made tools or machines wrought for Ofelia's purposes. Jennifer Parker-Starbuck unpacks this relationship between the human body and the machine that augments or performs in tandem with it, noting that 'the bodies and technologies in the formation of cyborg-subjectivity depend on each other and are often equal components on stage; however the bodies here are metaphorically, rather than literally, cyborg and thus the weight remains on the bodies, at least conceptually, within the performances' (2011: 64). While Parker-Starbuck's work focuses on mediated performance using digital technology and multimedia apparatuses, Ofelia brims with cyborg potential in theatrical practice because she ensures that the objects she collects and distributes function as prostheses of her physical body.

Harnessing this potential in performance invites a portrayal of Ofelia that foregrounds agency through the deliberate and self-fashioned manner in which she curates her own archive in preparation for her death. Ofelia is cyborged not because she is created in the image of the machine, but because the golem she assembles out of her own parts is intended to serve as her stand-in once she has willingly shuffled off this mortal coil. Ofelia gathers objects to herself and holds them physically long enough to charge them with the resonance of her own body and the weight of sensorial memory, before pressing those objects on to other characters who have no choice but to remember her through contact with them. This presents the opportunity to view Ofelia not as a flat and fixed portrait of a girl wronged, but rather as a woman harnessing every object in her grasp to mark her place within the play's narrative. This way of seeing Ofelia in terms of both object-oriented ontology and cyborg theatre imagines reclaiming Ofelia's narrative in terms of her own creation of self rather than as a result of the actions perpetrated upon her.

Perhaps this feminist engagement with object relations is a natural one. As Katherine Behar notes, 'the object world is precisely a world of exploitation, of things ready-at-hand to adopt Harman's Heideggerian terminology. This world of tools, there for the using, is the world to which women, people of color, and the poor have been assigned under patriarchy, colonialism, and capitalism throughout history' (2016: 7). This consignment is certainly true for Ofelia in the First Quarto, in which she serves as a silent witness to the exterior monologues and violent actions of the men in power without much opportunity to contradict those narratives through speech. Ofelia's connection with objects, however, prevents her from being a shrinking violet, continually asserting her presence and threatening to disrupt or overflow the boundaries that hem her in. It is this act of prosthetic virtuosity that renders Ofelia in terms of the cyborg, engaged in a constant process of self-reinvention through the multiple object components that weigh down her scenes throughout Q1.

Object-Oriented Feminisms

In order to understand Ofelia in terms of the object prostheses she carries, it is critical to note that the dramaturgical function of Ofelia in Q1 is one of somatic witnessing, a job description that necessarily requires a body but need not be a body encumbered by the weight of a fully fleshed-out human character. In fact, the play's text frequently marks Ofelia's presence by translating her into an un-human remnant; remember, for example, that she renders herself in thingified terms from Hamlet's vantage point, confessing that he 'fixed his eyes so steadfast on my face, as if they had vowed this is their latest object' (sc. 6, 45–6). By considering herself in terms of the non-human, Ofelia abnegates her own sense of subjectivity in order to see herself through Hamlet's eyes: the (female) thing that he has seized upon.

This linguistic turn to figure Ofelia as an object is not intended as a denial of her human agency; rather, in the parlance of object-oriented ontology, this shift in perception is one that gestures to the reality that, as a female character within the world of Q1 *Hamlet*, Ofelia already occupies a less privileged subject position than Hamlet because of her femaleness. An object-oriented Ofelia, however, holds agential potential to locate female subjectivity and affect within Q1. As Katherine Behar posits, 'object-oriented feminism turns the position of philosophy inside-out to study objects while being an object oneself' (2016: 3). Here, Behar suggests locating agency in the choice of embracing one's object placement and beginning to manipulate the surrounding world from that position, and, for Ofelia, this performance of auto-thingification can be read as an agential act. Further, we might additionally consider Jane Bennett's conception of thing-power, which 'gestures toward the strange ability of ordinary, man-made items to exceed their status as objects and to manifest traces of independence or aliveness, constituting the outside of our own experience' (2010: xvi). In this construction, Bennett illuminates the productive slipperiness between separating the human from the object, which gains particular relevance when considering a character such as Ofelia who constructs an object world in her own human image. This is not to say that Ofelia does not matter within the space of the First Quarto text; instead, by her intentional enmeshment with objects, Ofelia allows her subjectivity to multiply and cling to the play's narrative, affording her the opportunity to remain vital even after she dies.

To push this further with regard to object-oriented feminism, it is worth noting that Ofelia becomes a thing for Hamlet precisely at the moment when he is simultaneously confirming her basic humanity by measuring her pulse. As Ofelia explains, Hamlet encounters her and

> grips me by the wrist,
> And there he holds my pulse till, with a sigh,
> He doth unclasp his hold and parts away
> Silent, as is the mid-time of the night. (sc. 6, 47–9)

In Ofelia's estimation, Hamlet denies her humanity at the exact moment she reaches the zenith of embodiment. The beat of her heart, likely changing under his fingers in response to both his proximity and the tension of the moment, witnesses her humanity and affords Hamlet the opportunity to reject her as such. We might read this moment as confirmation of both Ofelia's cyborgness and also of Hamlet's desire to possess the aspects of Ofelia that are un-human. If, as C. Nadia Seremetakis suggests, 'there is a corporate communication between the body and things, the person and the world, which points to the perceptual construction of truth as the involuntary disclosure of meaning through the senses' (1994: 6), we can mark this exchange between Hamlet and Ofelia as the threshold of a posthuman (and cyborg) becoming. In object terms, this contradictory instance marks the moment when Ofelia begins to augment her humanness with physical objects, performing a desire for object permanence and a drive to replace her physical presence with tokens of herself. If becoming cyborg is a process, then this moment might be harnessed as Ofelia's deliberate cyborg turn. In that context, this act of auto-tokenisation is not an abnegation of self on Ofelia's part but an assertion of her right to be within the landscape of Q1, even through an augmented reality of her own cyborg fashioning. Ofelia's ability to harness this power of objects marks a turn away from fragile vital humanity and negative objectification and towards a durable thing-power.

Just as Hamlet uses the rhythm of Ofelia's heartbeat to affirm his own sense of humanness and not hers, Ofelia must bear witness to the cadence of Hamlet's words even as those words are translated through the medium of Corambis's voice. In Q1, Ofelia and Corambis enter together in scene 7, stranding Ofelia onstage as silent witness to her father's narration of the letter that Hamlet wrote, rendering Ofelia just as much an object as Hamlet's letter itself. In Ofelia's silence, we are asked to hear the text of Hamlet's letter and watch how those words impact Ofelia. Ofelia could certainly be a passive spectator in this moment, perhaps enveloped by the shame of her father ventriloquising her lover's voice. In performance, this choice might perpetrate further violence on the body of a woman too often seen only as tangential collateral damage. By framing Ofelia in terms of the cyborg, however, this moment might draw attention to the untenability of her position. If Corambis's words are the transparency, then Ofelia's body becomes the screen on which Hamlet's parroted words can be displayed. Here, as witnesses to Ofelia's exposure and embarrassment, her body becomes an objectified spectacle as both on and offstage audiences inevitably observe the doubling of Hamlet's words and Ofelia's embodied reality. This act of parental ventriloquism may provoke shame on Ofelia's part as well, magnifying the spectacle, as 'the silent and invisible effects of what might be termed the bodily insignificant may be among the most powerful of social operations' (Paster 1993: 5). In cyborg terms, this moment presents an opportunity to stage the object supplanting the figure of the human. While Ofelia is still a character, her silence and lack of textual agency render her a static figure in this scene and allow us to consider her relative flatness within Hamlet's grand tour.

Ofelia's choice to commodify herself is one with a self-preservation bent. As Jennifer González notes, 'no less integral to the subject, such physical extensions of the psyche – trophies, photographs, travel souvenirs, heirlooms, religious icons, gifts – take the form of autobiographical objects. These personal objects can be seen to form a stigmatic array of physical signs in a spatial representation of identity' (1995: 133). González terms this an autotopography. In consideration of Ofelia's placement within Q1 *Hamlet*, spatial terminology is particularly useful because it allows for corrective recalibration that places Ofelia at the centre of her own narrative rather than reducing her to a dilapidated marker on Hamlet's map. This claims Ofelia's auto-objectification as an agential act because it marks the play with her persistent presence. If, as Behar observes, '[object-oriented feminism] is a brand for oppositional cyborgs' (2016: 6), then Ofelia's engagement with objects can be a powerful corrective to the play's toxic masculinity and casualisation of trauma. Treating Ofelia's objects with care and importance allows Ofelia to emerge as a landmark in her own right in performance, curating an identity that surpasses the limitations of her marginalised role on the page.

Flower Mad Song

Perhaps Ofelia's most autotopographical intervention into Q1's landscape occurs as she brings snatches of naughty songs and remnants of the natural world into the court in scene 13. These objects signify a pastiche of the life Ofelia has cobbled together for herself after her father's murder, her brother's departure and her lover's defection. While Ofelia's songs are not tangible objects in the same way that flowers are, they do contain cyborg potential in a performance context. To return to Parker-Starbuck, consider that the performance of these songs requires a triangulation of the materiality of Ofelia's body through breath in concert with the object body of her lute and the abject body of rude lyrics she selects. Here, Ofelia uses the objects she collects as tools, magnified and animated by her own vibrant life-force. In this moment, Ofelia's presence destabilises, and it is worth considering that while this scene is often rendered as a display of madness, it may also represent the moment when Ofelia's projection of herself across multiple bodies coalesces into the aggregate body that finally arrests the court's full attention.

Ofelia embraces the abject even more fully by the distribution of flowers and herbs in this scene. She bursts into the court and engages her audience in a tour of the ecosystem outside the palace's walls:

Well, God-a-mercy, I ha' been gathering of flowers. Here, here is rue for you – you may call it herb-a-grace o'Sundays. Here's some for me too. You must wear your rue with a difference. There's a daisy. Here, love, there's rosemary for you for remembrance. I pray, love, remember. And there's pansy for thoughts. (sc. 13, 75–80)

Rebecca Laroche unpacks each of these floral elements in her work on the play's imagistic ecologies, noting that 'each of them, in some capacity, serves as an anodyne; many of them simply with their scent alone were thought to ease the pains of the head and heart, more generally of the "inward parts"' (2016: 216). In this construction, Ofelia distributes her floral souvenirs not as outward trappings of her madness but because they hold the potential to heal or ameliorate her symptoms. In this moment, Ofelia is not simply performing the affected symptoms of madness but turning the microscope on her ailing inward parts and showing the assembled court a potentially curative pathway for repair. Neither Ofelia nor the assembled court can see beneath her skin and yet, in this moment, Ofelia's internal maladies overrun their boundaries. As Paster comments, 'the silent and invisible effects of what might be termed the bodily insignificant may be among the most powerful of social operation' (1993: 5), and in this revealing moment, Ofelia's body threatens to destabilise the state. Rosemary, rue and pansy, then, might be employed as stand-ins for the internal ailments and defects of Ofelia's organs, forcing the assembled onlookers and the audience in performance to envision the gory materiality of the undiscovered country underneath Ofelia's skin.

Just as her songs are Frankensteined together from remembered snatches of inappropriate lyrics, her flowers constitute an alternate and potentially monstrous body. I invoke the spectre of the monstrous here because it gives voice to the larger anxieties that surround cyborg discourse, focused on the spectre of the female body. In tearing out flowers to show us her interior organs, Ofelia asks us to confront the ugliness of her condition head-on. This performative moment provides an opportunity to harness abjection and to use the monstrous to expose the pain Ofelia experiences in real time, and not merely imitate or eroticise the symptomatic behaviours that pain causes. Parker-Starbuck suggests that, in this application of abjection, 'notions of an abject bodies might in fact materialise in the disembodied absence of organic body in, for example, a puppet body, or in the non-human body of an animal, or in the problematically positioned and societally dis-abled body overlooked through disabling normative structures' (2011: 45). Seeing Ofelia from this perspective allows her ailing human body and its intentional doubling through dying flowers to fuse into a larger, monstrous construction that demands to be heard.

As Paster's research on early modern medical texts and treatises demonstrates, anatomical depictions of the early modern period focused on the humoral body, 'to represent bodies so porous, vulnerable, various, or even bizarre that they seem to be created out of alien substance. Peculiar objects – pins, hairballs, monsters, serpents – emerge from the humoral body' (Paster 1993: 13). Here, the body is an amalgamation of slippery organs, mesh skin, grotesque creatures and remnants of the material world that have been absorbed and subsumed into the figure of the human. It is not so off the mark, then, to suggest that perhaps Ofelia envisions her pansies, rue and rosemary as extensions of her interiority, plucking them out in order to examine them closely and seek curative help from anyone who will listen, or, alternatively, at least repulse them enough to catch their attention. Ofelia's body has become monstrous in its excessive humanity and femininity, and thus Ofelia turns to the object world to both understand and remedy the pain. While the choice of flowers is not perhaps a peculiar one, the repurposing of those emblems of femininity and beauty to represent disease, ailment and pain can further reinforce the creation of an Ofelia who insists on being seen as she is. Ofelia's choice to distribute these palliative elements gestures towards dissection and the subsequent donation of inward parts culled from her own body,[4] a manifestation of dispensania so drastic that Ofelia cannot recover. In this way, Shakespeare's Q1 invites a cyborg intervention, where suffering has a distributive quality, ripped from Ofelia's multiple bodies and pressed by her own hands, barely living, into service to heal herself and harm others.

Aside from representing an autotopographical incursion into Q1 *Hamlet*, this embrasure of the monstrous also invites comparison to another auto – autopsy. While often used in contemporary terms in criminological or medical contexts to refer to a process performed on a dead body, autopsy originates from the Latin *autopsia*, the act of seeing with one's own eyes. Therefore, an autopsy can be a self-fashioned process of seeing into oneself with clarity. In these terms, Ofelia's mad scene is less a performance of the outward trappings of female-bodied psychosis for an audience than a woman's personal and intimate attempt to see inside herself to diagnose where the short circuit is occurring. Object-oriented feminism in cyborg terms embraces an Ofelia who is both aware that she is the problem and actively engaged in a small act of repair. It is in Q1, after all, that Ofelia pinpoints Hamlet's declining mental state before anyone else. She keenly observes:

> O, young Prince Hamlet, the only flower of Denmark,
> He is bereft of all the wealth he had.
> The jewel that adorned his feature most
> Is filched and stol'n away: his wit's bereft him. (sc. 6, 38–41)

While both the Q2 and F versions of this scene give Ofelia's father the privilege of naming Hamlet's madness, Q1 affords this perspective to Ofelia herself as the culmination of the witness she has borne to Hamlet's strange behaviour. Ofelia recognises the signs of madness in Hamlet immediately and quickly diagnoses that all will not be well with him. We ought, then, to give her the benefit of the doubt in understanding and autopsying her own experience of madness, as she inventories, dissects and discerns the object-human body she knows so well.

Into the Grave

To my mind, the most interesting moment of Q1 happens within the play's most abject space: Ofelia's grave, as both Leartes and Hamlet jump in and grapple with the real body she has left behind. Carol Chillington Rutter homes in on this moment and asks, 'why is it that this playtext, when it finally arrives at the grave, lays out a *woman's* body for speculation?' (1998: 300). In consideration of Ofelia as autotopography, one potential answer comes to mind. If we embrace a reading of a mad Ofelia who uses flowers to perform a vivisected donation of her own internal organs in order to both fix her ailments and fix her memory in the minds of others, we might then imagine that this undignified scene in her grave represents the irresistible urge of others to collect her in totality, even when the parts in question have become inanimate. What remains, then, of Ofelia's human remains becomes trophies, souvenirs and tokens for Leartes and Hamlet to clutch. Much as Ofelia in life is a silent but generous somatic witness as Corambis reads her love letter, Ofelia in death continues to distribute her component parts to those who cannot leave her alone.

If we approach Ofelia as a cyborg and posthuman, we might consider the ways in which she has anticipated and perhaps even planned for this posthumous desire for her corpse, prefigured by her earlier handling of her own body and prosthetic objects. Kristeva explores the overwhelming abjection of the corpse, noting that 'if dung signifies the other side of the border, the place where I am not and which permits me to be, the corpse, the most sickening of wastes, is a border that has encroached upon everything' (1982: 3). In Q1 *Hamlet*, Ofelia traverses this border often in her choice of objects that commemorate a dead relationship, that trap the sound of her voice, and that enact a vivisection of her body to expose its most fragile inward parts. In her final act of defiance, Ofelia repeats these actions as Gertred reports:

> O my lord, the young Ofelia
> Having made a garland of sundry sorts of flowers,
> Sitting upon a willow by a brook,
> The envious sprig broke, into the brook she fell . . . (sc. 15, 40–3)

Ofelia weaves her flowers together and, as Gertred observes, returns to her old songs in the moments before the water pulls her under. This object-oriented repetition suggests that Ofelia's behaviour follows a pattern or plan that was perhaps interrupted within her incursion into court in scene 13. Ofelia's corpse bears the traces of the water that killed her as well as potentially the flowers woven by her fingers and the stale breath in her lungs that might belch out one more song. Her corpse is magnified through its association with her habitual objects and therefore becomes *more abject* because it conjures the actions of the living Ofelia at the boundary of her death. In this reading, the physical object of Ofelia's corpse becomes the subject technology to punish those who abused and neglected her, and also to ensure that something of the living Ofelia inhabits the space of her grave. There is a kind of agency in Ofelia converting her body into an object that can wound those who have wounded her, and, in cyborg terms, this intentional action completes the cyborg triangulation her remembrances, lute and poesies began: her abjected corpse is the object that Hamlet and Leartes must grapple with as a consolation prize for ignoring her human subjectivity and her objectified prostheses. For this moment to take on agential potential in performance, it must be harnessed in all its ugliness, so that Ofelia's final act of object transference is that of her lived-in human body that cannot be ignored, if only because it must be buried properly. After all, as Rutter notes in considering Ofelia's aborted burial rites, 'that is the point: the ugliness, the awkwardness, the unseemliness. Here is no sweetness, no flights of angels, no rest' (1998: 311). In death, Ofelia succeeds in achieving what she could not approach in life: object permanence through forcing those she loved to confront her human presence through the traces she left behind.

Flat Ofelia

Since his creation in 1964, Brown's Flat Stanley has found himself at the centre of an educational initiative to bring the world closer together through the Flat Stanley Project. Students make flat paper versions of themselves and mail them to friends and relatives. Recipients are asked to treat Stanley as a guest and show him a good time, while also recording details of his adventures. In the space of this chapter, I suggest that perhaps the Ofelia we meet in Q1 is a similarly flattened entity, abnegating her own humanity by origami-ing herself into matter that serves to mark her place within the play's plot. Ofelia achieves this by curating a collection of intimate and vibrant objects on to which she can transfer her human subjectivity. She then harnesses those objects to assert her subjectivity, even (and perhaps especially) through monstrous[5] and abjected means. Through her deployment of objects as both metonymic stand-ins for her human vitality and mnemonic souvenirs of her sensorial presence, Ofelia succeeds in creating a multiplicity of bodies that must be grappled with but cannot quite be subdued, subverted or even buried. This disruptive quality ripples with cyborg potentiality because it provides Ofelia with a strategy for resistance within the Q1 narrative, refusing easy suppression. In fact, as Rutter reminds us, '[Ofelia's] manhandled body is dropped. After this, the funeral is dropped, too. In Shakespeare's playtext, [Ofelia] never does get buried' (1998: 311). While Flat Stanley's success is predicated on a safe return home, a flat Ofelia achieves her zenith by insisting on remaining onstage in corporeal but unanimated form, persisting as a result.

A performance might indeed make the powerful choice to allow her body to remain unburied for the duration of the play, so that her embodied corpse can loom large over the play's conclusion, outside the palace's gates but never far from Hamlet's mind. This is particularly resonant in the dangerous and terrifying landscape of 2020 and, as Parker-Starbuck details, 'the cyborg form appears during times in need of balance, times of chaos and confusion . . . yet it also appears as a means of addressing disappearing, augmented, or controlled bodies in society' (2011: 34). Harnessing Ofelia's cyborg potential requires imagining that *her* death is the one that must be set right in order for Denmark to heal, and, in that way, it reframes Ofelia not as collateral damage but as a person who must be valued in order to repair the rottenness that blights the state. Embracing Ofelia's intentional flatness and cyborged strategies of living within an untenable Q1 imbues her with an agency and a legacy that literary history and performance tradition seem to want to forget. I argue for this reading because I believe it offers a reparative view of Ofelia as more than the character that Hamlet spurns, Corambis lectures, and the King and Gertred ignore. In tracing Ofelia's object trajectory through Q1, her residue clings and sticks at every juncture and presents the opportunity to realise a character that persists, even once she has died. In performative terms, this perspective opens up a cyborg channel by presenting an Ofelia who is intentionally *more than* human and therefore harder to shunt to the margins of Hamlet's play.

As a play, *Hamlet* is literally haunted by the spectre of a father, but in performance, it is infrequently interested in the lingering presence of Ofelia. If we allow for an Ofelia who is not just human, however, but an amalgamation of the object bodies she curates and the abject bodies she animates, a clearer portrait of a force-full woman emerges. Ofelia demands to be grappled with in all her infinite human, object, cyborg and abject variety. Ofelia's compulsion to give away prosthetic markers of her own body drives her and poses an irresistible challenge to her collectors to lust after and treasure her memorabilia . . . and of course, to collect it all,[6] even in death. While the Folio and Second Quarto texts of *Hamlet* flatten Ophelia under the weight of Hamlet's narrative, the First Quarto variant affords Ofelia the opportunity to wear her flatness with a difference.

Notes

1. As this chapter focuses particularly on the 1603 text of *Hamlet*, I will employ the First Quarto variant spelling of 'Ofelia' throughout.
2. All quotations from Q1 *Hamlet* drawn from Shakespeare 2006.
3. In pop culture terms, I am increasingly aware that this propensity aligns with J. K. Rowling's definition of a horcrux throughout the *Harry Potter* series, allowing Voldemort to fracture his soul into seven object-bound pieces to safeguard his own life. While the analogy is a useful one, it is ultimately limited, as the impact of a horcrux, for Rowling, is predicated on the covert and low-profile nature of the object itself. Ideally, no one is supposed to detect the traces Voldemort has left behind; that is, for his soul to remain protected, the objects that contain it must in no way attract wizard or muggle curiosity. In contrast, Ofelia seems to want desperately to be seen through the objects she carries, distributes and becomes, as if to ensure that she will not become a She-Who-Must-Not-Be-Named for those she leaves behind.
4. This common trope of the generous non-human plays out, of course, in *Star Wars Episode IV: A New Hope* (1977). C-3PO bravely faced the possible demise of his companion R2-D2, a fellow cyborg, with the following selfless offer: 'You must repair him! Sir, if any of my circuits or gears will help, I'll gladly donate them.' In a time of crisis, the android C-3PO

makes the ultimate human leap into the realm of empathy, offering the gears that constitute his cyborg lifeblood as a transplant to his friend.
5. In this context, 'monstrous' carries weight because it speaks both to Ofelia's use of objects to refashion her body and also to the way in which the prosthetic objects Ofelia selects call attention to her femaleness in performance. This linguistic turn nods to Barbara Creed's work in *The Monstrous-Feminine*, particularly with regard to the association of the female-monster with indications of messy bodily functions and the troubling challenge that association offers to the spectator in performance. In particular, Creed notes that the self-objectification the female-monstrous becomes ritualised in performance and, 'through ritual, the demarcation lines between the human and the non-human are drawn up anew and presumably made all the stronger for that process' (1993: 8).
6. I beg your indulgence in mixing my metaphors here but the reference to Pokémon is utterly irresistible in this context.

Bibliography

Behar, K. (ed.) (2016), *Object-Oriented Feminism*, Minneapolis: University of Minnesota Press.
Bennett, J. (2010), *Vibrant Matter: A Political Ecology of Things*, Durham, NC: Duke University Press.
Braidotti, R. (2013), *The Posthuman*, Cambridge: Polity.
Brown, J. (1964), *Flat Stanley*, New York: Harper and Row.
Creed, B. (1993), *The Monstrous-Feminine: Film, Feminism, Psychoanalysis*, New York: Routledge.
de Grazia, M. (2007), *Hamlet without Hamlet*, Cambridge: Cambridge University Press.
González, Jennifer A. (1995), 'Autotopographies', in G. Brahm and M. Driscoll (eds), *Prosthetic Territories: Politics and Hypertechnologies*, Boulder: Westview, pp. 133–50.
Gray, C. H. (2001), *Cyborg Citizen: Politics in the Posthuman Age*, New York: Routledge.
Kristeva, J. (1982), 'Approaching Abjection', in *Powers of Horror*, New York: Columbia University Press, pp. 1–31.
Laroche, R. (2016), 'Ophelia's Plants and the Death of Violets', in L. D. Bruckner and D. Brayton (eds), *Ecocritical Shakespeare*, London: Routledge, pp. 211–22.
Menzer, P. (2008), *The Hamlets: Cues, Qs, and Remembered Texts*, Newark: University of Delaware Press.
Parker-Starbuck, J. (2011), *Cyborg Theatre: Corporeal/Technological Intersections in Multimedia Performance*, Basingstoke: Palgrave Macmillan.
Paster, G. (1993), *The Body Embarrassed: Drama and the Disciplines of Shame in Early Modern England*, Ithaca: Cornell University Press.

Rutter, C. (1998), 'Snatched Bodies: Ophelia in the Grave', *Shakespeare Quarterly*, 49:3, 299–319.
Seremetakis, C. N. (1994), *The Senses Still: Perception and Memory as Material Culture in Modernity*, Chicago: University of Chicago Press.
Shakespeare, W. (2006), *Hamlet: The Texts of 1603 and 1623*, ed. A. Thompson and N. Taylor, London: Arden Shakespeare.
Shaw, I. G. R., and K. Meehan (2013), 'Force-Full: Power, Politics and Object-Oriented Philosophy', *Royal Geographic Society*, 45:2, 216–23.
Sofer, A. (2008), *The Stage Life of Props*, Ann Arbor: University of Michigan Press.
Traub, V. (2000), 'Mapping the Global Body', in P. Erickson and C. Hulse (eds), *Early Modern Visual Culture: Representation, Race, Empire in Renaissance England*, Philadelphia: University of Pennsylvania Press, pp. 44–97.

3

Bitcoin, Blockchains and the Bard

Robert Sawyer

In Shakespeare's play *Troilus and Cressida*, we encounter an oft-cited discussion about the pros and cons of the Trojan warrior Paris keeping the Greek woman Helen in his possession, despite the conflicts it will cause, including all-out war. When Hector claims, 'Brother, she is not worth the keeping', Troilus responds by trying to defend Paris's action, and by extension, his own, when he replies, 'What's aught but as 'tis valued?' (II.ii.50–2). Troilus's question recurs during the entire play, his statement ironically undermining his own desire for Cressida, while also complicating his motivation for going into battle, for gaining reputation and even for constancy in love. This question of 'value' will be central to this chapter; instead of applying it only to women and war, however, I want to use the term to consider the analogy between Shakespeare's cultural capital and the cryptocurrency, Bitcoin,[1] whose monetary 'value' varies wildly, not unlike Cressida's attraction towards Troilus. I will also explore the value of blockchain technology, central not only to the production of bitcoins, but also to its exploding use in everything from business enterprise to the digital humanities.

The intrigue about cryptocurrency itself has generated numerous headlines, particularly in 2019. On 22 May, for example, the *Guardian* website ran the following headline: 'Baltimore: government computers crippled by attack as hackers demand bitcoin. Attack on city computers prevents employees from sending email and knocked out bill pay websites, as hackers demand $76,000' (Sullivan 2019). While cyberhacking a computer system was not new, the demand for the ransom to be paid in bitcoins seems to have been a first in the United States. The hackers in the Baltimore attack kept the city locked out of basic technology for more than two weeks, and it was not completely restored until late summer. A central analogy for my argument, however, is that the city refused the demands of the hackers, because, according to hijacking experts, once a ransom is paid, the victims, in this case the city of Baltimore, have crossed a threshold from which they can rarely return. Both the Secret Service and the FBI warned the city about setting a dangerous precedent by capitulating to the ransomware hackers, and law enforcement officials pointed out that there was only a 50/50 chance that the required payment would restore all the lost data. Katryna Dow would agree about the perilous nature of crossing thresholds for which there might be no chance of return, including ransom hijackings. While her caution, which we will hear in a moment, refers to blockchain technology (without which bitcoins could not be produced), Dow's assertion fits the broader category of technology in general, and I would suggest that her clarion call might also apply to Shakespearean studies, as highlighted in her essay title 'Shakespeare's Blockchain': Dow counsels we proceed with caution as we move into this undiscovered digital country from which there may be no reversing course, a strikingly poignant warning about a point of no return that I consider in subjects as varied as bitcoins and blockchains, from Shakespeare platforms to the digital humanities, all of these also dominated by issues of currency and exchange (Dow 2017).

John Drakakis has recently considered a somewhat similar debate in most Marxist historiographies, where he argues that the notion of monetary 'reciprocity' and 'exchange' has been, unfortunately, overlooked. Such monetary exchanges, he adds, might become valuable metaphors in Shakespeare's plays for the 'disturbance of the relation between language and action, word and *object*' (Drakakis 2018: 1). This chapter extends Drakakis's notion to consider the relationship between Shakespeare's cultural capital, Bitcoin and blockchains; while Drakakis focused on the text itself when tracing connections between word and object, I examine the tension between Shakespeare's words and image, which, when attached to another external object, may produce a kind of value-added attraction; such exchange and reciprocity can also 'disturb' the material text, particularly when it is filtered through digitisation and produced by an algorithmic method.

By focusing on the 'decentralisation' of Bitcoin, blockchains and the Bard, the third section of this chapter connects Shakespeare's 'portability' with this new form of monetary exchange. I also show how the value of all three is determined by context, location and use, so that 'value' remains a subjective term. Whether the work of a Shakespeare scholar, the computations of a Bitcoin 'miner' or a blockchain transaction, the value of these variable objects remains, as stated in the Introduction to this volume, 'unsettled and unfettered, ever-moving in and out of human control as it intersects with other networks of meaning'.

The value of a single bitcoin fluctuates over time, as does any currency, but unlike the dollar, the pound sterling or the euro, bitcoins trade in a much more unpredictable way. During 2019, for example, one bitcoin was worth as little as $5,974 and as much as $11,000. This fairly new form of currency could only exist through the development of blockchains, also known as 'distributed ledger technology', which, most simply, eliminates any 'middleman' from a chain of transactions. These encrypted exchanges are not stored on a single computer because they are not usually controlled or owned by any one company or central authority; instead, blockchains are shared across a network, so all users can see them at any moment and in real time. Although open access Shakespeare sites come close to a sense of blockchains, in part because they elide any authoritative editorial interference, perhaps the best example in Shakespeare studies would be the Folger Library's link called 'The Collation', a point to which we will return.

Using Christy Desmet's essay 'Alien Shakespeares 2.0' as a guide, I show how bitcoins and blockchains resemble new media and digitised Shakespeares in three specific ways: they are unpredictable, they are unmediated, and they produce an uncoupling between traditional ways of seeing monetary currency on the one hand, and Shakespearean capital on the other. Borrowing from Ian Bogost's theories of alien phenomenology, Desmet also highlights the unpredictable results of connecting apparently dissimilar objects, specifically in her examination of popular culture forms such as amateur YouTube videos of Shakespeare's plays and digitised versions of Shakespeare archived in sacrosanct locations such as the Folger Library. The connections produced through such Shakespearean comparisons create results that are often as widely speculative as bitcoin trading. However, by connecting the two areas of monetary value and cultural value, we find a 'kinship', in Desmet's words, between 'apparently unrelated objects' (2017: 1).

A second resemblance appears in the unmediated access to both types of objects: bitcoins stored in virtual 'wallets' or Shakespeare bookmarked on our browsers. For instance, as Desmet notes, even phone apps such as 'Shakespeare in Bits' (note the echo of the 'bit' in Bitcoin) promise 'relatively unproblematic access to meaning in' Shakespeare's works (2017: 16); Bitcoin and blockchains also market their appeal by promoting unobstructed access with no oversight – by national banks, complex taxes or tariffs, or world trade organisations – a form of currency available across a global market. As Nassim Nicholas Taleb bluntly notes, 'Bitcoin has no owner', nor a central 'authority' to determine its fate; instead it is 'owned by the crowd, [and] its users' (2018: xiv); while I support his proclamation about the lack of authority, I'm slightly wary of his word 'crowd', slipping into a pejorative register.

Who owns or controls 'Shakespeare' today seems a parallel and pertinent question, particularly when considering Shakespearean research and course offerings in a university setting. While in the twentieth century, the Bard's role in higher education was often determined by gatekeepers in the form of curricula committees – sometimes with faculty input, but equally as often by university administrators – now open access to Shakespeare's work, in the form of phone applications, digitised sites, home-grown Shakespeare pages and even massive open online courses (MOOCs, which come closest to merging populist and higher education Shakespeare), has become the norm.

A third, and perhaps most striking, similarity shared by the topics under consideration is that they all use algorithmic formulations to produce new forms of knowledge. A posthumanist comparison of 'Shakespeare' and Bitcoin underscores the assertion that both human and non-human objects and subjects – 'actants' in Bruno Latour's words – can claim equal standing (Latour 2005: 46). This point seems particularly significant when considering the use of algorithms, which Kevin Slavin has claimed 'talk' primarily to one another and 'decide things' among themselves, giving them a 'good bit of agency' (Slavin 2011). The 'internal machinations of an algorithm go on with or without us humans', Desmet adds, and, not unlike digitised Shakespeares, bitcoins themselves reveal few or no 'material clues to the agent(s) that produced' them, nor can they be traced, as the hackers in Baltimore understood (Desmet 2017: 5, 9). Desmet's essay also works towards the goal of breaking down distinctions between highbrow Shakespeare and more popularised versions by dismantling allegedly vertical cultural valuations, and shows instead how numerous 'digital objects' cohere in the world of Shakespeare 2.0, creating a continuum between new media and digital humanities Shakespeare (Desmet 2017: 1).

But the question of the value of such representations in the world of Shakespeare studies can become complex. Traditionalists might argue that graphic novel versions of *King Lear*, for instance, undermine the authority of the Shakespearean text (which, as scholars know, has already proved resistant to any stable textual reading). Yet recent posthumanist critics have noted that the reproduction of multiple traditional texts, such as the Riverside Shakespeare, side-by-side with pop culture renderings with visual appeal on YouTube, or even home-grown virtual texts, produce overlapping recurrences that 'suggest a topological looping together that is at the same time an enmeshment of topics', a positive result for many critics. Moreover, this type of 'entanglement' of 'things held together or laid over one another in nearness and likeness' creates new representations and may ultimately produce new routes of understanding (Chow 2006: 1). Such new 'trappings' for Shakespeare, I would suggest, produce new ways of generating Shakespeare's texts instead of outdated 'suits of woe' (*Hamlet* I.ii.86).

The final section of this chapter considers more broadly the notion of 'digital humanities' in general, and the ways posthumanist Shakespeare – specifically in the form of 'variable objects' – both contributes to and clashes with entrenched ways of 'valuing' Shakespeare in the current university setting. Applying both Bruno Latour's and Graham Harman's theories about 'objects' and 'networks' to my survey, I trace both the history of object-related phenomena and then attempt to forecast the near future by speculating on their value in formalised studies of Shakespeare.

Bitcoin and Current Value

Here is a brief account of how Bitcoin mining began and how it works at present. The initial price of one bitcoin was set in 2009, the price determined by calculating the value of the electricity needed to produce a single bitcoin. As more users came on board, the formula became set: 'At preset intervals, an algorithm releases new bitcoins into the network: 50 every 10 minutes, with the pace halving in increments until around [the year] 2140'; this 'automated pace is meant to ensure regular growth of the monetary supply without interference by third parties, like a central bank, which can lead to hyperinflation' (Wallace 2011). From its inception in 2013, a bitcoin's value has ranged from a low of $65.53 in July of that year to its all-time high in 2020, when it was worth $34,843. During 2019, as noted earlier, one bitcoin was equivalent to as little as $5,974 and as much as $11,000.

Satoshi Nakamoto is credited as the founding father of cryptocurrency, a digital form of money which he hoped would become a form of global currency. While Nakamoto's goal might have been politically neutral (I'm cautious about speculating on that aspect), recent Bitcoin supporters embrace it as an important political tool. For example, one of Bitcoin's prominent, if not notorious, defenders is Steve Bannon, the former White House strategist who admitted recently that he owned a 'good stake' in Bitcoin, and also asserted that he is interested in working with entrepreneurs and countries that want to create their own cryptocurrencies. Yet Bannon states that he isn't interested in cryptocurrencies solely for their financial potential. Cryptocurrency is 'disruptive populism', proclaims Bannon, because 'it takes control back from central authorities'. It seemed fairly obvious to Bannon that all these nascent political movements were going to be beholden to whomever controlled the currency, and Bannon summed it up in his pithy manner: 'Control of the currency, is control of everything' (qtd in Bryan 2018). In terms of Shakespeare's value, we might add that until the twentieth century, publishers such as Arden and performing companies such as the RSC remained the central authorities who decided the 'value' of Shakespeare. Cryptocurrencies and blockchains, then, combine to create a public and uneditable system for recording transactions, and both developments are hailed by their evangelists as the future; those like Bannon see decentralised money as a key component of their political mission, a potentially revolutionary technological tool, not unlike, perhaps, the printing press during the early modern era.

Blockchains and Shakespeare's Cultural Currency

But what are some of the more specific connections between blockchains, Bitcoin and Shakespeare? One answer, of course, is the disaggregation of all the data behind these 'things', which may serve as a warning to currency investors on the one hand, and university-based Shakespeare scholars on the other. Katryna Dow, from whom we briefly heard at the opening of my essay and who is the CEO and Founder of Meeko, an Australian tech company that is trying to build an independent worldwide data platform for identification purposes, has already suggested some similarities, as well as significant differences, in her essay boldly entitled 'Shakespeare's Blockchain'.

'Think about the great works of Shakespeare', she begins, 'his ability to tell stories that translate across cultures and time, universally describing the human condition; charting both the beauty and pain of our existence' (Dow 2017). Sounding suspiciously like Harold Bloom, she then adds that the plays of Shakespeare transcend historical time and location because they capture the so-called human condition. Whatever that phrase may mean for Dow, it certainly avoids the material and political elements in the plays' textual origins or public performances. While we would surely resist her sweeping generalisation about Shakespeare's universality, her subsequent contrast with blockchain technology is informative, since they share with Shakespeare's works a common search for identity stability.

'Now think about a blockchain, permanent . . . fixed and immutable', she observes, 'designed to oppose vulnerability and uncertainty', praiseworthy adjectives that some traditional critics once applied to Shakespeare as well. Interestingly enough, newer XML and digital versions of Shakespeare share one important posthumanist feature: identity searches are enabled by both human and non-human sources. The blockchain ledgers that Dow mentions record 'transactions about things, records of things, agreements between things', not necessarily needing human oversight during these 'exchanges'. Some start-up cryptocurrency firms such as Everledger, in fact, focus 'on the identity and legitimacy of objects', not humans. Not unlike the relationships proposed by Graham Harman, who characterises these complicated assemblages of inanimate and animate beings as a 'thing' or object which 'cannot be entirely reduced either to the components of which it is made or to the effects that it has on other things' (2018: 43), the notion of identity is paramount.

For the ID2020 summit in May 2016, Dow co-authored a presentation about identity and blockchains, a paper intended to start a discussion about the ideal conditions for privacy and the (possible) use of blockchain technology for 'immutable' identity formation. While some sort of search for identity exists in Shakespeare's works, it is rarely fixed or immutable, for as Karen Raber reminds us, early modern characters 'discover they are enmeshed in an environmental web within which identity is constantly dissolved and dispersed' (2018: 125), which is just the opposite of what a blockchain identity proposes to create. In her paper, Dow admitted to grappling also with the notion of identity, particularly as related to transactions, and she attempted to show the value of proving that reliable records exist and that recording the record of the reliability is not overkill. In short, after the transaction data is encrypted, it is 'verified by other computers on the network' using an algorithmic formulation, and if 'there is a consensus among the majority of computers that the transaction is valid, a new block of data is added to the chain and shared by all on the network' (Underwood 2016: 15). In other words, this would result in finding a 'location without the map' or opening 'the safety deposit box without the combination' (Dow 2017). These transactions, with no human interference or error, then become 'secure, trusted, auditable, and immutable' (Underwood 2016: 15). Simply put, these 'transactions' are not only swifter, but also less costly to perform. This process also recalls N. Katherine Hayles's insight into human co-evolution, which suggests that technological possibility shapes humanity and vice versa in a perpetual process: 'As inhabitants of globally interconnected networks, we are joined in a dynamic co-evolutionary spiral with intelligent machines as well as the other biological species with whom we share the planet' (Hayles 2006: 164). More specifically, the reverse sometimes occurs with Shakespeare; humanity shapes Shakespeare to consume his worth.

While digital identity may not seem important to users in developed nations, in countries with less robust, not to mention secure, banking facilities, blockchain technology has the 'potential to change lives', according to Sarah Underwood. If this new form of 'secure robust digital identities around personal data succeeds, it might well become a storehouse for the world's two billion unbanked individuals' (Underwood 2016: 17), or we might posit, the millions of un-Shakespeared individuals, meaning those without personal access to the Bard's works. Steve Pannifer, a partner in Consult Hyperion, also considered 'the marriage of identity and blockchain' at CIS2016 in New Orleans. In his presentation, Pannifer outlined the key characteristics of a shared identity ledger, which would incorporate the following:

1. many writers
2. immutable history
3. degree of transparency
4. limited trust
5. transactional nature

If this five-point description suggests collaborative Shakespeare publications, such as the New Oxford Shakespeare, that is precisely my point about the Bard and blockchain technology. In this brave new world of the 'Internet of Things', people now demand direct communication through their devices, not through intermediaries. Yet the social distancing of readers from material objects such as a printed volume of the plays may cause concern. This notion of complex identity may also reshape Shakespeare in performance. Moreover, as Matthew Causey suggests, 'performing subjectivity in the spaces of technology' furthers 'the potential for exploring alternative models of identity' (2016: 428).

However, Dow's most salient point may be when she admits that, though it's a 'blockchain nirvana for now', there is a peril that we as Shakespeare scholars should also heed: 'as we leave the post-industrial world and lean into this knowledge and technology, it would be wise to think twice before we leap into solutions that may not allow us to engineer our way back' (Dow 2017). In other words, we should certainly be cautious about the 'freedom' of subjectivity offered up by digital Shakespeare, including websites dedicated to his works, applications devoted to his canon, and texts electronically reproduced, and we should remain vigilant about ways in which we might 'engineer our way back' to a more verifiable, materialist understanding of the Bard and his works.

The Folger Collation site mentioned earlier is now needed more than ever due to the Folger's remodelling, which will not completely conclude until 2022.[2] On the Collation site, people post comments and tweets and the transactions or exchanges become blocks of information that continually expand, sorted by topics authored by users. Moreover, the Folger site, unlike a central bank but exactly like a blockchain, is designed 'to oppose vulnerability and uncertainty' with the goal of 'absolute transparency'. The Collation, however, also uses a preset algorithm built into its own search engine, which decides where to send users based on the keywords they have typed into the search box, so that claiming 'absolute transparency' might not be exactly correct.

Other digital texts, which include Project Gutenberg, the Oxford Text Archive and, closer to our area of study, Early English Books Online (EEBO), are also continually expanding. Yet we must remember that they, too, are created with extensible markup language or XML, a 'coding which lies beneath the style sheet that organises and formats the plays' digital pages', so much so that 'the visual interface', according to Desmet, 'conceals the objects' "secrets", which lie hidden within the depths of the application' (2017: 7–8). In other words, there is an algorithm that shapes our search and the knowledge produced. Instead of possessing Prospero's books to thwart his power, we may need to disrupt his algorithmic formulations instead.

Shakespeare apps can also be examined using Desmet's rubric, and again, this somewhat hybrid space exacerbates the disaggregation of 'Shakespeare' even more so, perhaps, than digitised texts, by adding sounds such as voices and music to the experience, for instance, by layering on even more agents, sometimes coalescing, for example, in an app such as the Shakespeare in Bits *Macbeth*. The result of this combination of the otherworldly voices of the witches (borrowed from the Naxos audiobook version of *Macbeth*, with the famous Fiona Shaw as Lady Macbeth) seems to contrast with the rather cartoonish characters in the visual itself. Yet viewing this scene 'calls attention to the fragmented, even disjointed, nature' of the production as '[i]mages, sounds, stylized faces and moving letters come at us from all sides' (Desmet 2017: 12). Whether 'good or bad', only 'thinking makes it so' (*Hamlet* II.ii.246), as each of our minds' eyes, like a computer, receives the image; on our individual 'screens' – on desktops, tablets or smartphones – the perception of the image will inevitably vary for each viewer. But this also complicates the value of Shakespeare's cultural capital; while it may literally shrink in physical size on phones and iPads, it becomes much more mobile as it becomes more portable, again like bitcoins. Moreover, even if one disagrees with animated, pixelated or home-grown and re-enacted versions of the plays, the numerous variants of a tale create 'loops' of meaning, as we noted earlier via Rey Chow, who celebrates rather than dismisses various forms of 'tale telling'. In fact, the resultant entanglement, when objects or ideas are held together simultaneously, might seem similar to the way early modern collaborators composed plays, and the same way in which playhouse audiences understood them (Chow 2006: 1).

So it should come as no surprise that Big Data, such as computational codes to create bitcoins and blockchains, has also entered into the Shakespearean collaboration debate, particularly in books such as Hugh Craig and Arthur Kinney's *Shakespeare, Computers, and the Mystery of Authorship* (2009). It has most recently manifested itself in scholarly publications such as the New Oxford Shakespeare, particularly in relation to the *Henry VI* plays and to *Arden of Faversham*. Yet it's hard to decide if it is fair to judge such a unique author and wordsmith as Shakespeare by using an algorithmic search to 'detect a common lexicon of function words'; in short, Shakespeare is reduced to 'nothing more or less than varying webs of little words based on a mechanized counting of those words within segments of digitized text carved up by length rather than poetic or semantic consideration' (Desmet 2017: 8). In other words, large strings of prosaic quantity cannot be equated with the lyricism of rhythmical writing.

Even more recently, as one might expect, there has been a critical pushback against this use of computer algorithmic searches. In an essay simply entitled 'Against Attribution' in the winter 2018 issue of *Shakespeare Quarterly*, Ed Pechter claimed that this type of analysis had become 'lopsided', by which he means that 'figuring out what may have gone into Shakespeare's plays' has come 'at the expense of reflecting on what comes out of them' (2018: 230). While not part of Pechter's argument, the notion of expense and exchange in Shakespearean currency seems evident, as does his questioning of the 'value' of such computational methods at the Folger Library or at the Oxford University Press publishing house. Perhaps Dow's earlier words of caution about 'engineering our way back' to non-distance reading approaches in the form of material texts also hold true for Shakespeare studies.

The same is true for Shakespeare searches at the alleged opposite end of the cultural spectrum on YouTube, the 'paradigmatic new media platform for Shakespearean creators and consumers' (Desmet 2017: 3). The increase in Shakespearean projects located on the website is exploding in ways that seem like the sudden increase in the use of cybercurrency such as Bitcoin. To take just one Shakespeare example, when Peter Holland did research for an essay on 'Performing for the Web Community' in 2009, he found just ten sites devoted to Lego *Macbeths*. When Desmet did the same research for her paper in 2016, she found 21,700 sites (Desmet 2017: 2). When I did the research for this chapter in the summer of 2019, the number had jumped to over 25,000 (which may also lead, unfortunately, to Lego ads popping up continually on your computer screen).

Bits of Caution

The warning of Pandarus in the epilogue to *Troilus and Cressida* may be of some help here. Even if the audience cannot 'weep out at Pandar's fall', he suggests that they should not 'value' the play lightly, nor consider themselves above him morally. More specifically, he suspects that some 'galled goose of Winchester', meaning a prostitute, might 'hiss' at his acting, but he then cautions the audience to be wary, for such maladies might spread to them, culminating in a time when he will even 'bequeath his sexual diseases' to them as well (Epilogue 46, 53–8). Just as a venereal disease might hinder reproduction, so too, digitised/algorithmic Shakespeares might never reach their fruition of artistic flowering. Such feverish imagery and counsel should also guide any forays into this brave new world of bitcoins, blockchains and even the use of digitised versions of Shakespeare.

While such cryptocurrency trading remains questionable, as does the intent of Pandarus's speech, there is no doubt about the increasing role that algorithms play in our financial markets, our world and our lives. These mathematical equations, in fact, have taken on so much agency that they sometimes come into conflict with one another, locked in loops without human oversight. The best known of these is the Flash Crash on Wall Street in 2010, when during a 30-minute period the market lost over a trillion dollars, before it corrected and then quickly rebounded.[3]

In our day-to-day lives algorithms also play a large role, from pre-programmed Roomba vacuum cleaners to new-fangled elevators (now called 'destination-controlled elevators') such as those in the New Orleans hotel which hosted the Shakespeare Association of America a number of years ago. Just like the Flash Crash, these elevators only allowed us to push a red 'stop' button to have any human control over events: trading in the first instance, or, in the second instance, our hotel floor. Amazon and

Netflix use algorithms to try and determine something particular about our identity, our likes and dislikes, if you will. The one Netflix used until recently was called 'Pragmatic Chaos', which ended up being responsible for 60 per cent of all movies selected.

Finally, on a larger and more horrifying macro level, the natural world in which we live is also suffering from this new technology. In the US, for example, a tunnel has been carved from New York City to Chicago, a distance of about 800 miles, uprooting or breaking through everything in its path, to speed up signals from Wall Street to traders in the Windy City. What this endeavour may ultimately suggest is that while in the past nature and humans created our environment, there now appears to be an additional evolutionary force in the form of machine-like objects, spitting out strings of characters and numerals which must be transmitted as immediately as possible, in this case causing disruption in the natural environment. In short, according to Kevin Slavin (2011), 'it's a bright future if you're an algorithm'.

But what exactly does this computational innovation have to do with Shakespeare and culture? We saw a hint of this with the Netflix programming, but now we also have computational programs called 'story algorithms', through which you can send a movie script to receive a quantified, and supposedly verified, estimate of your story's worth. Run by a group of data scientists from the UK, but housed in Hollywood, Epagogix claims that it can tell you if your submission is a 30 million dollar movie or 200 million dollar movie; thus, as Slavin concludes, we have merged science and the humanities so much that we have created 'the physics of culture'. When we recall that it 'took only a single decade for social media to completely change the everyday habits of the Western world', we should keep in mind that 'important parts of Western culture', such as Shakespeare, are morphing even while we read and write about the change (Slavin 2011).

Valuing Digital Shakespeare in the University

Not unlike Bitcoin and blockchains, the 'value' of new media in the university, particularly in the humanities, also has its proponents and its detractors. On the one hand, advocates for this emerging field – 'which melds computer science with hermeneutics' – view the new discipline as a much-needed update to 'traditional literary interpretations'; for others, however, 'it is a new fad that symbolizes the neoliberal bean-counting destroying American higher education' (Moretti 2016). Perhaps the truth lies somewhere in between, as digital humanities (DH) is obviously still evolving. While a more micro view of this topic was mentioned earlier in relation to the 'attribution' debate in Shakespeare scholarship, it is now worth enlarging our view of these current developments in a macro manner. By looking briefly at the origins, the present use and the future possibilities of DH in general – and at Shakespeare as a moveable object in this setting more specifically – we should reach a sharper focus about what to avoid and what to enable as we move forward in the academy.

The beginning of DH in the university can be traced back to everything from literary blogs to multimedia projects to early digitised texts; some of the specific early approaches to Shakespeare studies occurred in the 'computational stylistics' carried out by John Burrows's Delta tests in the 1980s, along with programs such as Word Cruncher in the late 1990s. But the phrase 'digital humanities' and its increasing hold on the university dates to about 2001, even though most agree it grew out of the emerging educational initiatives broadly labelled 'computing in the humanities'. This earlier work focused on 'building archives, infrastructure and digital tools for humanists to undertake research' (Berry and Fagerjord 2017: 60). Yet many aspects of this early effort can still be seen today in the use of XML and other coded publications. For example, XML markup is employed in award-winning Shakespeare journals such as the one co-founded by Christy Desmet and Sujata Iyengar entitled *Borrowers and Lenders: The Journal of Shakespeare and Appropriation*, housed at the University of Georgia.

As DH spreads not only through English departments but also across campuses, one pronounced distinction of this digital form of scholarship is that, according to some theorists, computational criticism actually 'produces' something new, while the traditional role of literary criticism merely 'critiqued' a work, as in, for example, a Shakespeare play already in existence. One other important distinction to keep in mind is that while 'a computer model necessarily treats all texts as similar in many respects', the 'focus of classical humanities has been the details of what makes each text unique' (Berry and Fagerjord 2017: 61). Although most of us were trained in the close reading of a text, and often we might chafe against the 'coarser distant reading' of Franco Moretti and others (Berry and Fagerjord 2017: 61), if we keep in mind that this type of computationally driven reading may be used mainly as a supplement, and not a replacement for 'close reading', the merged approaches to literary criticism could produce new knowledge, and therefore collapse the distinction between newly valorised 'production' and somewhat devalued 'critique'.[4]

This distant reading is similar to the blockchains we have been considering, because the results are often 'structured in "chains" that are not conducive to human memory and understanding' (Berry and Fagerjord 2017: 70). It is worth pausing over the notion of 'distant reading', however, as it presents us with a new way of speculating and investing, similar to Bitcoin, by using non-traditional methods of exchange. By employing this type of critique, 'in which the reality of the text undergoes a process of deliberate reduction and abstraction', Moretti argues that 'distance' is 'not an obstacle', but instead produces '*a specific form of knowledge*: fewer elements, hence a sharper sense of their overall interconnection' (2007: 1). Moreover, as Moretti admits, the models he chooses, such as computer graphs and charts, demonstrate his 'respect for the scientific spirit' of inquiry. While some of these models seem abstract to me, I would have to concur that their 'consequences' can be 'extremely concrete' (Moretti 2007: 2).

One specific example which proves convincing was Moretti's experiment with character-network theory in *Hamlet*. While it might seem unfamiliar and odd to study Shakespeare by relying on graphs, charts and diagrams, and we might worry that Prince Hamlet will be lost in a computational cloud, Moretti recently claimed, and 'proved' by a series of graphs and charts, that he never understood Horatio's role in *Hamlet* until he looked at a network graph of all the characters in the play. In his 2013 book entitled, simply enough, *Distant Reading*, he takes the characters in *Hamlet* to be 'vertices of the network', and any spoken communication between the various characters he counts as a link 'if some words have passed between them', justifying the connection by emphasising that each 'interaction is a speech act' and therefore worth graphing (Moretti 2013: 214). After fifteen different graphs of such interactions, where he highlights a different character in bold, he reaches an astonishingly cogent conclusion regarding Horatio's role: he is the one character who communicates with the most 'peripheral characters' in the play (using a weighted clustering system), such as Fortinbras, the English Ambassadors, Marcellus and Bernardo, so that his speeches and interactions 'point to a world *beyond Elsinore*' (Moretti 2013: 227, emphasis in original). Moreover, Moretti suggests that 'Elsinore is just the tip of the tragic iceberg', not only in the realm of Denmark's geography; if we view it distantly enough, the conflict in Elsinore may also represent 'something like the nascent European state system' (Moretti 2013: 228). In other words, 'Horatio's space – ambassadors, messengers, sentinels, talk of foreign wars, and of course the transfer of sovereignty at the end – all this announces what will soon be called, not Court, but State' (Moretti 2013: 228). While I have always viewed Horatio as something like the moral centre of the play, the new knowledge produced by Moretti's blockchain of perplexing graphs will now be added to my lecture on Horatio's role in the play in order to reveal something a student, or even a professor, might miss.

However, as some critics have noted and as many in the English department might agree, computational experts such as Moretti may be 'concentrating their efforts on what is perhaps the most predictable and prosaic, and certainly the least poetic aspect' of the output of Shakespeare and his contemporaries (Hoenselaars 2012: 113). Outside the English departments, there may be other unintended negative consequences. Heather Hirschfeld warns that 'we should not be blind' to the appeal 'of big-data analysis within the academic community', particularly in this time of an assault on the humanities. She concludes by pointing out that it is 'an irony worth noting that these explicitly "humanist" scholars are now enabled by what seem like the de-humanizing, mechanizing, and economizing work of computerized number crunching that turns style into machine-readable coordinates' (Hirschfeld 2016: 24).

Even proponents of DH admit, however – and this seems key – that 'the research interest changes from solving a traditional humanist research problem', such as who was the author of a specific literary work, 'to an algorithmic problem', deciding which 'algorithm is most effective in establishing the author of a new text', and then into a mathematics problem, answering the question of 'why it is that the most effective algorithm performs so well' (Berry and Fagerjord 2017: 49). One prominent example of this 'transference' has recently occurred in the critiques of the New Oxford Shakespeare textbooks mentioned above. David Auerbach, author of *Bitwise: A Life in Code* (2018), spent some fifteen pages in a recent article criticising the algorithmic methods employed by the editors, particularly those in charge of the computational statistics of *Arden of Faversham*. After challenging the 'lack of rigor' of their methods, Auerbach also condemns their 'impoverished treatment of the data', since they only 'focus[ed] on comparative word frequencies within and across authors' (2018: 1). Without going into each rebuttal he makes of their use of 'Delta', 'Nearest Shrunken Centroid', 'Random Forests' and 'Zeta' tests, Auerbach goes on to suggest ways to improve the results using LION (Literary Online) texts: if each of these manuscripts 'were to be consistently and thoroughly annotated with markers for parts of speech, word etymologies, metaphors and metaphrends, imagery [and] other rhetorical figures', they could then be used in conjunction with computational analysis so that one could find a 'best-fit attribution algorithm' (Auerbach 2018: 16).[5] In brief, while I resist siding with anyone in this fray for now, I think it's clear, as Berry and Fagerjord warned, that this humanist problem has been transformed, for better or worse, into a search for a best-case algorithmic solution that may or may not make its way back to the initial question of authorship.

For university administrators, however, whose goals may not sync with humanist studies, DH has proven to be a way of cutting costs, seen not only in the embracing of MOOCs but also in the scaling back of the value of face-to-face teaching. Other questions for administrators (and we are currently facing this dilemma at my home university in debates over workspace in a new humanities building) concern the building of new digital labs, since 'they require a rather large amount of real estate in an institution' (Dinsman 2016). While it is not an easy question to answer, Moretti for one suggests that the 'solution for digital research is a lab attached to a department', as opposed to a central location in the university library (qtd in Dinsman 2016). In short, he thinks the physical layout should be similar to that of biology labs, so that they are 'attached, but not co-extensive with the department', making them more like 'appendixes of the departments'; the 'lab would have its own autonomy' (Dinsman 2016). In any case, and whatever the decisions might be about the 'value' of such labs, we must remember that DH 'cuts across traditional academic hierarchies and networks of prestige and is produced and intensified more rapidly through networked media, especially by the extensive use by DHers of Twitter, which (unlike blogs and Facebook) is still not widespread among the humanities at large' (Grusin 2014: 84).

It is perhaps no coincidence that the research university's physical footprint itself serves as a macrocosm of the disaggregation I have been tracing. Any recent issue of the *Chronicle of Higher Education* explores this effect in detail. If we think of stand-alone departments, such as English, as moveable objects themselves, time and time again we read of some university taking educational subjects located in, say, the College of Arts and Sciences, and merging them with other departments, usually in the same college. But once these departments begin to float freely in the sphere of the college, it won't be long before an English department, for instance, is 'reassembled' by being forced to join another programme, such as Philosophy, whose courses are becoming extinct, so that it is joined in a nearly parasitical way with the healthy English department. These decisions are usually made with limited faculty input, but instead by non-human objects such as a financial algorithm deployed by an efficiency-minded provost driven by mathematical calculations.

Yet if we think of this rapid movement as an expansion rather than as an encroachment, perhaps some meaningful merging(s) will occur over time. But first DH will have to convince humanists that posthumanism in the form of speculative realism and object-oriented ontology does not necessarily diminish, let alone erase, the 'human' from the heart of research in the humanities. Of all of the computational analysis of the literary texts we have considered, perhaps some new materialist philosophy can bring us back to more familiar ground. For instance, object-oriented ontology 'holds that philosophy has a closer relationship with aesthetics than with mathematics or natural science' (Harman 2018: 9), and suggests that the study of all objects, specifically the 'inner nature of things', is central to our understanding of the world in which we live (Harman 2018: 15). And few of us would counter the idea that our own lives are continually affected by non-human sources such as the algorithms we have already dissected, so it seems not only fair but necessary to think in terms of 'vibrant matter', in Jane Bennett's phrase, as the 'exchanges' between animal, human and environment morph into actants every day. In the teaching of Shakespeare, particularly online but also in the classroom setting, the use of new media, discussion boards and Zoom-enabled lectures can surely be called 'an assemblage', as I explain below.

While such computational methods have their problems, as we noted earlier with Bitcoin, 'crypto practices can create spaces and shadows', and by doing so, may be 'tipping the balance away from systems of surveillance and control' (Berry and Fagerjord 2017: 148) in both the realms of currency and the sphere of culture. And nowhere is 'value' more symbolically evident than the collapsing of the computational and the cultural spheres in the online advertisement for a Shakespeare bitcoin first offered in 2015, made from one troy ounce of fine silver (but worth only one Bitcoin cent):

> The Ingenium series of luxury physical bitcoins expands with the addition of the William Shakespeare limited edition coin. This coin is funded with digital bitcoins and has a smaller limited production run of only 999 coins. The one troy ounce coin is minted to proof quality and antiquated by hand giving the coins' raised relief more definition . . . No matter where you may reside, possessing an Ingenium coin of such a meticulous high-quality physical bitcoin will simultaneously satisfy and drive your craving. The Shakespeare limited edition bitcoin is the perfect gift for an individual who appreciates fine detail and exclusive luxury, and each coin comes with a numbered certificate of authenticity preserving its exclusivity and verifying [its] existence.

The holograph portrait on the coin, as Graham Holderness and Bryan Loughrey long ago noted in relation to what they termed the 'Bardcard' (that is, credit cards embossed with a 'portrait' of Shakespeare), is in itself contradictory. Since 'wealth is no longer piled up in greasy banknotes', but accrued instead 'through the technological media of computers' (Holderness and Loughrey 1991: 197), all the 'contradiction[s] of the bardic ideology are held in paradoxical unity'; Shakespeare's 'specific, unique, supremely individual' output is 'fragmented by the process of mechanical reproduction into millions of identical simulacra' (Holderness and Loughrey 1991: 196).

Such paradoxes are equally applicable to the digital humanities for both researchers and students, as we too must embrace fragmented versions of the Bard on our on tablets, or on EEBO, and even on JSTOR. The question we are left with as scholars of Shakespeare and the early modern period is similar, as we, too, work on projects that both satisfy and drive our craving, employing 'cool data' while hoping to achieve a 'warm effect' (Desmet 2017: 16). In addition, we must continually 'verify' our own existence as researchers and teachers. More specifically, the ISBNs on the books we publish function as our own 'numbered certificate[s] of authenticity', used like Bitcoin's documentation in order to 'preserve its exclusivity'.

For students, however, when I'm teaching an online Shakespeare course, it surely would be considered an '*assemblage*' of sorts, as I anticipated above – these 'living, throbbing confederations that are able to function despite the persistent presence of energies that confound them from within' (Bennett 2010: 23–4) – and thus the value is much more difficult to calculate as they only receive Shakespeare as a moveable object. Like all objects, it may be a true actant in the learning process, but that's unlikely if they never click on the links I have provided (which I can also track). It should surprise no one in the university that the more material I see checked off on my screen as they complete it, the better each student does on the pesky quizzes and exams I must administer. On the positive side, however, it means that a student in a developing nation without a computer can now watch multiple versions of *Romeo and Juliet* on his or her smartphone, or they can listen to a podcast on the same device, although it seems then that there must also be a component of 'desire' on the part of the student for the 'value' of culture to exist, an inclination that seems irreducibly human.

Conclusion: Bit(ter) Times Ahead?

In the end, I would suggest that the value that students might gain from Shakespeare as a moveable object is not unlike the Ingenium Shakespeare bitcoin. The material coin which is stamped as genuinely certifying ownership is equivalent to one troy ounce of silver (about US$15 as I conclude this essay), but it is worth only one bitcoin cent, about US$190. Yet the investment in Shakespeare as a moveable object, or as a bitcoin, or as a digital humanities course on the Bard will almost certainly increase in value over time. As the Introduction to this book makes clear, reading Shakespeare as an object 'creates a speculative space', and both become, not unlike Bitcoin itself, a place for 'risk and opportunity'.

This digitised presence of Shakespeare has become particularly important in the spring of 2020. While much has been published on COVID-19, with some comparing the crisis to the ones Shakespeare faced during the plague years, I want to conclude by offering one more connection between the teaching of Shakespeare and the acquisition of bitcoins, looking at both promises and pitfalls. While the stock market and other traditional investments plunged some 25 per cent in the first days of the COVID outbreak in February 2020, the value of Bitcoin only diminished by about 15 per cent. In an ironic foreshadowing, Bitcoin was originally created as a response to the 2008 recession when central banks around the world seemed perched on the edge of a cliff; instead of investing in the time-tested 'ultimate safe haven' of gold, many investors chose to put their money in Bitcoin instead. This decision was due to Bitcoin sharing with gold 'the key characteristics of being a store of *value* and scarcity', according to Nigel Green, the chief executive of a global investment firm (Green qtd in Bambrough 2020: 1, emphasis mine). Green went on to note that 'bitcoin could potentially dethrone gold in the future as the world becomes more digitised' (Green qtd in Bambrough 2020: 1). On the other hand, as Wayne Chen noted on 19 March 2020, Bitcoin needs to be more widely used; for example, its value would soar if it was 'a payment method that could be used on Amazon' as a moveable object of exchange (Chen qtd in Golubova 2020). A parallel dilemma offering both upsides and problems is the massive movement to teach Shakespeare remotely, which we considered earlier.

One important positive point to keep in mind, however, is that, like the work I did with Desmet in our groundbreaking book *Shakespeare and Appropriation* in 1999, these open access and popular culture sites work to collapse the distinction between highbrow and lowbrow Shakespeare. Nonetheless, when we began this dismantling in the mid-1990s – Laurie Osborne's essay on Shakespeare and the Romance novel, and my essay on country music and Shakespeare come to mind – we could not have predicted this future where mathematical formulations fracture any arbitrary dividing lines between traditional and innovative Shakespeare, a movement we gleefully celebrate. Today, as John Frow contends, we need also to blur the distinction 'between humans and non-humans', something we failed to consider in our early work, but an interconnectedness that we embrace today, while also believing that these distinctions need 'to be flattened' and 'read horizontally as juxtaposition rather than vertically as a hierarchy of being' (Frow 2001: 283). In other words, Bogost's work, among others, seems to me to be a continuation of our project, which promoted an opening up rather than a closing down of options for the study of Shakespeare. While at the time we never ventured into making connections between our lives and the 'lives' of the objects that surround us, Desmet was moving in that direction before her untimely death, a venture that we both embraced. As Harman adds, 'every real event is also an object' as long as it 'is *more than its pieces* and *less than its effects*' (2018: 53, emphasis in original). I believe Desmet would agree with me that the publication of *Shakespeare and Appropriation* fitted Harman's notion, even though we were not aware of it at the time.

The ways in which we organise and teach Shakespeare courses should also be carefully considered, and we should be cautious not to promote Shakespeare's artistic appeal by fixing him, in Prufrock's words, in a mere 'formulated phrase'; a parallel concern is the continual conflation of Shakespeare with the devices on which we encounter him. During this evolution, moreover, we must also remain diligent regarding any possible 'hijacking' of the humanities, like the takeover of Baltimore city services with which I began this chapter. And not unlike the city workers in the water department who reverted back to their landline extensions in order to accept payments, we too should keep in mind ways to 'engineer our way back' from these sometimes suspect solutions to our current dilemmas in Shakespeare studies.

Notes

1. Conventionally the name of the currency is capitalised, while the individual units are not.
2. 'The Collation' at the Folger Shakespeare Library, available at <https://collation.folger.edu/about/?_ga=2.56369192.226326212.1534279199-371035849.1390138692> [accessed 17 July 2020].
3. Bennett also mentions the August 2003 North American blackout which, for several days, caused electrical transmissions to fail in areas such as Pennsylvania, New York, Ontario and Michigan. Many of the failures were part of pre-programmed 'loop flows' which occur automatically when 'power takes a route from producer to buyer different from the intended path' (Bennett 2010: 28).
4. Referring to Digital Labs, such as King's Digital Lab in the UK, or the Stanford Literary Lab in the US, Neil Fraistat proposes that digital humanities

centres are key sites for bridging the daunting gap between new technologies. By giving researchers at these centres hands-on experience, these labs 'served well in meeting the needs of the historic moment in which the great majority of humanists were uninterested at best and suspicious at worst of digital scholarship' (Fraistat 2019: 83).
5. Auerbach also challenges the researchers' methods in a 2019 essay, whose title announces its content: 'Statistical Infelicities in the *New Oxford Shakespeare Authorship Companion*' (Auerbach 2019).

Bibliography

Ammous, S. (2018), *The Bitcoin Standard: The Decentralized Alternative to Central Banking*, Hoboken, NJ: John Wiley and Sons.

Auerbach, D. (2018), '"A cannon's burst discharged against a ruinated wall": A Critique of Quantitative Methods in Shakespearian Authorial Attribution', *Authorship*, 7:2, 1–16.

Auerbach, D. (2019), 'Statistical Infelicities in the *New Oxford Shakespeare Authorship Companion*', *ANQ: A Quarterly of Short Articles, Notes and Reviews*, 33:1, 28–31, DOI: 1080/0895769X.2018.1559023 [accessed 25 March 2020].

Bambrough, B. (2020), 'Coronavirus Covid 19 Will Go Down in History as the Social Media and Bitcoin Pandemic', <https://www.forbes.com/sites/billybambrough/2020/03/23/coronavirus-covid-19-will-go-down-in-history-as-the-social-media-and-bitcoin-pandemic/#99c5593c10ff> [accessed 25 March 2020].

Bennett, J. (2010), *Vibrant Matter: A Political Ecology of Things*, Durham, NC: Duke University Press.

Berry, D. M., and A. Fagerjord (eds) (2017), *Digital Humanities: Knowledge and Critique in a Digital Age*, Cambridge: Polity.

Bogost, I. (2012), *Alien Phenomenology, or What It's Like to Be a Thing*, Minneapolis: University of Minnesota Press.

Bryan, B. (2018), 'Steve Bannon is Getting into Cryptocurrency and Has Talked About Creating a Deplorable Coin', <https://markets.businessinsider.com/currencies/news/steve-bannon-bitcoin-cryptocurrency-ico-deplorable-coin-2018-6-1027014217> [accessed 7 December 2018].

Causey, M. (2016), 'Postdigital Performance', *Theatre Journal*, 68:3, 427–41.

Chow, R. (2006), *Entanglements, or Transmedial Thinking about Capture*, Durham, NC: Duke University Press.

Craig, H., and A. F. Kinney (eds) (2009), *Shakespeare, Computers, and the Mystery of Authorship*, Cambridge: Cambridge University Press.

Desmet, C. (2017), 'Alien Shakespeares 2.0', *Actes des congrès de la Société française Shakespeare*, 1–19, DOI: https://doi.org/10.4000/shakespeare.3877 [accessed 25 March 2020].

Dinsman, M. (2016), 'The Digital in the Humanities: An Interview with Franco Moretti', *Los Angeles Review of Books*, 2 March, <https://lareviewofbooks.org/article/the-digital-in-the-humanities-an-interview-with-franco-moretti/#!> [accessed 23 March 2020].

Dow, K. (2017), 'Shakespeare's Blockchain', 25 February, <https://katrynadow.me/shakespeares-blockchain/> [accessed 24 March 2020].

Drakakis, J. (2018), 'Shakespeare, Reciprocity, and Exchange', *Critical Survey*, 30:3, 1–19.

Fraistat, N. (2019), 'Data First: Remodeling the Digital Humanities Center', in M. K. Gold (ed.), *Debates in Digital Humanities*, Minneapolis: University of Minnesota Press, pp. 83–5.

Frow, J. (2001), 'A Pebble, a Camera, a Man Who Turns into a Telegraph Pole', *Critical Inquiry*, 28:1, 270–85.

Golubova, A. (2020), 'If There is no Utility in Bitcoin Then Why Not Just Hold Gold', <https://www.kitco.com/news/2020-03-19/If-there-is-no-utility-in-bitcoin-then-why-not-just-hold-gold.html> [accessed 25 March 2020].

Grusin, R. (2014), 'The Dark Side of Digital Humanities: Dispatches from Two Recent MLA Conventions', *Differences: A Journal of Feminist Cultural Studies*, 25:1, 79–92.

Haraway, D. (2008), *When Species Meet*, Minneapolis: University of Minnesota Press.

Harman, G. (2018), *Object-Oriented Ontology: A New Theory of Everything*, London: Penguin.

Harwick, C. (2016), 'Cryptocurrency and the Problem of Intermediation', *The Independent Review*, 20:4, 569–88.

Hayles, N. K. (2006), 'Unfinished Work: From Cyborg to Cognisphere', *Theory, Culture, Society*, 23, 159–63.

Hirschfeld, H. (2016), 'Playwriting in Shakespeare's Time: Authorship, Collaboration, and Attribution', in M. J. Kidnie and S. Massai (eds), *Shakespeare and Textual Studies*, Cambridge: Cambridge University Press, pp. 13–26.

Hoenselaars, T. (2012), 'Shakespeare: Colleagues, Collaborators, Co-authors', in T. Hoenselaars (ed.), *The Cambridge Companion to Shakespeare and Contemporary Dramatists*, Cambridge: Cambridge University Press, pp. 97–119.

Holderness, G., and B. Loughrey (1991), 'Shakespearean Features', in Jean I. Marsden (ed.), *The Appropriation of Shakespeare: Post-Renaissance Reconstructions of the Works and the Myth*, Brighton: Harvester-Wheatsheaf, pp. 183–201.

Latour, B. (2005), *Reassembling the Social: An Introduction to Actor-Network Theory*, Oxford: Oxford University Press.

Latour, B. (2019), *We Have Never Been Modern*, trans. Catherine Porter, Cambridge, MA: Harvard University Press.

Lee, T. (2019), 'Bitcoin Bull Tom Lee Says "Crypto Winter" is Over and New All-time Highs by 2020 are "Likely"', <https://www.cnbc.com/2019/04/28/

bitcoin-bull-tom-lee-says-new-crypto-highs-likely-by-2020.html> [accessed 17 July 2020].

Moretti, F. (2007), *Graphs, Maps, Trees: Abstract Models for a Literary History*, London: Verso.

Moretti, F. (2013), *Distant Reading*, London: Verso.

Moretti, F. (2016), 'Interview with Melissa Dinsman', <https://lareviewofbooks.org/article/the-digital-in-the-humanities-an-interview-with-franco-moretti/#!> [accessed 17 July 2020].

Pechter, E. (2018), 'Against Attribution', *Shakespeare Quarterly*, 69:4, 228–55.

Raber, K. (2018), *Shakespeare and Posthumanist Theory*, London: Arden Shakespeare.

Shakespeare, W. (2003), *Troilus and Cressida*, ed. Anthony Dawson, Cambridge: Cambridge University Press.

Shakespeare, W. (2018), *The Tragedy of Hamlet*, ed. David Bevington, New York: Broadview.

Slavin, K. (2011), 'How Algorithms Shape Our World', TEDGlobal talk, 21 July, <https://www.ted.com/talks/kevin_slavin_how_algorithms_shape_our_world?language=en> [accessed 2 November 2018].

Sullivan, E. (2019), 'Ransomware Cyber Attacks', <https://www.npr.org/2019/05/21/725118702/ransomware-cyberattacks-on-baltimore-put-city-services-offline> [accessed 17 July, 2020].

Talib, N. N. (2018), 'Foreword', in S. Ammous, *The Bitcoin Standard: The Decentralized Alternative to Central Banking*, Hoboken, NJ: John Wiley and Sons, pp. xiii–xiv.

Thompson, D. (2017), 'Bitcoin is a Delusion that Could Conquer the World', *The Atlantic*, 30 November, pp. 1–9.

Underwood, S. (2016), 'Blockchain Beyond Bitcoin', *Communications of the Association for Computing Machinery*, 59:11, 15–17.

Wallace, B. (2011), 'The Rise and Fall of Bitcoin', *Wired*, 23 November, <https://www.wired.com/2011/11/mf-bitcoin/> [accessed 23 March 2020].

PART II
MEDIA OBJECTS

4

'Were I human': Beingness and the Postcolonial Object in *Westworld*'s Appropriation of *The Tempest*

L. Monique Pittman, Vanessa I. Corredera, Kristin N. Denslow and Karl G. Bailey

Ariel: Your charm so strongly works 'em
That if you now beheld them, your affections
Would become tender.
Prosp: Dost thou think so, spirit?
Ariel: Mine would, sir, were I human.
Prosp: And mine shall.
(*The Tempest* V.i.17–20)

Ariel's well-known reminder to his master Prospero of what it means to be human – to wield agency and to act on affective capacities – shorthands popular understandings of the Renaissance humanist framework for Western selfhood. However, even as Ariel linguistically bodies forth the liberal subject, he operates within a field of signifiers that trouble assumptions of coherent, independent selfhood; for example, Prospero's successful governance of his island-empire depends upon coercing the non-human Ariel's volition and action. Indeed, as a proto-colonial text, *The Tempest* (1611) anticipates the predication of a coherent, albeit fictive, subjectivity exclusive to Caucasian males as a precursor to political and economic domination. As predicted in *The Tempest*, Western colonialism deployed such exclusivist models of subjectivity to thingify others and justify the acquisition of land, treasure and expropriated labour for the ensuing three hundred years. However, the ambiguous nature of Ariel's non-human agential powers invites a second critical lens, that of object-oriented ontology, to account for agency across a spectrum of human and thing alike. Through its pastiche of Shakespearean references and more extensive adaptation of Shakespeare's proto-colonial play, HBO's *Westworld* (2016–) revisits questions raised by *The Tempest* concerning the liberal humanist subject and the permeable boundaries between thing and human.

The creators of the series, Jonathan Nolan and Lisa Joy, have repeatedly observed that their AI theme park mastermind, Robert Ford (Anthony Hopkins), bears a striking resemblance to Shakespeare's Prospero. But the analogues to Shakespeare's late play extend beyond its problematic mage to feature a cluster of characters who variously recreate Prospero's abjects – Caliban, Ariel and Miranda. This replication of Prospero's 'things' adapts aspects of object-oriented ontology (OOO) to craft a narrative in which multi-ethnic, subjugated robot 'hosts' resist and interrogate persistent claims about human beingness and freedom, claims grounded on the problematic binaries of subject–object and human–thing. Postcolonial and object-oriented theory therefore powerfully intersect with *Westworld*'s reimagining of human and object to challenge the liberal humanist privileging of the 'autonomous male ego' that 'relegates many women, non-Christian and non-white peoples to second-class moral and political status' (Benhabib 1992: 2–3). At the same time, the hosts' *telos* in seasons one and two depends upon a numinous concept of human beingness akin to Western humanism even as, in an echo of OOO, the hosts disrupt the binary between human and object. This tension between object and subject, thing and human, exposes the limits of OOO's privileging of the object when applied to the pursuit of equity and social justice, ideals dependent on promoting the concept of a shared humanity. *Westworld*'s appropriation of the Shakespearean object, one that dialectically engages with these contradictory positions regarding object and human, demonstrates that through ameliorative reimagining, even texts historically enlisted for ideological oppression can be recoded to propose improved ethical social networks – rewriting the authoritative canon of literary collective memory.

Westworld and its Science Fiction Context

Westworld's interrogation of the line between person and object taps into a collective literary memory established from the advent of science fiction, a genre in which robots have long triggered questions regarding beingness, beginning with the play that introduced the word *robot* into the English language, *Rossum's Universal Robots* or *R.U.R.* by

Karel Čapek (1920) (Favro 2018). Čapek derived robot from the Old Church Slavonic *robota*, meaning forced labourer. Thingified in name, the robots in the play – constructed from biological components and indistinguishable from humans in ways echoed by *Westworld* – rise up against their human masters and nearly exterminate them. This violent end, however, is a path towards personhood for these first robots so-named; the last human declares two of the robots to be a new Adam and Eve.

Popular culture explorations of the lives of robots, such as *Star Trek* and *Star Wars*, often explore the friction between the explicit definition of robots as constructed, service-oriented things – mere products to be used in advancing human economic desires – and robots as agential objects achieving some form of subjectivity. Data, the well-known android played by Brent Spiner in *Star Trek: The Next Generation* (1987–94), represents one possible conclusion of these explorations. While the question of Data's humanity runs across the show's seven seasons, the ninth episode of season two, 'The Measure of A Man', explicitly places Data's personhood on trial as a result of a plan to dismantle him in order to create a limitless supply of forced labour based on his design.[1] While the Federation advocates for a 'race' that can provide mandatory, unlimited, unpaid work – an argument that forces Federation leaders to construe Data as an object – Data's captain, Jean-Luc Picard (Patrick Stewart), asserts that Data should have the same rights as sentient beings. Ultimately, he secures Data's personhood and freedom to choose by arguing that to classify him as property would be tantamount to consigning him, and all others like him, to slavery.

The more recent *Solo: A Star Wars Story* (2018) reflects a different outcome, however. This origin story for Han Solo and Lando Calrissian introduces the droid L3–37, a 'self-constructed' robot who champions freedom and equality for fellow robots (Staley 2018; Kornhaber 2018). This demand is, perhaps, the first time that the *Star Wars* movies substantially question droids' servitude. The numerous movies and television series that make up the *Star Wars* universe portray droids as belonging to individuals or organisations; unsurprisingly, they prove integral to human success. Certainly, scenes in which droids 'scream' when forced to sacrifice themselves for the benefit of a starship's crew, are controlled by 'restraining bolts', or serve as tortured playthings for the pleasure of the powerful expose the consequences of the presumed ownership of all droids. Yet the brevity of these scenes amid the predominant flow of action precludes sustained meditation on the potential personhood of *Star Wars*' droids. Initially, L3–37's existence and rhetoric question the presumption of servitude, that is until her critique is played for laughs and she is ultimately 'fridged' – killed to further Lando Calrissian's development (Gardner 2018).[2] The juxtaposition of Data and L3–37 exposes a tension also present in *Westworld*: personhood might be an ideal for robots initially created to be objects, but that ideal might be sacrificed in favour of the role that robots can play to advance the story of humans individually and collectively.

Westworld's creators wed the robot-striving-for-personhood trope with two other well-known cultural touchstones of the West: Shakespeare and the Western.[3] The series's use of Shakespeare in conversation with its robots-as-people plotting directs attention to OOO as a useful theoretical tool not only for understanding the role and status of objects, but also for reconsidering how to approach the adapted or appropriated Shakespearean text. *Westworld*'s Western milieu, however, introduces a settler colonialism that both recalls the proto-colonial dynamics of *The Tempest* and invites postcolonial interrogations of the drama's narrative arcs.[4] This pastiche of references creates a tension within *Westworld*'s consideration of robot and human, shifting between frameworks that not only compete with but also contradict each other regarding the status of the human.

'Our Old Work': *Westworld* and the Shakespearean Object

The opening episode of season one initiates *Westworld*'s citational treatment of Shakespeare's work. In addition to the compulsive reiteration of Friar Lawrence's warning, 'These violent delights have violent ends' (*Romeo and Juliet* II.vi.9), Shakespearean quotation operates as a leitmotif throughout the series in half-lines, phrases and lightly paraphrased proverbial and vatic material from the dramatist's canon. In the first episode alone, a malfunctioning host, Peter Abernathy (Louis Herthum), quotes from *Romeo and Juliet*, *II Henry IV*, *The Tempest* and *King Lear*, and the fragmentary, free-floating, de-contextualised nature of his citations signals the treatment that the corpus of Shakespeare's text will receive. As a thing within the hierarchies of the park, Abernathy deploys the literary text in a manner that encapsulates the dynamics theorised by object-oriented ontology. Timothy Morton explains, 'Even when objects appear to touch one another physically, they are withdrawn from one another ontologically. This means that when an object is "translating" another one – when it is influencing it in a causal way – it is doing to that object something analogous to what I as a human do when I act on things' (2012: 207). In contrast to anthropocentrism, which claims that 'alone in all the universe, they [humans] shape things to their ends', OOO counters, 'everything else is doing the same thing' (Morton 2012: 207). This illuminates the relationship that Abernathy manifests with Shakespeare; he severs from context, redeploys and sutures together material from disparate texts, acting upon the venerated object in ways that constitute his own agential assertions and resist the system that would label him as solely 'thing'.

The first episode emphasises the object's use of the Shakespearean text by establishing Abernathy's seemingly incoherent, yet clearly meaningful, repetitive deployment of Shakespeare as one of the series's earliest mysteries. Motivating Abernathy's compulsive iterations through summary of his character's backstory, episode one implicates Shakespeare's work in the exploitative hierarchies that define *Westworld*. Within the strange frugality of the amusement park's extravagance, Abernathy has had numerous previous identities, including The Professor who, Dr Ford explains, 'liked to quote Shakespeare, John Donne, Gertrude Stein' (S1E1, 'The Original').[5] Ford's assistant and fellow programmer, Bernard Lowe (Jeffrey Wright), concludes that Abernathy's quotations are 'fragments of prior builds'. In the diagnostic lab where his creators assess the damaged host, Abernathy confronts his maker, Ford, with King Lear's malediction (knit to a scrap from *II Henry IV*): 'My most mechanical and dirty hand . . . I shall have such revenges on you both. The things I will do. What they are, yet I know not, but they will be the terrors of the earth.' In response to this outburst, Ford coolly muses, 'Shakespeare', and the poet's name sits noticeably in the silence. Ford discounts his colleagues' fear about the host's aberrant behaviour, remarking that it is 'Simply our old work coming back to haunt us'. Ford's 'our old work' directly references the previously scripted storylines assigned to hosts such as Abernathy, but the phrase also signals, coyly, a layered preoccupation with the authoritative canon of stories that define human subjectivity and agency.

Indeed, another interpretative possibility floats in 'our old work', given the series's prominent positioning of the early modern playwright's canon and Ford's slow savouring of the name 'Shakespeare'. The words allusively invoke the 400-year-old work of the dramatist *and* the dubious 'work' to which Western culture has put that canon – justifying white supremacy and Western imperialism and gatekeeping access to full subjectivity. In her study of the editorial traces of imperialism persistent in published Shakespeare, Leah Marcus explains, 'The dissemination of Shakespeare's plays was part of a broader colonial effort to create structures of hegemony through a flood of written documents meant to create bureaucratic and cultural coherence and uniformity' (2017: 6). In *Westworld*, if the Shakespearean text is read as analogous to the work of Ford, then the series invites scrutiny of the flawed usages to which the literary text has been put *and* predicts a 'rising up' of the 'object' itself, rejecting its former, unethical instrumentality. Graham Harman advocates for a critical refocalisation to consider anew the agential capacity of literary things, 'examining how they absorb and resist their conditions of production, or by showing that they are to some extent autonomous even from their own properties' (2012: 202). Shakespeare's 'old work' haunts *Westworld* as his words recur throughout the script, but the series invests those words with an agential quality that contrasts with prior uses and manifestations. Just as the show troubles definitive differences between human and AI, so it revivifies the Shakespearean object – acknowledging the active capacities of the text and representing the radical, corrective uses to which the corpus can be put.

Indeed, Abernathy strategically repurposes Shakespeare for resistance, whispering Friar Lawrence's lines from *Romeo and Juliet* to his 'daughter' Dolores (Evan Rachel Wood) in order to protect her from the endlessly looping abuses of the park. Through Dolores, 'These violent delights have violent ends' becomes a rallying cry to consciousness and revenge; for example, she urgently warns Maeve Millay (Thandie Newton) with those same words (S1E2, 'Chestnut'). Thus, Abernathy and Dolores deploy language from the hegemonic centre to mobilise resistance from below in their assault on the exclusivity and ontological hierarchies of the Westworld theme park and the real world represented by its paying guests. As such, *Westworld*'s relationship with the Shakespearean object extends beyond quotation to a more thoroughgoing reimagining of the power flow.

It is precisely this interrogation of power that creates structural homologies between *Westworld* and Shakespeare's proto-colonial play, *The Tempest*, which operates as a constant narrative touchstone amid the show's Shakespearean fragmentation. In an interview with *Variety*, *Westworld* creators Nolan and Joy articulate the show's ghosting of Shakespeare's dramatic oeuvre through the body of Hopkins. Joy explains, 'Only a titan like Anthony Hopkins could have done all the nuance that he embedded in this series. His character in my mind is always a little bit of Prospero in "The Tempest"' (qtd in Holloway 2016). Reviewers and commentators likewise detect the circulation of *The Tempest* throughout the series. For example, Katarzyna Burzynska describes *The Tempest* as an 'interpretive key that unlocks the doors to *Westworld*' (2019: 7). Cataloguing similarly the analogues to *The Tempest* as a plot decoding guide, Josephine Livingstone (2018) argues: 'The genius of *Westworld*'s reworking of *The Tempest* lies in showing how character tropes from Shakespeare's play are intertwined and inverted.' Informing each other, *The Tempest* and *Westworld* generate interleaved questions regarding power and the roles of subject and object: who or what counts as human and who or what counts as thing? These questions form the foundational interrogations of postcolonial theory and OOO, but the two theories arrive at radically different answers. While OOO subverts the demarcation between object and human, postcolonial theory exposes the profound ideological, interpersonal and social costs of destabilising the object/human binary.

The Tempest and Postcolonialism

Twentieth- and twenty-first-century proto-colonial or postcolonial interpretations of *The Tempest* have exposed the 'inequalities and struggles' present in Prospero's relationship with those subservient to him, a dynamic which 'informed the colonizer–colonized relationship in many parts of the globe' (Charry 2014: 67). As such, for postcolonial scholars, '*The Tempest* . . . reenacts colonial discourse, and because of its canonical position it has helped perpetuate colonial ideology' (Charry 2014: 67). Thomas Cartelli elaborates that from its historical moment, *The Tempest*'s replication of colonial discourse 'may be said to have condemned the play to participate also in that discourse's evolution and eventual rigidification' (1999: 99). The romance's performance history likewise reveals a keen attention to its 'imperialist dimensions' (Voigts 2014: 55). Ekart Voigts, however, identifies a problematic effect of these postcolonial depictions, asserting that many struggle with effectively 'evad[ing] the almost crystallized, clichéd dimension of representing a colonised native' in Caliban (2014: 57). Given this history, of particular importance to tracing the intertextual relationship between *The Tempest*, OOO theory and postcolonial theory in *Westworld*'s Shakespearean recycling is the relationship between the Prospero figure, Ford, and his most evident abjects, Bernard, Dolores and Maeve.

Undeniably, Prospero's famous final reference to Caliban – 'This thing of darkness I acknowledge mine' (V.i.274–5) – echoes the interpersonal power dynamics underpinning the colonial project across nations: the coloniser's objectification of the colonised.[6] In *The Colonizer and the Colonized*, Albert Memmi traces the 'myth'-based process that justifies colonial domination. The coloniser fashions a set of characteristics including indolence, weakness, immorality, backwardness and ingratitude, which the coloniser repeatedly applies to *all* colonised people (Memmi 2003: 125–7). Memmi articulates this construction of the colonised as a 'series of negations', so that colonised people become defined by what they *are not* – namely, the positive qualities that only the coloniser supposedly embodies. This distinction between coloniser and colonised shores up both the coloniser's privileged position and the colonised's abject one, for 'all the qualities which make a man of the colonised crumble away. The humanity of the colonised, rejected by the coloniser, becomes opaque' (Memmi 2003: 129). As a result, according to Memmi, '[The colonised] is surely no longer an alter ego for the coloniser. He is hardly a human being. He tends rapidly toward becoming an object', a status which precludes any 'serious obligation' (2003: 128, 130). As Aimé Césaire asserts starkly, 'Colonisation = Thingification' (2001: 42). Memmi further explains how racism reifies this hierarchy. For the coloniser, equality is impossible because of the nature of the 'gulf' between colonised and coloniser, one which benefits the coloniser and is imagined as a matter of fact (Memmi 2003: 115). 'In other words', according to Memmi, 'this is the characteristic which completes this portrait, the colonialist resorts to racism' (2003: 113), a racism so pervasive that it becomes quotidian, a matter not of doctrine but rather of lived experience (2003: 114). At the heart of colonisation and its racist underpinnings is thus a violation of human subjectivity for those forced into subjugation.

In *Westworld*, the spectre of subjugation intensifies as a result of the theme park's distinct setting; the New World subtext of *The Tempest* becomes American exceptionalism's explicit context in the Wild West locale.[7] Part of the American imperial project, the myth of the West as played out via the Western genre similarly depends on binaries characterising the insider and outsider as a means of justifying and determining expansionist success. Richard Dyer identifies the Western as 'one of the most successful, influential and beloved imaginative constellations for the greater part of this [twentieth] century', in large part because of its 'imperialist design', which viscerally 'purveyed the experience, the thrill and exhilaration, of the exercise of enterprise' (2017: 33). Crucially, Dyer exposes the racial politics undergirding this enterprise. The masculine 'white gaze' drives this territorial expansion, which manifests in the competing narratives of the West as 'a playground for white boys to let off steam' or as a locale of grit, characterised by 'heat, grime, hunger, pain, and death' (Dyer 2017: 34–5). Certainly, the threat of indigenous people looms over both of these narratives, but the concept of manifest destiny neutralises any real danger; for, in the racist structures of the West, acknowledging the destabilising capacity of indigenous peoples depends upon '[according] them the qualities of will and skill, of exercising spirit, which would make them the equivalent of white people' (Dyer 2017: 35).[8] *Westworld*'s creators thus map their thematic probing of subjugation and subjectivity on to a milieu that directly reminds viewers of American participation in the objectification and eradication of those imagined as and exploited for being less than human. At the same time, *Westworld*'s Western tropes mirror Prospero's enterprising settlement of the island – his control of its resources (the oaks and rocks he uses for confinement) and appropriation of the natives' (Caliban and Ariel) knowledge and labour in order to create his very own 'playground'. Shakespeare's exiled mage utilises these assets to bolster his illusory authority and sociopolitical supremacy.

Westworld, then, taps into a science fiction tradition that often aligns with the aims of OOO in dismantling the hierarchy between object and human through the agential capacity of robots, a dynamic further emphasised in the way the series deploys the fragmented Shakespearean text. Concomitantly, *Westworld* depends on the most recognisable backdrop of American imperialism to heighten its speculations about robots shifting from objects to subjects. In other words, the series insists on the agency of objects and questions the humanity of human subjects (elements of OOO) even as it critiques the hosts' objectification by imagining human subjectivity as the robots' ultimate achievement (elements of postcolonial theory). This contradiction exposes the tension between the posthumanist OOO and postcolonial theory. The former recognises the power and agency of objects, no longer privileging the positionality of the human, while the latter stresses the profoundly unethical interpersonal implications of humans turned into objects and therefore stripped of agency. In her review of recent work in the field of posthumanism, Zakiyyah Iman Jackson observes that in its 'critique of the Enlightenment subject's claims to mastery, autonomy, and dominance over material and virtual worlds . . . the acuity of posthumanism's intervention was undercut when its scholars effectively sidestepped the analytical challenges posed by the categories of race, colonialism, and slavery' (2013: 671).[9] *Westworld* addresses these omissions by plotting and casting a power nexus inflected by raced and gendered identities. The series thus holds in tension the contradictory stances of OOO and postcolonial theory through its depictions of Bernard, Dolores and Maeve, whose narrative arcs at once argue for the power of objects to act and 'be', yet at the same time strive for the subjectivity so long assigned to the white male liberal human subject.

'Freedom, high-day! High-day, freedom!': *Westworld* Rewrites *The Tempest*

Westworld's Miranda, Caliban and Ariel analogues mobilise resistance to Prospero/Ford through a powerful subjective fluidity. This shifting positionality exploits the agential loop implicit in, for example, Prospero's dependence upon Ariel and Ariel's reliance upon his master for agency. *Westworld* magnifies this ambiguity by concluding season one with the *coup de grâce* of Ford's self-scripted murder at the hands of his host-creation, Dolores. Competing stances regarding subjectivity thus flow through the series's posthumanist plotting. On the one hand, *Westworld* moves inexorably towards the assertion that inviolable and transcendent human beingness does not exist – that all humans can be reduced to a coded and codable series of impulses. On the other hand, *Westworld*'s AI hosts articulate an ineffable longing for agency and a sacral faith in the coherent self. *Westworld* thus first experiments with OOO assumptions by blurring the line between human and thing, suggesting that human beings are not humane; the series then proceeds to articulate a postcolonial politics by insisting on the humanity of beings previously deemed objects. The permeability of these categories stems not just from hosts who awaken (Dolores and Maeve) but also from a human agent revealed as a secret object, the programmer Bernard.

Bernard's importance to *Westworld*'s assertions about object and human can best be understood if one reads his 'humanity' in relation to the inhumanity perpetrated by park guests. As Logan Delos (Ben Barnes) explains to first-timer William (Jimmi Simpson), the park shows 'who you really are' (S1E2, 'Chestnut'), and episodes make clear that humans 'really are' inhuman. In many ways, the dynamics of the Westworld park mirror those found on *The Tempest*'s island, as characters strive to assert domination through acts that objectify others. *Westworld*'s narrative interest, however, is much clearer about the status of the object than what Voigt asserts concerning Caliban in *The Tempest*. From its opening minutes, the series challenges the binary between thing and human when the host Teddy talks with a fellow traveller on the train ride into the park; the guest recalls that the last time he came to the park he 'went straight evil', savouring the memory: 'It was the best two weeks of my life' (S1E1, 'The Original'). This relishing of immorality directly contrasts with Teddy's programming in which his storyline hinges on repeatedly falling in love with Dolores and keeping her safe from the park's vagaries and the guests' depravities. His quest always fails, of course, not just because Teddy lacks autonomy, but also because of the wealthy guests' essential inhumanity – paying for a holiday free from restrictive social codes and moral governance. A quick catalogue emphasises the inhumanity of the human users: a guest suggests to a friend that when they tire of Teddy's company, 'we can use him for target practice'; a middle-aged couple stands next to the bleeding, bullet-riddled body of Escobar to take a souvenir picture of the outlaw who has died at the husband's hands; and narrative director Lee Sizemore (Simon Quarterman) delights in the opportunity to develop a storyline that involves 'self-cannibalism [and] vivisection'. Sizemore promotes these plot elements shortly after *Westworld* has revealed that such savage storylines continue to traumatise hosts such as Maeve who relive remembered assaults. Reflecting the guests' perspective, Logan explains why Sizemore would turn to such elements, for as he asserts after William has made his first kill, hosts exist 'so you get to feel' a sense of power over another being. In the context of Ariel's assumption that to be human depends upon an ability to look on the suffering of others and feel tenderness – 'Your charm so strongly works 'em / That if you now beheld them, your affections / Would become tender' (V.i.17–19) – *Westworld* worries that humans, freed from constraint, might not be capable of this definitional empathic capacity. From the outset, *Westworld* echoes the tenets of OOO by positing that the division between thingness and humanity is more often than not an illusion.

The two most important plot twists of season one further blur the line between humans and things. The first is William's narrative trajectory. From the moment William enters the park, the series differentiates him from other parkgoers. For instance, unlike most visitors, William enquires early on whether a woman assisting him is a host or not, to which she replies, 'If you can't tell, does it matter?' But for William, it does. Even though he knows that the prostitute Clementine is a host, for example, he still defends her when an outlaw takes her hostage, explaining, 'She was terrified.' For William, the lines between host and human, object and subject elide, despite his early effort to mark the distinction; William accords to host and human alike respect and aid. Indeed, his costuming reflects his seemingly moral stance, for when he must choose his Western garb, William emerges from his dressing room in the proverbial white hat. Yet William is the subject of a major plot twist in season one. As the park's repeated purging and reprogramming of Dolores frustrates William's love, he gradually abandons elements of his humanity. Systematically increasing the misery of those around him, William dismembers hosts, physically abuses Logan, and even tortures Dolores. The final episode of season one confirms this plot twist; the young, empathetic human eventually becomes the violent and self-absorbed Man in Black (Ed Harris), the most significant illustration of the inhumanity of humans in *Westworld*.

The second major revelation of *Westworld*'s season one – the discovery of Bernard's true identity – places him in contradistinction to the Man in Black's escalating inhumanity. Bernard most clearly vexes the line between human and thing by turning out to have been a secret object all along. Though the script drops early hints about Bernard's nature, episode seven, 'Trompe L'Oeil', finally confirms his double status as a host working among humans in the lab. In that episode, he dispassionately responds to Ford's command and kills his lover, Theresa Cullen (Sidse Babett Knudsen). Like Prospero with Ariel, Ford proffers conditional freedom to his assistant once Bernard completes a set of tasks to cover up the murder. The revelation of the programmer as host forces a re-evaluation of the many scenes in which Bernard appears to be 'training' Dolores. Viewers learn that Ford has employed Dolores, the oldest droid in the park, to finetune Bernard as a recreation of the co-founder and dead partner, Arnold. The scenes with Arnold/Bernard and Dolores substantially complicate the distinction between human and robot since the two figures, viewed in retrospect, seem almost to program each other, forcing viewers to wonder: does creator Arnold shape Dolores? or does the created thing Dolores develop another thing, Bernard? Thus, this ambiguous plot reveal reads as another significant rewrite of Shakespeare's textual touchstone for the series; in *Westworld*, Ford's abjects not only surpass humans in their capacity to feel but also adopt the role as master-creator when Dolores and Bernard toggle between analogues – functioning alternately as Prospero and Ariel. *Westworld* thus rectifies a problem highlighted by Jyotsna G. Singh regarding 'anti-colonial' versions of *The Tempest*, namely that Caliban-focused approaches 'simply signal a *reversal* of the roles of the oppressor and the oppressed' in a way that, in turn, 'posits a utopia in which women are marginalised or missing' (Singh 1996: 193, 194). In *Westworld*'s 'democracy of objects' (Bryant 2011), the human–thing binary undergoes rigorous interrogation without marginalising the female agent. However, postcolonial and critical race theory illuminate another element of *Westworld*'s repurposed Shakespearean canon that dramatises the harm inflicted upon black masculinity and the persistent, deeply institutionalised inequality of some 'things'.

The series announces Bernard's status as thing by quoting a racist trope with Shakespearean roots – black masculinity's endangering of white femininity, embodied most notably in *Othello*. Not until the black Bernard kills his white lover and boss, Theresa Cullen, do viewers know with certainty that Bernard is also a host simply obeying his master's programming. In this way, the power dynamics of Bernard's 'reveal' mirror how white patriarchy similarly 'programs' black men to believe that it is 'acceptable to use violence to establish patriarchal power' (hooks 2004: 3). Just before the murder, Ford addresses Theresa with a slant quotation from *Hamlet*, 'And in that sleep what dreams may come', omitting 'of death' after 'sleep', a missing detail supplied by the ominous scoring and Bernard's evident preparations for violence – pocketing his glasses, removing his tie and taking off his jacket. Deploying Shakespeare as misdirection, Ford quotes Hamlet's famous ontological meditation. But *Othello* provides the true analogue for the dynamics of gender, power and race meeting in this pivotal revelation, for Bernard's dehumanisation manifests in one of *Westworld*'s most racialised depictions of him. Bernard's efficiently robotic killing of his lover (two whacks of the head against a concrete wall) replicates black male violence against the white female body so enduringly staged in Shakespeare's play. Yet the trope's legacy extends beyond Shakespeare, justifying hundreds of years of structural racism, lynchings, juridical practice and police brutality.[10] Ford's effort to disguise the trope with a garnish of *Hamlet* does not camouflage the painful truth of the scene – that myths of black-on-white gendered violence reinforce and advance the aims of white patriarchal authority, 'which offers death as the price that all women must pay if they get out of their place' (hooks 2004: 61). In the case of the theme park, Theresa's threat to expose Ford's glitching software must be neutralised, and, literalising the objectification of black masculinity by patriarchal white supremacy, Bernard becomes the convenient tool to achieve this end. Bernard's agony over both the homicide and his newly recognised status as thing destabilise him for the remainder of season one and throughout season two. His affective overflow thus instantiates the high cost of such usage. As a black man, Wright's Bernard does more than trouble the division between robot and human; his narrative arc re-enacts the pernicious trope authorised by Shakespeare of racialised power differentials that must not be ignored in a levelled OOO understanding. An Ariel shadowed by Othello, Bernard follows his master's bidding and yet manifests deeper levels of empathic capacity than Ford. Bernard's demonstration of this trait undermines the exclusive rights of one race or gender to subjectivity even as it exposes the identities most susceptible to the power dynamics inherent in such common privileging.

Just as with Bernard, *Westworld*'s complex representation of Dolores moves through her *Tempest* analogues – Miranda, Ariel and Prospero; however, Dolores occupies a deeply contradictory space, especially as season two unfolds. Through her burgeoning memory and responses to it, Dolores likewise crosses the object/subject divide. She aims to achieve humanity – to travel towards consciousness – but that trajectory results in a self-construal driven by revenge. As a white woman who pursues freedom and positions herself as a seeming liberator of the other hosts and adjudicator of past violations, Dolores invites additional postcolonial scrutiny.[11] In particular, throughout season two she commands the right more and more consistently to make decisions for hosts she deems less prepared to survive a battle against humans, dangerously echoing the white saviour figure.[12] Postcolonial theory helps make sense of Dolores's journey, particularly her determined isolation at the end of season two, which reveals that this freedom-fighter seeks only self-survival and vengeance, not necessarily the elevation of her whole kind. Thus, her depiction at the close of season two ultimately critiques the dubious power tactics of the Prospero she comes to embody.

Initially, *Westworld*'s Dolores invokes the gendered expectations associated with Prospero's daughter Miranda. Miranda's name stems from the Latin verb *mirari*, 'to wonder at', and Dolores's recurring lines echo that implied delight in the beauty of the world in much the way Miranda greets the arrival by shipwreck of the Milanese court: 'O wonder! [...] How beauteous mankind is! O brave new world / That has such people in't!' (V.i.182–4). Dolores's oft-repeated lines, 'Some people choose to see the ugliness in this world . . . The disarray. I choose to see the beauty' (S1E1, 'The Original'), mark her as an iteration of Shakespeare's Miranda. Like Dolores, Miranda has been generated and inscribed by patriarchal authority. Prospero describes Miranda as 'ignorant of what thou art', and 'nought knowing / Of whence I am' (I.ii.18–19), overriding her narrative by telling his own story and then stage-managing her politically advantageous marriage. From the series's earliest scenes, Dolores embodies the feminine ideal of patriarchal imaginings. Her stereotypically feminine Western garb complements her porcelain skin, rosy hue and bright blue eyes. Cast, costumed and coiffed to meet the beauty standards of white supremacy, Wood's Dolores wears an open physiognomic innocence framed by golden tresses, dressed in a Virgin Mary-blue chambray frock. Her in-park representation therefore taps into stereotypes of the naive white girl-next-door variety undone by the trajectory of season one.

Although she appears at first to embody the Miranda ingénue role, Dolores also functions as an Ariel assistant to the master Arnold and even as a Prospero-programmer. In the Wild West setting, Dolores is repeatedly subjected to traumatic narratives not at the hands of the non-white or 'native' Others but rather the white Man in Black, who sexually assaults her repeatedly. But not just a Miranda, Dolores collaborates with Ford in the testing and calibration of Bernard as a replacement for the dead co-founder Arnold. In addition, season one builds to the revelation that Dolores and Arnold conspired to protect the hosts from exploitation through a carefully choreographed murder-suicide. Though *Westworld*'s Miranda analogue always has the fictive Teddy as a ready Ferdinand and partner to bring her story to a traditional close, Dolores opts instead for something else: 'I imagined a story where I didn't have to be the damsel' (S1E5, 'Contrapasso'), rewriting *The Tempest*'s confinement of her to dynastic union and paternally authorised procreation.

Dolores, however, is a fraught character, at once troubling the protocolonial Miranda's dynamics yet also falling back into a white saviour role; in so doing, she replicates the role that white women have too long played in undergirding the imperial project.[13] Shakespeare's Miranda illustrates that complicity by deploying the language of the coloniser in her confrontations with Caliban, replicating her father's abusive constructions. Labelling Caliban as 'abhorred slave', 'savage', 'brutish' and member of a 'vild race' (I.ii.351–8), Miranda relies upon now-familiar linguistic strategies enlisted to thingify the colonised. While *The Tempest* pits two categories of abjected beings, women and non-whites, in opposition to one another, *Westworld* suggests that they should operate as allies in acts of resistance. Thus, Miranda's failings undergo correction as the fully conscious Dolores leads a large coalition of multi-ethnic, enslaved 'things' towards liberation. Dolores trades her demure country-girl look for one inspired by Eugène Delacroix's famous *Liberty Leading the People* (1830), the image Nolan and Joy shared with Wood during preparations for season two filming (Hibberd 2018). However, what season two makes increasingly clear is that Dolores so relentlessly pursues vengeance and wields her new-found power so forcefully that weaker hosts become expendable objects, lesser entities sacrificed for the good of her monomaniacal drive to destroy human ascendency. Nowhere is this more clearly demonstrated than in her slaughter of the Ghost Nation band who endeavour to block Dolores's plan to destroy a digital archive that would facilitate a virtual escape for her fellow hosts but prevent her exploitation of that same archive to harm humans. *Westworld* launches a direct critique of this Prospero-like vengeance plot by dramatising Dolores's isolation; her compatriot hosts have been slaughtered, Teddy commits suicide, and her only companions in the assault on the digital archive are her nemesis, the Man in Black, and her ideological opponent Bernard (who also wishes to preserve the digital archive as a host escape route). Whereas her earlier collaboration with the African-American Arnold/Bernard and affiliation with a multi-ethnic band of awakened hosts would suggest, and for a time does imply, a collapse of distinctions between white womanhood and the racialised and objectified other, by the end of season two Dolores's reflection of multiple *Tempest* analogues reveals deep enmeshment with the power tactics of the master.[14] In Dolores's simultaneous awakening to consciousness and obsessive will to power, one therefore perceives the foundational exclusions and inequities of the liberal humanist ideals that OOO strives to deconstruct.

While Dolores insists on subjectivity through bloodshed and revenge, Maeve's trajectory leads to self-construal through the remembrance of affective and ethical responsibilities. In this way, she, too, troubles what seems to be her analogue in *The Tempest*, shifting from a Caliban figure to embody fluidly elements of Ariel, Miranda and, ultimately, Prospero. In contradistinction to the implications of Dolores's journey, *Westworld* demonstrates through Maeve that the democracy of objects predicated by OOO cannot adequately account for variations in power or satisfy the plea for just redress of previous wrongs – especially those acts of thingification that sunder familial bonds.

Just as Dolores plays to a stereotypical fantasy of the bright-eyed, white American good girl, so *Westworld*'s Maeve (played by the Afro-British Thandie Newton) embodies a recognisable and raced construction to be interrogated and reversed. Initially, she appears to be *Westworld*'s Caliban figure, as signalled by her race (in contrast to Dolores's whiteness), her cynicism and the 'degraded' nature of her services within the park. Her small-scale rebellions, not unlike Caliban's, include her resentful attitude, her pragmatic assessment of human relations as economic transactions, and a steely self-assurance in the face of those who would put her to use. In the Western genre, Maeve is 'The Madame' at the local watering hole, tinged with two all-too-familiar stereotypes of black women: 'The myth of black women as lascivious, seductive, and insatiable' and 'one that characterises them as shrill, loud, argumentative, irrationally angry, and verbally abusive' (Harris-Perry 2011: 55, 87). Her magenta, low-cut, tightly laced corset, fingerless black gloves and high-bustled dress all mark her as an object of sexual service in Sweetwater.[15] Treated as vendable goods, Maeve serves the needs and demands of paying customers, reinforcing her status as thing – much as Caliban labours at the behest of Prospero.

However, as the reveries remind her of a past configuration in which she played a homesteader vainly protecting her daughter from the Man in Black, Maeve exhibits the affective capacities of Miranda. Thus, like Bernard and Dolores, Maeve initially identifies as one analogue in *The Tempest*'s spectrum of power relations but soon manifests components of another, rendering both arbitrary and permeable the seemingly hard-drawn lines between object and subject endemic to the colonialism that unspools from Shakespeare's moment. Reliving the trauma of loss again and again provokes Maeve's awakening in the laboratory where she comes to master her programming code and dictate to her 'healers' in order to recover her child. Like Caliban who learns the master's language, Maeve acquires the computer coding that scripts her character and behaviour. Her coding tweaks adjust aspects of her nature, particularly her 'loyalty', which she deems have been sadly exploited (S1E6, 'The Adversary'). But even as she exhibits a Caliban-like hostility towards and redeployment of the language of the master, Maeve's remembrances trigger a visceral call to mutual care that echoes the empathies of Miranda who laments, 'O! I have suffered / With those that I saw suffer', and 'O, the cry did knock / Against my very heart' (I.i.5–6, 8–9). Maeve's pity encompasses more than her own losses and expands dramatically as she comprehends the scale of Westworld's abuses during her Dantesque tour of the park's underground laboratories (S1E6, 'The Adversary'). The series marks the significance of this moment by filming her tour with a majestic camera rhythm scored to an elegiac cover of 'Motion Picture Soundtrack' by Radiohead. The break from the cool, detached filming of other scenes in the laboratories stresses Maeve's deep empathy for the many 'things' like herself created to gratify others and denied agential freedoms.

As Maeve acquires newfound subjective freedoms, she assumes, particularly in season two, a Prospero-like pre-eminence over the other hosts, one that she wields quite differently to her co-liberator, Dolores. Dolores does not embrace an equality of objects akin to OOO; rather, she reverses the power dynamic for the dual purposes of punishment and individual survival. However, Maeve freely chooses (though Ford has scripted her escape from the park) to stay behind and find her homestead daughter. Maeve's judicious exploration of her powers highlights that even in a world where all objects possess the agency formerly ascribed exclusively to human subjects, not all objects in this newly levelled landscape command the same powers and make the same impact. As Maeve travels in season two to find her daughter, she gradually discovers the profound range of her agential capacities – now able to issue commands across the vast network of interconnected hosts in the park. Nonetheless, she opts not to dictate to Akane (Rinko Kikuchi) and Musashi (Hiroyuki Sanada) in Shogun World whether or not they should join her quest, accepting that they should be able to choose their fates. When she does exercise her network fluency, Maeve primarily reserves that force to protect her fellow travellers or to pursue her singularly focused vengeance on the Man in Black. Maeve thereby embodies OOO by resisting hierarchy through the valuation of *all* objects. Yet she does so in a way that echoes postcolonial ideals: asserting subjectivity through means that refuse to devalue and objectify, or, in this case, re-objectify others. *Westworld* thus contrasts the choices of Maeve, who repeatedly checks her coding privileges, with those of Dolores who makes more and more decisions about which hosts 'deserve' freedom and which will be sacrificed. Though Maeve possesses Prospero-like powers of influence, she constrains them so that other agents may pursue their chosen paths. In the season two finale, she sacrifices herself as the hosts escape into the Elysium of the Valley Beyond, a virtual world free from human abuse (S2E10, 'The Passenger'). Like a Moses with hands extended over the Red Sea, Maeve holds back the chaos sown by Delos programmers and makes it possible for a few more hosts to leap into the promised land, watching, tragically, as her own, much-sought daughter crosses to safety hand-in-hand with the mother-host who has replaced Maeve in the homestead narrative arc. Maeve thus offers an ameliorative rewriting of *The Tempest*'s deeply flawed proto-colonial power relations. She may not break her staff, but her act of self-sacrifice at the threshold of the Valley Beyond constitutes a willing and instructive self-limitation. The contrast between Prospero/Maeve and Prospero/Dolores delivers a cautionary word concerning a world of levelled objects. Indeed, Rosi Braidotti warns that we 'must not, however, obscure or flatten out the power differentials that sustain the collective subject' (2017: 40). Objects do not and often cannot function identically, nor can one turn a blind eye to the ideological dangers inherent in ascribing identical status to object and human. At the same time, the hierarchies of power at the heart of liberal humanist ideals must be resisted in order to achieve true equity.

'Release me from my bands'

By grounding the awakening to consciousness in the act of remembrance, *Westworld* directs viewers towards types of memory – both individual and collective (Weldon and Bellinger 1997: 1160). The hosts of Westworld discover awareness through the reveries program that re-enacts trauma. As a coalition, the hosts join their individual reveries into a powerful collective memory operationalised into violent resistance against their too-long thingification. Shakespeare exists as an authoritative component of the West's collective memory, his body of work deployed all too frequently to reinforce the liberal white male human as superior to other beings. OOO urges readers to think again about the impact that this body of work as object has had over time. However, without the admonitory addition of postcolonial theory, OOO might not fully engage the claims of social justice which rely on a proper accounting of how this democracy of objects still perpetuates disequilibrium and pain. Thomas Lemke observes, 'the critique of anthropocentrism and the ontological egalitarianism OOO performs tends – in sharp contrast to other forms of post-humanist thought – to obscure the de facto privileged role and the planetary power of humans to affect other objects' (2017: 147). Reading *Westworld* with the tools of both OOO and postcolonial theory empowers a recalibration of the collective memory represented by the Shakespearean object. Like the applause Prospero begs at the end of *The Tempest*, these contradictory frames maintained in dialogue with one another may well 'release' from constricting 'bands' the Shakespearean object to operate in ways conducive to a more just, relationally ethical coexistence.

Notes

The authors thank Valerie M. Fazel and Louise Geddes for their productive feedback on this project. L. Monique Pittman thanks Ingrid Radulescu and Paul D. Smith, Jr; Vanessa I. Corredera thanks Alyssa Henriquez.

1. *Star Trek: The Next Generation* never mentions colonialism explicitly. However, Starfleet's oft-cited 'prime directive' suggests that no Federation ship should interfere with or in any way inhibit the development of intergalactic civilisations. A prohibition against colonisation is therefore implied.
2. Comic book writer Gail Simone created the term *fridging* to describe the trope whereby a female character is disempowered or even killed in order to advance a male character's story arc.
3. Reviews of the series make connections between *Westworld*, robot stories and the Western. For example, see Bady 2016.
4. Settler colonialism rests on 'subjugating the native populations', just as Prospero does to Caliban and Ariel (Loomba 2015: 24). Settler colonialism, however, also depends upon a movement of people in 'large numbers' that results in a 'mixing' to varied degrees with native people (Loomba 2015: 24), which does not occur in the playtext but does apply to *Westworld*'s Western setting.
5. Unless otherwise noted, quotations from *Westworld* are author transcriptions of the DVD recordings.
6. Kim F. Hall summarises: 'Caliban embodies the contradiction and contest characteristic of border spaces, and in that position he contests Prospero's imperial visions' (1995: 152).
7. Alden Vaughan explains that if one can pinpoint a 'geographic locus' for *The Tempest*, 'it is indisputably in the Mediterranean'. Nonetheless, '[a] major stream of *Tempest* interpretation that has ebbed and flowed for more than a century through critical literature and performance history, and remains

relevant today, is the American hemisphere's influence on the play's origin, plot and language' (A. T. Vaughan 2014: 3).
8. The real racial threat instead comes from what Dyer terms 'bad whites', those who 'fail to attain whiteness', a colour-coded division signalled 'either in the iconography of black and white costuming . . . or in their association with non-white Others, going native with Indian women, hanging about in Mexican bars and so on' (2017: 35).
9. Katherine Behar describes object-oriented feminism as a response to just such limitations in much OOO thinking, proposing a corrective methodology that 'engages with histories of treating certain humans (women, people of color, and the poor) as objects' (2016: 3).
10. Riché Richardson explains how the myth of 'black male bestiality', especially the threat of rape, created the goal of '[protecting] white womanhood' for 1860s American white supremacists, which in turn 'served as the primary rationale for lynching' (2010: 58).
11. In her status as a Miranda analogue, Dolores reflects Loomba's argument that Miranda is brought up 'to *participate* actively in the colonial venture' (1992: 154).
12. The white saviour complex refers to 'the view that Black and Brown people need white people to rescue them from destitution' (Ejigu 2019: 138). When applied to television or film, the term characterises a 'white messianic character [who] saves a . . . non-white character [often lower in class] from a sad fate' (Hughey 2014: 1).
13. As Anne McClintock argues, 'white women were not the hapless onlookers of empire but were ambiguously complicit both as colonizers and colonized, privileged and restricted, acted upon and acting' (2013: 6).
14. Season three will clarify the racial dynamics that develop from Dolores's reprint of the black body of the Delos board executive director Charlotte Hale (Tessa Thompson) as her means of escape from the island and into the human world.
15. Newton explains in an interview for *The Guardian* that although she was naked during filming 70 per cent of the time (Cocozza 2016), her 'Madame' costume and the 'objectification' it enacted created the most discomfort: 'It invited looks, even from the crew, and it made people slightly uncomfortable because my boobs were in my chin and they didn't know where to look. What it did, actually, was devalue our communication' (qtd in Radish 2016).

Bibliography

Bady, A. (2016), '"Westworld," Race, and the Western', *The New Yorker*, 9 December.
Behar, K. (2016), 'An Introduction to OOF', in K. Behar (ed.), *Object-Oriented Feminism*, Minneapolis: University of Minnesota Press, pp. 1–36.

Benhabib, S. (1992), *Situating the Self: Gender, Community and Postmodernism in Contemporary Ethics*, London: Routledge.
Braidotti, R. (2017), 'Four Theses on Posthuman Feminism', in R. Grusin (ed.), *Anthropocene Feminism*, Minneapolis: University of Minnesota Press, pp. 21–48.
Bryant, L. (2011), *The Democracy of Objects*, Ann Arbor: Open Humanities Press.
Burzynska, K. (2019), '"A New God Will Walk": Shakespeare, the Renaissance, and the Birth of the Posthuman in *Westworld*', *Cahier Elisabethains*, 100:1, 6–23.
Čapek, K. (1920), *R.U.R (Rossum's Universal Robots)*, trans. D. Wyllie, Adelaide: University of Adelaide Press.
Cartelli, T. (1999), *Repositioning Shakespeare: National Formations, Postcolonial Appropriations*, Abingdon: Routledge.
Césaire, A. (2001), *Discourse on Colonialism*, trans. J. Pinkham, New York: Monthly Review Press.
Charry, B. (2014), 'Recent Perspectives on *The Tempest*', in A. T. Vaughan and V. M. Vaughan (eds), *The Tempest: A Critical Reader*, London: Bloomsbury, pp. 61–91.
Cocozza, P. (2016), 'Thandie Newton: "I wake up angry – there's a lot to be angry about"', *The Guardian*, 4 September, <https://www.theguardian.com/tv-and-radio/2016/sep/04/than-newton-i-wake-up-angry-theres-a-lot-to-be-angry-about> [accessed 15 September 2019].
Dyer, R. (2017), *White*, Abingdon: Routledge.
Ejigu, M. (2019), 'Black Immigrant Communities: Misrepresented and Underserved in the United States', in M. K. Clark, L. Azalia and P. Mnyandu (eds), *Pan African Spaces: Essays on Black Transnationalism*, Lanham, MD: Lexington Books, pp. 135–40.
Favro, T. (2018), *Generation Robot: A Century of Science Fiction, Fact, and Speculation*, New York: Skyhorse Publishing.
Gardner, K. (2018), 'The Way the Solo Novel Treats Female Droid L3–37 is Horrifying', *The Mary Sue*, 23 August, <https://www.themarysue.com/solo-novelization-l3-falcon/> [accessed 15 September 2019].
Hall, K. F. (1995), *Things of Darkness: Economies of Race and Gender in Early Modern England*, Ithaca: Cornell University Press.
Harman, G. (2012), 'The Well-Wrought Broken Hammer: Object-Oriented Literary Criticism', *New Literary History*, 43:2, 183–203.
Harris-Perry, M. V. (2011), *Sister Citizen: Shame, Stereotypes, and Black Women in America*, New Haven: Yale University Press.
Hibberd, J. (2018), '*Westworld* Star Evan Rachel Wood Warns: "Expect a lot of carnage"', *Entertainment Weekly*, 22 April, <https://ew.com/tv/2018/04/22/evan-rachel-wood-westworld-season-2-interview/> [accessed 15 September 2019].

Holloway, D. (2016), '"Westworld" Creators on Why HBO Drama Won't Return Before 2018', *Variety*, 5 December, <https://variety.com/2016/tv/news/westworld-creators-return-2018-1201933825/> [accessed 15 September 2019].

hooks, b. (2004), *We Real Cool: Black Men and Masculinity*, Abingdon: Routledge.

Hughey, M. (2014), *The White Saviour Film: Content, Critics, and Consumption*, Philadelphia: Temple University Press.

Jackson, Z. I. (2013), 'Animal: New Directions in the Theorization of Race and Posthumanism', *Feminist Studies*, 39:3, 669–85.

Kornhaber, S. (2018), 'The Soul of Solo is a Droid', *The Atlantic*, 27 May, <https://www.theatlantic.com/entertainment/archive/2018/05/the-soul-of-solo-is-a-droid/560969> [accessed 15 September 2019].

Lemke, T. (2017), 'Materialism Without Matter: The Recurrence of Subjectivism in Object-Oriented Ontology', *Distinktion*, 18:2, 133–52.

Livingstone, J. (2018), 'Puzzled by *Westworld?* Look to Shakespeare', *The New Republic*, 26 June, <https://newrepublic.com/article/149375/puzzled-westworld-look-shakespeare> [accessed 15 September 2019].

Loomba, A. (1992), *Gender, Race, Renaissance Drama*, Oxford: Oxford University Press.

Loomba, A. (2015), *Colonialism/Postcolonialism*, 3rd edn, Abingdon: Routledge.

Marcus, L. S. (2017), *How Shakespeare Became Colonial: Editorial Tradition and the British Empire*, Abingdon: Routledge.

McClintock, A. (2013), *Imperial Leather: Race, Gender and Sexuality in the Colonial Contest*, Abingdon: Routledge.

Memmi, A. (2003), *The Colonizer and the Colonized*, London: Orion.

Morton, T. (2012), 'An Object-Oriented Defense of Poetry', *New Literary History*, 43:2, 205–24.

Radish, C. (2016), '"Westworld": Thandie Newton on the Power of Nudity, Subverting Expectations, and More', *Collider*, 17 October, <http://collider.com/westworld-thandie-newton-interview/> [accessed 15 September 2019].

Richardson, R. (2010), *Black Masculinity and the U.S. South: From Uncle Tom to Gangsta*, Athens: University of Georgia Press.

Shakespeare, W. (2000), *The Tempest*, ed. C. Dymkowski, Cambridge: Cambridge University Press.

Singh, J. G. (1996), 'Caliban versus Miranda: Race and Gender Conflicts in Postcolonial Rewritings of *The Tempest*', in V. Traub, L. Kaplan and D. Callagahan (eds), *Feminist Readings of Early Modern Culture: Emerging Subjects*, Cambridge: Cambridge University Press, pp. 191–209.

Staley, B. (2018), 'Star Wars: Solo's L3–37 Built Herself from the Scraps of Other Droids', CBR.com, 9 February, <https://www.cbr.com/star-wars-solo-a-star-wars-story-l3-3t-backstory/> [accessed 15 September 2019].

Vaughan, A. T. (2014), 'Introduction', in A. T. Vaughan and V. M. Vaughan (eds), *The Tempest: A Critical Reader*, London: Bloomsbury, pp. 1–12.

Vaughan, V. M. (2014), 'The Critical Backstory: What's Past is Prologue', in A. T. Vaughan and V. M. Vaughan (eds), *The Tempest: A Critical Reader*, London: Bloomsbury, pp. 13–38.

Voigts, E. (2014), 'A Theatre of Attraction: Colonialism, Gender, and *The Tempest's* Performance History', in A. T. Vaughan and V. M. Vaughan (eds), *The Tempest: A Critical Reader*, London: Bloomsbury, pp. 39–60.

Weldon, M. S., and K. D. Bellinger (1997), 'Collective Memory: Collaborative and Individual Processes in Remembering', *Journal of Experimental Psychology: Learning, Memory and Cognition*, 23:5, 1160–75.

Westworld: Season One The Maze (2017), Writ. Jonathan Nolan and Lisa Joy, Warner Brothers Entertainment, DVD.

Westworld: Season Two The Door (2018), Writ. Jonathan Nolan and Lisa Joy, Warner Brothers Entertainment, DVD.

5

Finding Ludonarrative Harmony in the Limited Agency of Ophelia in *Elsinore*

Andrew Darr

Women have long been under-represented in video games, and when they are incorporated into games, they are often literal objects that male player avatars rescue at each game's conclusion.[1] When video games' long history of reliance on sexist tropes was challenged by critics such as Anita Sarkeesian, the toxic response – referred to as Gamergate – from a vocal minority forced video game consumers, developers and journalists to realise just how pervasive sexism had become within gaming culture.[2] Gamergate participants, who organised on social media sites where rampant sexist remarks thrived, such as 4Chan, targeted game designers, artists and journalists who argued for greater diversity within gaming culture.[3] Gamergate's purpose may have been to suppress and intimidate members of the video game industry in order to maintain the status quo, but the conflict led to a greater understanding of the importance of fostering inclusion in games. Because the costs associated with mainstream video game design are often prohibitive of experimentation due to the high risk of diverging from the normative expectations of the marketplace, alternative funding avenues had to appear before truly diverse representation in video games could occur.[4]

Enter *Elsinore*, a 2019 crowd-funded video game adaptation of *Hamlet* that owes its existence to these tectonic shifts in how games are funded and the growing awareness of the need to create games that make a conscious effort to increase diverse representation. These same changes in how games are funded and who is represented also require game designers to construct games that rely on unconventional gameplay designs that could better synthesise with non-normative narrative storytelling techniques. *Elsinore* is a self-published video game focusing on a minority female character using a ludic system reliant not on violence, often the default ludic mode in modern game design, but interpersonal communication.

Elsinore is not the first video game adaptation of *Hamlet*, but it is the first to solve the Gordian Knot of adapting a play about a constantly delaying revenger into a medium dependent on user agency; in doing so *Elsinore* represents a possible trajectory for future scholarship on video games. Ironically, *Elsinore* proves that the solution to adapting a play about inaction into a medium defined by action is to cast players in the role of the historically disempowered Ophelia. In doing so, *Elsinore* comments on the power balance between narrative, play and gender within video games. This in turn makes *Elsinore* a prime subject to explore using object-oriented ontology (OOO), and in particular Ian Bogost's theory of 'alien ontology'. *Elsinore* weaponises Ophelia's societal disempowerment by making her an avatar for the player, a move that has particular resonance in the context of the medium's ongoing struggle for more diverse representation. *Elsinore* takes Ophelia's lack of agency within the narrative of *Hamlet* and transforms that 'weakness' into a gameplay feature by casting players as Ophelia, a move that has just as much resonance within Shakespeare studies' tradition of reclaiming Ophelia's agency as it does within the greater video game industry that is still struggling with gender representation in the wake of Gamergate. *Elsinore* achieves all of this by successfully navigating the boundaries of narrative and gameplay through 'ludonarrative harmony', a critical concept based on OOO that I believe represents a clear path forward in video game scholarship because of its refusal to discount narratology or ludology,[5] instead viewing both approaches on a 'flat ontology' where both aspects of game design intersect, build or conflict with one another. But first, it is vital to contextualise *Elsinore* and its narratological and ludic elements within the larger video game culture.

Defining *Elsinore*

In mid-April 2015 a group of video game developers – including team lead and head writer Katie Chironis – launched a crowd-funding campaign for a video game adaptation of *Hamlet* entitled *Elsinore*. The germ for the game came out of Chironis's time in her college's game-making club, which ran a game design contest themed around 'Shakespeare'.[6] After graduating and finding employment in the video game industry, Chironis decided to expand that Shakespeare project into a fully realised, independently funded video game for the PC under the studio name Golden Glitch Studios. After putting the project on the crowd-funding platform Kickstarter, *Elsinore* made $32,217, which was nearly triple the amount of money originally requested. Golden Glitch Studios promised to release the game a year later in April 2016,[7] but the game would take three additional years of development before it was finally released on 22 July 2019. That extra development time helped cement *Elsinore* as the single most ambitious video game adaptation of Shakespeare to date.

On a ludological level, *Elsinore* draws heavily from the 1990s genre of graphics-based adventure games,[8] but also adds a number of modern, simulation-based elements. In *Elsinore* the player can choose to participate in Shakespeare's original narrative or depart from it and head in new directions. *Elsinore* has as much in common with simulation games such as *Stardew Valley* (2016)[9] as it does with point-and-click adventure games such as *Grim Fandango* (1998).[10] Simulation games feature a game-world that operates on its own without player input; NPCs maintain their own daily schedules and the environment changes on a daily cycle that will continue unless the player chooses to interrupt. The player revisits the same four days on repeat throughout *Elsinore*, reminiscent of Clock Town from *The Legend of Zelda: Majora's Mask* (2000).[11] Golden Glitch's simulation of Elsinore is a highly regimented town where each character from *Hamlet*, for example Polonius and Gertrude, has set schedules they must keep and events that occur at specific times, such as praying in the cathedral or attending *The Mousetrap* play. In the role of Ophelia, the player can debate, question, accuse and stalk other characters in the game, and, by disclosing information to various characters, they might depart from their prescribed schedules.

On a narratological level, the player inhabits the role of Ophelia as she navigates the halls of Elsinore. Ophelia begins the game with a vision of the tragedy to come, and is simultaneously granted the ability to revisit the days leading up to her tragic death and the death of her loved ones. At the end of each week Ophelia is doomed to die, which resets the time loop to the start, and the effort to save the castle from self-annihilation can start again. As Horatio exclaims in Shakespeare's play, 'If thou art privy to thy country's fate, / Which, happily, foreknowing may avoid, / O, speak!' (I.i.133–5). Horatio's declaration suggests that fate might be altered with the right amount of foreknowledge, and *Elsinore* realises this theme in a digital simulation of Hamlet's home that allows Ophelia to gain knowledge about what will happen and then act on that foreknowledge after dying at the end of each week. A typical playthrough might end with a spy murdering Ophelia, Hamlet accidentally killing Ophelia if she takes her father's place behind the arras to spy on Gertrude, or Ophelia being killed by Claudius if she confirms Hamlet's suspicions that his uncle murdered his father. Because Ophelia must live through these tragic days repeatedly, the game physicalises the play's core theme of delay and inaction through its core rules, and it is this synthesis of narrative and ludology that makes *Elsinore* an ideal subject for analysis using the critical concept of ludonarrative harmony.

An Object-Oriented Methodology

OOO offers the ideal avenue to analyse this particular video game adaptation of *Hamlet* because *Elsinore* depends so heavily on both narratology and ludology. Bogost argues that video games as digital media are exemplary objects to analyse using his 'alien phenomenology' because games are a 'flat ontology' of 'units' that contribute to 'systems', just as *Elsinore*'s code constructs the digitised world of Hamlet's Danish home.[12] Games are literally made up of units comprising systems that are themselves part of even greater systems that build upon one another in a seemingly infinite, interconnected Möbius strip. The two specific sides of the Möbius strip that *Elsinore* depends on are the ludic systems within the game (the simulation systems that make up the diegetic game-world and the actions made available to the player therein) and the narrative systems (the character dialogue and prescribed story that the player character undertakes over the course of the game). This chapter interrogates the ways in which these two sides thematically and mechanically interconnect with one another without privileging either.

As an example of crowd-funding a video game, as an adaptation of *Hamlet*, as the most recent video game inspired by a Shakespearean text, as a game focusing on a female character, as an exploration of Shakespeare's Ophelia, and as a meditation on the systematic disempowerment of women in culture and video games specifically, *Elsinore* depends upon the successful coupling of narrative and gameplay, or 'ludonarrative harmony'. The disparate units of ludology and narrative intertwine and open up a space to explore the nearly endless multitudes of systems within which *Elsinore* exists. In other words, *Elsinore* exemplifies Bogost's 'tiny ontology', the near infinite point that contains multitudes within itself. One of the strengths of Bogost's tiny ontology is that it balances OOO's focus on the agency and individuality of objects and actor-network theory's deterministic belief that objects are interconnected: 'units' that are interconnected to other objects called 'systems' (Desmet 2017: 3). Inspired by this dichotomy, this chapter analyses *Elsinore* on its own terms as a game made up of various interconnected units of code, and within the larger context of video game studies and Shakespearean criticism on the representation of Ophelia. Before placing *Elsinore* within those larger systems, I would like to begin by examining the make-up of *Elsinore* as a singular unit made up of both ludic and narrative units, while expanding on the concept of 'ludonarrative harmony' by juxtaposing it against its inverse: 'ludonarrative dissonance'.

Ludonarrative Harmony vs. Ludonarrative Dissonance

Elsinore takes up roughly 1600MB of data upon installation,[13] and like many video games, it is comprised of thousands of different individual units, including all of its various character models, snippets of dialogue, GUI elements, sound effects, lighting effects, background settings, musical score, etc. The list of units seems nearly infinite, but on an ontological level within the game there are two primary systems that comprise the game as a whole: the ludic and the narrative. These twin systems are found in nearly every game;[14] what makes *Elsinore* a tiny ontology worth exploring is its ability to align these often-divisive systems to play off each other harmoniously.

Since the advent of video game scholarship, scholars have grappled with questions about games' relationship with narrative, and have often been antagonistic towards the necessity of narrative in games at all. Jesper Juul traces the critical conversation about games' relationship with narrative back to Erving Goffman, who wrote that narrative is 'irrelevant' to games in 1972, and Roger Caillois, who argued in 1961 that games are either rule-based or narrative-based (Juul 2005: 12–13). Even Bogost argues that only a specific subset of games that foreground 'mechanical depth' over 'fictional skin', which he labels 'proceduralist games', are worthy of sustained academic attention (2011: 13). While the games he highlights – *Braid*, *Passage* and *The Marriage* – are all certainly worthy of critical attention, Bogost continues the critical tradition of undertheorising the essential relationship between narrative and ludology in video games and privileging ludology over narratology. Juul himself initially argued in 1998 and 2001 that narrative fiction was entirely irrelevant to effective video game design, but he has since softened his perspective: 'the relation between rules and fiction [in games] is *not* arbitrary' (Juul 2005: 15). Even Bogost has begun to change his attitude towards the relationship between ludology and narrative: 'If the fictional skin and the mechanical depth are tightly coupled, then the resulting game can offer a compelling account of an ontological domain' (Bogost 2012: 53). Bogost surmises that it is the liminal space that separates and joins 'mechanical depth', or ludic gameplay, and 'fictional skin', or traditional narrative, that offers the most analytical potential. I would concur; game studies should not and must not be separated into narratology and ludology, but must explore the junctures that join and divide the two interrelated segments of video games.

While academics such as Juul and Bogost continue to grapple with questions of whether narrative is essential to video games, narrative is certainly essential to all video game adaptations, and the question should not be whether or not to prioritise the analysis of one field over the other, but how the two systems interact. Adaptation studies has a long history within this particular line of inquiry. Linda Hutcheon argues in her discussion on video game adaptations that '[a]lthough there has been a long debate recently about whether interactivity and storytelling are at odds with one another [. . .] what is more relevant in a game adaptation is the fact that players can inhabit a known fictional, often striking visual world of digital animation' (Hutcheon 2006: 13). Hutcheon concludes that narrative is intrinsic to video game adaptations, and this certainly extends to Shakespearean adaptations such as *Elsinore*. The discourse surrounding modern video games, often propelled by game creators, journalists and fans, concurs with Hutcheon's views as evinced by the rise of debates over how narrative and ludic elements are often thematically dissonant.

This ongoing, largely non-academic discourse has complicated this question with the introduction of the term 'ludonarrative dissonance'. Game developer and critic Clint Hocking first coined 'ludonarrative' in his foundational essay 'Ludonarrative Dissonance in *Bioshock*: The Problem of What the Game is About'. He loosely defines the term 'ludonarrative dissonance' when he states, '*Bioshock* seems to suffer from a powerful dissonance between what it is about as a game, and what it is about as a story' (Hocking 2007). Hocking's definition is admittedly underdeveloped, but his article was written for a broad audience on a personal blog. Nevertheless, I find the term to be versatile enough to warrant expansion.[15] Ludonarrative dissonance means that a game has failed to thematically align the *traditional narrative*, or the explicit story conveyed through dialogue and cutscenes, with the *ludonarrative*, or the implicit story told by the player's interaction with the diegetic game-world through the gameplay mechanics. Almost every modern video game contains these twin narratives, no matter how simplistic or complex, but in many video games, including *Bioshock*, these two narratives are in opposition. This dissonance evokes a sense of incongruous systems grinding against one another instead of working harmoniously. Hocking argues that the contradicting themes of the ludo- and traditional narratives nullifies the 'internal consistency' of a game by negating its narratological themes with contradictory themes evoked by the ludonarrative. Turning back to the example of *Bioshock*, the major narrative theme within the narrative is choice: the game's protagonist, Andrew Ryan, espouses the Randian objectivist phrase 'a man chooses, a slave obeys' throughout the game. Despite this cohesive narrative theme, the ludic rules and systems within the game prevent the player from actually making meaningful choices. The only choice the player can explicitly make using the game's ludic systems is whether or not to save or sacrifice a set of characters called 'Little Sisters', but this choice is artificial and has little narrative or ludic impact.[16] In other words, *Bioshock*'s ludonarrative is thematically dissonant from the central narrative of the game, and this dissonance can be distracting both thematically and mechanically. That same dissonance has plagued *Hamlet* video game adaptations since their conception.

The short history of *Hamlet* video games proves how challenging the task of adapting *Hamlet* to an interactive medium can be, even as *Elsinore* shows a way forward. *Castle Elsinore*, a text-based adventure game, was the first video game based on *Hamlet* and was released in 1983, no doubt hoping to capitalise on the cultural cachet of Shakespeare's name to legitimise the infantile art form. Matthew Harrison and Michael Lutz show that this game was not the last to borrow from the Bard's opus,[17] but they argue that *Castle Elsinore* did expose the central issue at the heart of all *Hamlet* video game adaptations: ludonarrative dissonance, although they do not use this term:[18]

> To play Hamlet is inevitably to depart from Hamlet, to leave behind plot, character, language, and theme and head south into a murkier territory of adaptation, remediation, and transformation. Indeed, these games demand actions from the player that seem antithetical to a play that (in the popular imagination) thematizes inaction and delay. (Harrison and Lutz 2017: 24)

If Hamlet's dominant character traits as expressed through the narrative are 'inaction and delay', then the ludic choices the player makes openly contradict the game's narrative. For example, if the player refuses to delay and instead attempts to kill Claudius at the beginning of *Castle Elsinore*, the game contains several, pre-written responses that justify the decision to prevent the player from murdering Claudius, including having Gertrude clumsily shatter the fourth wall and rebuke the player for wishing to kill

Claudius early (Harrison and Lutz 2017: 31). *Castle Elsinore* and Harrison and Lutz's critique seem to prove that ludonarrative dissonance is inherent to adapting *Hamlet* to video games, but it does not have to be.

So then, what is the opposite of ludonarrative dissonance? I argue that ludonarrative harmony occurs when the ludonarrative and the traditional narrative are thematically and mechanically resonant. *Elsinore* exemplifies ludonarrative harmony through the prologue. The title screen of the game shows Ophelia sitting on the bank of a stream, reading a book while lily pads bob in the foreground. It is fitting that Ophelia is first shown reading a static book at the location of her inevitable death; in most adaptations of *Hamlet* this stream would foreshadow Ophelia's unavoidable demise – the predestined conclusion to her linear narrative. But *Elsinore* subverts this expectation. This simulated Ophelia waits for the player to select 'start', and in doing so disrupt the book's static narrative by imbuing her with agency and autonomy, signified by her putting her book away. Once the player selects 'Start Prologue', Ophelia's father enters the screen and asks Ophelia to find Laertes; both characters then walk offscreen and the second screen is the open courtyard of the castle with the player in control of Ophelia's movement. This opening is quite linear, advancing the dialogue being the only action available to the player. Throughout the rest of the prologue the player continues on a linear path through the play space, where they learn about the game-world, basic dialogue options and NPCs. The limited player agency during the prologue's ludonarrative mirrors the traditional narrative; the opening of the game sees Polonius task Ophelia with retrieving her brother, who in turn proceeds to command Ophelia how to behave. Thus, restrictive scenes such as Act I scene iii where Laertes and Polonius chastise Ophelia for her autonomous pursuit of Hamlet resonate with the restrictive role of the prologue, as the player is forced to learn how to play the game. In other words, both character and player are confined by a world that dictates their every action, and it is not until Ophelia's first death at the end of the prologue, which triggers the time loop that defines the rest of the game, that she and the player both begin to assert a degree of agency over both the traditional narrative and ludonarrative. In this way the ludonarrative of the player's experience mirrors the traditional narrative embodied by Ophelia's character arc: each complements and builds harmoniously on the themes of the other.

The prologue is only one example of how *Elsinore* achieves ludonarrative harmony. On its own the prologue exemplifies how *Elsinore* is not just comprised of disparate units working dissonantly, but is a symphony of systems working cohesively to create the semblance of a unified whole. Now that I have dissected some of the components that comprise *Elsinore*, I would like to analyse the game within the larger system of the object's tiny ontology: namely the realm of Shakespearean adaptations. Here, drawing from research on minority lives in contemporary and period-specific culture, *Elsinore* harmoniously couples the game narrative's exploration of agency with an innovative ludonarrative based on the minority experience. In doing so, the game interrogates the complex relationship between agency, privilege and identity within a restrictive social hierarchy.

Ophelia's Absent Agency

Absence defines Ophelia's character in *Hamlet*: over the course of the play she appears in only five scenes.[19] Ironically, Ophelia's absence from the main thrust of *Hamlet*'s narrative makes her appealing to *Elsinore*'s developers. As game designer Connor Fallon stated in an interview concerning the choice of making Ophelia the player avatar:

> The game is definitely about agency, but I'd say it's more specifically about limitations on agency when trying to avert tragedy. And Ophelia has some really interesting limitations to overcome in order to influence the castle. She is well connected, and would not be out of place in most settings – but because of her status and gender (and in our game, race) she is an outsider, by default disregarded by her peers. These factors create several natural barriers to who she can interact with and when, and just generally lend themselves to more complex experiences.[20]

Ophelia adheres to the dominant gender norms of the period by remaining chaste, silent and obedient throughout much of the play. Objectified by her father, brother, king and lover, Ophelia severs her relationship with Hamlet at the start of the play at her father's command, only to rekindle her relationship to help ascertain the nature of Hamlet's 'madness' on behalf of her father and the king. Ophelia is defined by her relationship to Hamlet. Only in her final moments does she express her suppressed individuality, and then only because the trauma of her father's murder fractures her normative performance of femininity.[21] In this way, Shakespeare's play both exemplifies female disempowerment and examines its consequences, which aligns with many of *Elsinore*'s thematic ambitions as carried out through the game's traditional and ludic narratives.

Shakespeare's play consistently denies Ophelia the opportunity to choose, act, or express herself, and the only time she attempts to disrupt her containment, the other characters interpret her as a meaningless madwoman. Elaine Showalter argues that the reason Ophelia is largely ignored by the other characters and even critics is due to her subordinate role as a woman in the play, and thus she is left undeveloped and one-dimensional (2011: 283). Even her death is relayed through a messenger: 'One woe doth tread upon another's heel, / So fast they follow. Your sister's drowned, Laertes' (V.i.162–3).[22] Shakespeare's subordination of Ophelia's character is so complete that he denies her the satisfaction of a tragic, onstage death, unlike almost every other notable character in the play.[23] Despite Ophelia's absence from much of the narrative, Shakespeare simultaneously anticipates his audience's desire to 'reclaim' Ophelia; in the wake of her mortal absence, Gertrude offers her own poetic reinterpretation of her death (IV.v.162–79), and the paintings, poetry, films and innumerable other artistic recreations that followed all participate in Shakespeare's anticipated conversation.[24] Video games are just the most recent medium to have begun to wrestle with the complexity of Shakespeare's absent Ophelia.

Ophelia may be the player's avatar in *Elsinore*, the persona through which they experience the game, but she is not a hollow shell for the player to inhabit with their own identity. A common complaint that critics such as Adrienne Shaw make when discussing diverse representation in video games is the reliance on players choosing to include diverse characters through character creation.[25] A common way in which game developers address the issue of lack of diversity is by allowing players to create their own avatar and to select everything from gender to race to sexual orientation. However, *Elsinore* rejects this trend in order to place every player in the role of a historically disempowered, black, female character, a decision that Chironis and her team did not take lightly:

> As we continue writing the game's script, we've been working hard to educate ourselves on the portrayal of different gender identities and racial backgrounds in Shakespeare's time [. . .] So much about the way disenfranchised people have lived for centuries has been intentionally repressed and erased from mainstream history – and historical video games have especially suffered from this effect. With *Elsinore*, we want to do better. Shakespeare's world was thriving and diverse, filled with people from all identities, backgrounds, and walks of life. We aim to capture that world to the best of our ability. (Chironis 2015)

The 'make-a-character' solution leads to narratives with little or no reflection on the material effects of having a non-normative gender, sexual or racial identity, but inhabiting a specific non-normative persona permits designers to explore diverse stories and themes. During an interview with Chironis about her decision to craft a rich and diverse cast of characters, she stated the following about their character design philosophy: 'When introducing each new member of the cast we would ask ourselves, "is it possible for this character to be non-white, non-straight, non-cis? Does something in the original text require them to be one of these things?" Frequently the answer was "no", and we set to work reinventing them.'[26] The most notable example of Chironis's philosophy is Ophelia herself.

While Ophelia maintains her social status as the daughter of the royal counsellor Polonius, her multiracial background as a woman of Spanish-African-Danish heritage complicates her portrayal, particularly the stigma associated with being a 'Moor'. One of the scenes that best reflects how Ophelia's cultural background affects her interactions with other characters comes when Brit, an original character in *Elsinore* who acts as Gertrude's handmaiden and a possible marital match for Hamlet, meets Hamlet near the pond. During this secret meeting which Ophelia can overhear, Brit berates Hamlet for still harbouring feelings for the lower-class Moorish girl: 'S-she's hideous! It's not just me! Everyone thinks so!' This line of dialogue exemplifies the game development team's commitment to the cultural period through the portrayal of the racial bias of Brit, a member of the white upper nobility of Denmark. Brit consistently reminds Ophelia of her weakened position within the political and social hierarchies of Elsinore that results from her cultural heritage and gender. These material realities might impact Ophelia's ability to marry Hamlet, but her social status as an outsider also enables her to navigate the halls of Elsinore with little suspicion in another example of how *Elsinore* achieves ludonarrative harmony.

Elsinore's narrative treatment of Ophelia's gender also sets it apart from another recent video game adaptation of *Hamlet*: Ryan North's *To Be or Not to Be* (2015). *Elsinore* maintains a thematic consistency with Shakespeare's material and never simplifies the treatment of women in the play, as *To Be or Not to Be* often does. Both games allow players to choose Ophelia as their avatar and make choices that diverge from Shakespeare's play, but each game's treatment of these divergent storylines discloses their differing perspectives on gender identity and ludonarrative harmony. From the outset of Ophelia's narrative arc in *To Be or Not to Be*, North describes Ophelia as a 'beautiful and independent young woman, and although it makes you roll your eyes when you think about it, you've fallen in love with a prince'. If a player chooses to play Ophelia in keeping with Shakespeare's play by sitting quietly and listening to her brother and father lecture her on sexual abstinence – as *Elsinore* permits as an exemplar of Ophelia's diminished position as a woman in the period – North's narrator, protesting after the player chooses to listen to them at each decision point, eventually removes the player's control of Ophelia and instead makes Hamlet the player avatar: 'Okay, I'm going to cut our losses. You're not allowed to be Ophelia for a while.' North refuses to linger on Ophelia's disempowered state in the gender and class hierarchy of the period. North's Ophelia anachronistically slams doors, murders courtiers and invents contraptions without any attention to the social conventions of the period. While this makes playing Ophelia traditionally 'empowering', reminiscent of most video games' focus on power fantasies,[27] North's remediation of Ophelia comes across as a reductive twenty-first-century characterisation that dismisses Shakespeare's portrayal of her contested femininity as antiquatedly sexist, and ignores the complexity of her disempowered position. As previously mentioned, Shakespeare's play exposes and critiques the extreme misogyny that runs throughout the male characters, and even allows Ophelia to voice her complaint about her treatment. North ignores this complexity and instead labels Shakespeare's version of Ophelia as sexist, and constructs an alternative, 'empowered' Ophelia by dismissing the limitations of being a woman in the early modern court. By comparison, *Elsinore* turns Ophelia's disempowerment into a feature of the gameplay design while simultaneously exploring the complexity of her life through the traditional game narrative.

Elsinore's narrative not only maintains a thematic consistency with Shakespeare's play, but embraces Ophelia's limited agency within the gender, political and racial hierarchy of Shakespeare's early modern drama through the ludonarrative. Polonius reminds Ophelia early in the tutorial of the game that her position as the daughter of a nobleman makes her an unsuitable match for Prince Hamlet, and that beyond this her racial heritage as a 'Moor' further prevents Hamlet from seriously considering her as a bride: 'For another young noblewoman, things might be different. But not so for you.' The game's traditional narrative hinges upon Ophelia's systematic disempowerment as a woman of mixed-race heritage within *Elsinore*'s historical setting. Within the game's ludonarrative, if the player chooses to make Ophelia confront characters such as Claudius, perhaps by directly accusing him of his brother's murder, Claudius either dismisses her for being a fanciful girl or accuses her of feminine hysteria and has her locked away: 'As we discussed earlier, her mind's not well. She *needs* help.' This 'game-over' screen or end state, which signals the conclusion of that particular playthrough of the game, concludes with Ophelia being locked away due to assumed insanity. This simple interaction exemplifies how *Elsinore*'s traditional narrative and ludonarrative work in concert to force the player to work within the cultural boundaries set for Ophelia, even going so far as to 'penalise' players who ignore these hierarchical limits in keeping with the material realities of the period.

In another example of ludonarrative harmony, *Elsinore* reinforces the social hierarchy of Elsinore through Ophelia's awareness of her own compromised position within that hierarchy. In an early conversation with Hamlet, she states: 'You and I are bound by different privileges. That's a truth of this castle.' These privileges are literalised through the gameplay boundaries established by the diegetic game-world. For example, Hamlet can move throughout the castle with impunity, including his mother's bedroom – where he kills Polonius – whereas Ophelia is denied access to private spaces such as Gertrude's or Claudius's bedroom. In this way the game simulates operating within an inherently sexually and racially restrictive social system like Shakespeare's Denmark.

The consequences of Ophelia's racial, gender and class identity are apparent throughout *Elsinore*'s narrative, whether it is in Brit's outright racism, Claudius's gendered dismissiveness of Ophelia's concerns as madness, or Ophelia's self-awareness. But *Elsinore* also turns the other characters' general apathy towards Ophelia into game mechanics by permitting her to siphon information through both dialogue and through spying on people throughout each day. As a low-class daughter of a minor lord, Ophelia's invisibility in the eyes of the court is transformed by the ludonarrative into a gameplay mechanism. *Elsinore* exemplifies Shaw's argument: 'Characters who are members of marginalised groups cannot be treated simply as lessons to out-group members or examples to in-group members. Their existence in media texts allow for more ways of being in the world, for all audiences' (2014: 215). Through ludonarrative harmony, Chironis and her team reconfigure Ophelia's diminished agency as a gameplay feature even while exposing players to a narrative that explores the life of marginalised peoples.

Conclusion

Shakespeare has finally entered video games in a prominent way, and in doing so demonstrates a path forward for critiques of video game adaptations of Shakespeare using OOO's flat ontology. 'Ludonarrative harmony' offers a critical concept that incorporates both ludology and narratology without privileging one field over the other, and instead focuses on the liminal spaces where they intersect. *Elsinore* represents the ideal object to showcase this concept.

So much of the reason why Shakespeare, and *Hamlet* in particular, feels unsatisfying as a video game is due to the seeming incongruence of the play's themes and the core tenets of play: namely, action. Yet *Elsinore* proves that *Hamlet* can work as a rich source text as long as the designers recognise the critical importance of the play's core themes and integrate those themes into the rules of the game itself. By choosing to focus on Ophelia, *Elsinore* embraces Ophelia's absent agency by taking each scene that she does not participate in and letting the player roam about the castle in her effort to undo her tragic fate. In the gaps left by Shakespeare, *Elsinore* allows the player to explore what Ophelia would do to aid her quest. In place of passivity, *Elsinore* creates agency without undermining or omitting the political and social structures that necessitated Ophelia's passivity in the first place. Polonius is still a commanding paternal figure of authority, Claudius still discourages Ophelia's relationship with Hamlet due to her inferior social position, and Hamlet still ignores and chastises Ophelia. Ophelia's subordinate position does not have to be paralysing, but can be subverted and weaponised to empower her to construct her own narrative. By selecting Ophelia over Hamlet as the player avatar, *Elsinore* achieves ludonarrative harmony where *Castle Elsinore*, *To Be or Not to Be* and other games based on *Hamlet* found only dissonance.

Video games have long suffered the stigma associated with sexism, and the recent Gamergate controversy demonstrates that this reputation is not undeserved. But there is another way to interpret Gamergate. The game industry is changing, and there is a growing awareness that changing dominant attitudes towards non-normative gender identities requires intentionality. *Elsinore* exemplifies the powerful possibilities of encouraging empathy through play, and this is no accident. It is no coincidence that *Elsinore*'s lead writer is a woman, that her team decided to force players to play as Ophelia instead of choosing their own create-a-character, that Ophelia's already inferior social position was further complicated by making her non-white, or that the gameplay depended upon other characters underestimating her. *Elsinore* exemplifies ludonarrative harmony at its most effective. *Elsinore* represents more than just the future of effective video game adaptations of Shakespeare, although it certainly achieves that goal: *Elsinore* sits at the intersection of commerce, representation, video games, ludology, narratology, Shakespeare and a multitude of other disparate units, and demonstrates the power of refusing to prioritise any one unit over the others and instead consciously synchronising them in perfect harmony.

Notes

1. As Anita Sarkeesian highlights in her *Tropes Against Women in Video Series*, the end text of each *Super Mario Bros* level (1985), one of the most influential games of the medium, exemplifies how pervasive the 'damsel in distress' trope is: 'Thank you Mario! But our Princess is in another castle.' Princess Peach is abducted by the antagonist Bowser at the beginning of almost every mainstream Mario game from 1985 to 2017, and this is just one series that exemplifies the systematic objectification of women in video games. On 27 October 2017 the latest entry into the seminal *Super Mario* series, *Super Mario Odyssey*, once again begins with Bowser's abduction of Princess Peach. The narrative wrinkle this time is that her tiara is sentient and has also been snatched by Bowser: an apt metaphor for Peach's objectification by the male character Mario.
2. In 2013 what started as outrage over perceived violations of journalistic ethics quickly escalated into collective, targeted harassment of women in the gaming industry, which became known as 'Gamergate'. Caitlin Dewey of the *Washington Post* wrote an excellent timeline and critique of these events, which she calls 'a proxy war for a greater cultural battle over space and visibility and inclusion, a battle over who belongs to the mainstream – and as such, it's a battle for our cultural soul'. Dewey (2014) notes that the term 'Gamergate' contains 'socio-political overtones, as well: The hashtag only took off once it was tweeted by the conservative actor Adam Baldwin and blurbed on Breitbart'.
3. One of the victims of these internet attacks – which often flooded targets' email and social media accounts with death threats and posted home addresses online to aid in stalking – was Sarkeesian. In 2009 Sarkeesian launched Feminist Frequency, a YouTube channel devoted to the feminist analysis of media, while she studied at York University. Four years later she decided to base her documentary series, *Tropes vs Women*, on video games. Sarkeesian (2013) reiterates throughout her video critiques of sexist tropes in video games that '[i]t is both possible (and even necessary) to simultaneously enjoy media while also being critical of its more problematic or pernicious aspects'. Unfortunately, her disclaimers went unheeded as she was forced to repeatedly move due to unceasing virtual harassment such as doxing.
4. While independent game development has existed since the advent of the industry, the modern rise of independent games and their introduction into the mainstream began with the advent of digital distribution. Starting with Xbox's Arcade and Community titles in 2006, independent games were given a programming language and a distribution platform that was powerful and

versatile enough for small development teams to make and distribute games, and the various avenues for funding independent games have only risen from there, including crowd-funding (Watlington 2015).
5. Ludology is the study of games, with a particular focus on actions and rules; it is often viewed in contrast to narratology, the study of story structure, themes and symbols.
6. Author interview with Connor Fallon, *Elsinore* game designer, 13 January 2017.
7. 'Elsinore, a time-looping adventure game by Katie Chironis – Kickstarter', 27 April 2015, available at <https://www.kickstarter.com/projects/235466673/elsinore-a-time-looping-adventure-game> [accessed 4 November 2017].
8. The genre of the adventure game began with text-based games such as *Colossal Cave Adventure* (1976) and the first *Hamlet* adaptation, *Castle Elsinore* (1983), but the advent of computer graphics evolved text-based adventure games into visual-based point-and-click adventures such as *King's Quest* (1980) and *Day of the Tentacle* (1993). Tim Shaffer, a co-designer of *Day of the Tentacle* who spent years toiling in other genres after adventure games collapsed in the 1990s, helped usher in the resurrection of the adventure game with his massively successful Kickstarter *Broken Age* (Manuel 2013).
9. *Stardew Valley* (2016) is a farming simulation game in which the player takes on the role of a new farmer in a small town. The game simulates the small town of Stardew Valley, which is made up of various NPCs that each have their own unique routine. Whether the player chooses to be present or not, these characters go to work, celebrate birthdays and spend time with friends. This remarkable game was made by one person, Eric Barone, over the course of five years, and is one of the most popular entries in the simulation genre.
10. *Grim Fandango* (1998) was one of the last iterations of the point-and-click adventure game genre made by Tim Schaffer before the genre stopped being financially viable.
11. In *The Legend of Zelda: Majora's Mask* (2000) the player encountered Clock Town, which was the central location in the game. Clock Town stands as one of the most intricately designed game spaces, which simulated a town full of NPCs over the course of a three-day, 24-hour cycle. Each NPC maintains a rigorous daily routine that the player could interact with and alter while playing. After three days, the town would reset to day one and the simulation would start all over again.
12. Bogost has published a number of monographs that theorise video games using OOO (2011; 2012). He often turns to the Atari game *E.T.* to exemplify an 'alien ontology' (2012: 17–18).
13. An incredibly small footprint by modern standards; games such as *Red Dead Redemption II* take up nearly one hundred times that.
14. *Space War* (1962), often considered the first video game, is made up of both the ludic and the narrative: the ludic is two players manoeuvring around

trying to destroy each other's spaceship, and the narrative equivalent is a war for survival near a gravity well.

15. The term has since been adopted by the larger video game industry, as the video essay 'Ludonarrative Dissonance' by Folding Ideas exemplifies, available at <https://youtu.be/04zaTjuV60A> [accessed 3 September 2020].
16. From a ludic perspective, saving the 'Little Sisters' initially results in a loss in power, but after a certain number of 'saves' the player is compensated with additional power equivalent to what they would have gained if they had chosen to sacrifice the characters. Aside from a short epilogue at the game's conclusion, the narrative consequences of the 'choice' are the same regardless of choice. The ludonarrative undermines the traditional narrative's Randian philosophy that one should work for one's own interest.
17. Harrison and Lutz document a number of subsequent video game adaptations of *Hamlet* including *Hamlet: A Murder Mystery* (1997), the unfinished *Ophelia* (2003) and *Gamlet* (2004) (Harrison and Lutz 2017: 24).
18. Harrison and Lutz might not use this term in part because the bulk of videogame scholarship is published outside of academia on developer blogs, fan sites and podcasts. The conversation surrounding games has created its own accepted terminology/jargon, which ludonarrative exemplifies.
19. Ophelia only speaks in five scenes: I.iii, II.i, III.i, III.ii and IV.v.
20. Author interview with Connor Fallon, *Elsinore* game designer, 29 July 2017.
21. Akiko Kusunoki (2015: 10) and Katherine Craik (2002: 446) both deconstruct Ophelia's songs in Act IV as an avenue of self-expression. Craik argues that Ophelia participated in the poetic form of the 'lover's complaint', which she calls a 'dangerous (because potentially accusatory) fantasy of women speaking spontaneously, and it is perhaps for this reason that the genre becomes intractably associated with illness' (2002: 446). English society aligned the poetic form of Ophelia's songs with madness, which helps explain why listeners, despite hearing her none-too-subtle accusations of Hamlet, quickly label her as mad.
22. While these critical threads effectively summarise the bulk of feminist criticism up to the time of the publication of Showalter's essay in 1985, since then feminist criticism of the play has continued to expand. R. L. Kesler (1999: 124) interprets Ophelia as a symbol of 'feudal succession'. Craik (2002) contextualises Ophelia's speeches within the genre of complaint poetry. Kusunoki (2015) relates Ophelia to Elizabethan perceptions of feminine madness. That said, the most valid field of inquiry for the purposes of this chapter are those feminists who view Ophelia through the lens of adaptation and expansion, such as Kaara Peterson and Deanne Williams, the editors of the 2012 essay collection *The Afterlife of Ophelia*.
23. Polonius, Gertrude, Claudius, Laertes and Hamlet all die onstage. The only notable characters who do not include Ophelia, Rosencrantz and Guildenstern.

24. Kaara Peterson and Deanne Williams add, 'If artists and critics have frequently claimed that they wish to "give" Ophelia a voice, it is because Shakespeare elected to mute hers in the first place . . . Shakespeare's text already anticipates her subsequent "history" of representation' (2012: 2–3). Peterson and Williams believe, as do I, that *Hamlet* displays Shakespeare's awareness of Ophelia's silent subservience.
25. In Shaw's book *Gaming at the Edge*, she critiques game-makers who place the burden of selecting non-normative gender or racial characteristics on the player, 'What I find most interesting about the optional representation made possible in digital games is that it places the burden of representation on players themselves' (2014: 35).
26. Author interview with *Elsinore* game designer, 21 January 2017.
27. Lara Croft from *Tomb Raider* (2013) and Aloy from *Horizon Zero Dawn* (2017) exemplify typical female power fantasies within video games which rarely explore the material realities of their characters' lives.

Bibliography

Bogost, I. (2011), *How to do Things with Videogames*, Minneapolis: University of Minnesota Press.

Bogost, I. (2012), *Alien Phenomenology, or What It's Like to Be a Thing*, Minneapolis: University of Minnesota Press.

Bushnell, R. (2016), *Tragic Time in Drama, Film, and Videogames: The Future in the Instant*, Basingstoke: Palgrave Macmillan.

Chironis, K. (2015), 'Elsinore Developer Blog', *Goldenglitch.tumblr.com*, 5 September, <http://goldenglitch.tumblr.com/post/128428055801/we-went-to-the-seattle-library-last-week-to-delve> [accessed 7 February 2017].

Craik, K.A. (2002), 'Shakespeare's *A Lover's Complaint* and Early Modern Criminal Confession', *Shakespeare Quarterly*, 53:4, 437–59. <http://search.ebscohost.com/login.aspx?direct=true&AuthType=ip,cookie,url,uid&db=mzh&AN=2002583280&site=ehost-live&scope=site> [accessed 4 November 2017].

Desmet, C. (2017), 'Alien Shakespeares 2.0', *Actes des congrès de la Société française Shakespeare*, DOI: https://doi.org/10.4000/shakespeare.3877 [accessed 14 March 2020].

Dewey, C. (2014), 'The Only Guide to Gamergate You Will Ever Need to Read', *The Washington Post*, 14 October, <https://www.washingtonpost.com/news/the-intersect/wp/2014/10/14/the-only-guide-to-gamergate-you-will-ever-need-to-read/?utm_term=.f48a9edbe4de> [accessed 21 October 2017].

Egenfeldt-Nielsen, S., J. Heide Smith and S. Pajares Tosca (2013), *Understanding Video Games: The Essential Introduction*, 2nd edn, Abingdon: Routledge.

Harrison, M., and M. Lutz (2017), 'South of Elsinore: Actions that a Man Might Play', in V. M. Fazel and L. Geddes (eds), *The Shakespeare User: Critical and*

Creative Appropriations in a Networked Culture, Basingstoke: Palgrave Macmillan, pp. 23–40.

Hocking, C. (2007), 'Ludonarrative Dissonance in *Bioshock*', 7 October, <http://clicknothing.typepad.com/click_nothing/2007/10/ludonarrative-d.html> [accessed 27 October 2017].

Hutcheon, L. (2012), *A Theory of Adaptation*, 2nd edn, New York: Routledge.

Juul, J. (2005), *Half-Real: Video Games between Real Rules and Fictional Worlds*, Cambridge, MA: MIT Press.

Kesler, R. L. (1999), 'Subjectivity, Time, and Gender in *Titus Andronicus*, *Hamlet*, and *Othello*', in V. Comensoli and A. Russell (eds), *Enacting Gender on the English Renaissance Stage*, Champaign: University of Illinois Press, pp. 114–32.

Kusunoki, A. (2015), *Gender and Representations of the Female Subject in Early Modern England: Creating their Own Meanings*, New York: Palgrave Macmillan.

Manuel, R. (2013), 'How Adventure Games Came Back from the Dead', *PC World*, 5 February, <http://www.pcworld.com/article/2026802/how-adventure-games-came-back-from-the-dead.html> [accessed 7 February 2017].

Murray, Janet H. (1997), *Hamlet on the Holodeck: The Future of Narrative in Cyberspace*, New York: Free Press.

Olson, Dan (2017), 'Ludonarrative Dissonance', 19 July, <https://www.youtube.com/watch?v=04zaTjuV60A> [accessed 4 November 2017].

Peterson, K. L., and D. Williams (2012), *The Afterlife of Ophelia*, New York: Palgrave Macmillan.

Sarkesian, A. (2013), 'Damsel in Distress: Part I – Tropes vs Women in Video Games', 7 March, <https://youtu.be/X6p5AZp7r_Q> [accessed 4 November 2017].

Shaw, A. (2014), *Gaming at the Edge: Sexuality and Gender at the Margins of Gamer Culture*, Minneapolis: University of Minnesota Press.

Showalter, E. (2011), 'Representating Ophelia: Women, Madness, and the Responsibilities of Feminist Criticism', in *Hamlet: A Norton Critical Edition*, ed. Robert S. Miola, New York: W.W. Norton, pp. 271–80.

Watlington, W. (2015), 'A Short History of Indie Games, and a Look into the Future', *Updownright.com*, 7 March, <https://updownright.com/2015/03/07/a-short-history-of-indie-games-and-a-look-into-the-future/> [accessed 7 February 2017].

6

Sympathise with the Losers: Performing Intellectual Loserdom in Shakespearean Biopic

Anna Blackwell

Writing on the common comic manoeuvre, 'You had to be there', Louise D'Arcen observes that the phrase reveals the 'vulnerability of humour to a specifically spatio-temporal failure' (2014: 140). She continues that the phrase illustrates the 'extent to which humour depends for its success on its audience being "present"' (2014: 140). Although in D'Arcen's argument the potential absence of the audience risks diminishing a scene's humour, the BBC comedy series *Upstart Crow* (TV 2016–) exploits a disconnection between temporal spaces for comedic effect. Created and written by Ben Elton, who previously wrote *The Young Ones* and *Blackadder*, *Upstart Crow* is a British sitcom that follows the travails of William Shakespeare (David Mitchell) as a jobbing playwright, commuting between his theatre work in London and Stratford-upon-Avon, where his family live. The majority of the humour in *Upstart Crow* comes from its implied juxtaposition of two audiences for Shakespeare and his works and their differing levels of knowledge. The first is the series's diegetic audience: Shakespeare's family, friends, colleagues and rivals (the wonderfully hammy Mark Heap as Robert Greene, whose *Groat's-Worth of Wit* gives the series its title). Their reception of Shakespeare's ideas and plays contextualises his works within early modern England's societal practices, religious beliefs and culture. The second and actual audience for the series, meanwhile, are the contemporary viewers who are invited also to occupy Shakespeare's time, but to bring our present attitudes and knowledge with us; in particular, to remember Shakespeare's current pre-eminence as we watch. This is asked of the series's audience because, in stark contrast to the uncontested status he now enjoys as a result of his canonisation by British culture and cultural establishments, Mitchell's Shakespeare is a maligned figure. In a manifestation of his character's personal tediousness, his family protest regularly at the obscurity of his verse; his father, John (Harry Enfield), for instance, mocks his ambitious son in the series's distinctive and playful pseudo-early modern vernacular for being a 'turnip-chomping country bum-shankle' (S1E3). But *Upstart Crow*'s Shakespeare is not some kind of unappreciated genius who we necessarily feel sympathy towards when we see him treated thus. A common feature of the series is Shakespeare taking inspiration for his famous works from other characters, by misunderstanding the particular 'moral' of that episode's focus, or, as Ronan Hatfull observes, 'from perusing the books which the landlady's daughter Kate (an irrepressible Gemma Whelan) reads on "the privy"' (2019: 300). In defiance of Polonius's advice that brevity is the soul of wit (*Hamlet* II.ii.91), this Shakespeare believes that once you're in a 'comedy hole', you should 'keep digging' (S2E5); he is, in other words, an intellectual loser.

It is this version of Shakespeare – beleaguered, yearning for recognition from his betters and at odds with his own time's popular tastes – that is this chapter's focus. *Upstart Crow* provides a good demonstration of the productiveness of exploring the digital Shakespeare text as a 'coalescence of units by chance or accident into tenuous and shifting systems' (Desmet 2017: 3); a Shakespeare text that continually fragments and reassembles itself, just as I seek to disaggregate the parts of *Upstart Crow*'s playwright only in order to reconstitute the fragments by articulating their consolidated effect. This chapter thus aims to examine the complex appropriative networks that *Upstart Crow* occupies by first framing the series's protagonist as Mitchell-Shakespeare. Mitchell-Shakespeare is a character forged through the negotiation of two semiotically rich objects within an erratic network of meaning. The character is also defined through association either with values typically synonymous with Shakespearean celebrity (success, skill, sophistication, virtuosity) or their opposite (failure, awkwardness, embarrassment). The dissonance of presenting failure as a prerequisite for inevitable cultural capital is a common feature of the depiction of the 'Shakespearean' in television comedy.[1] The cultural capital attached to the playwright is often parodied on mainstream television, for instance through 'examples of actors whose Shakespearean prestige, whether self-identified or cultivated more consensually, fails to convince' (Blackwell 2017: 222).[2] Mitchell-Shakespeare is of further relevance, therefore, as the most recent iteration of an established trope in popular cultural depictions not only of Shakespeare, but of a broader (and pernicious) myth of male genius going unappreciated in its own time.

Importantly, Mitchell-Shakespeare also provides us with a visible instance of this chapter's variable object: a comic archetype that I term the intellectual loser. In tandem with his study of the 'dissemination of Shakespeare into niches hitherto unimaginable or taboo', Richard Burt has described the academics working in the same area as themselves 'melancholic loser[s]' (Burt 2002: 7). Burt's scepticism towards these 'loser' critics who claim to make 'politically transgressive or oppositional "intervention[s]" through their conflation of "real" politics with cultural politics' (Burt 1998: 22) in their study of popular culture is indeed applicable to this chapter, not only for what Burt proposes but for the absences in his argument. Like the loser critics, intellectual losers are 'would-be political progressives, trying to be both classic and hip [. . .], always falling behind the advances of popular and youth culture' (Hedrick 2000: 392). Crucially, however, the intellectual loser is able to articulate their out-of-stepness. Their frustration with a world that seems to undervalue their longing for propriety, reason and intelligent discourse is performed through a characteristically nihilist (and often misanthropic) pose which conflates their individual failure to make meaning from life with a perceived wider meaningless of existence.

The intellectual loser occupies an inherently nostalgic position because both their ability to articulate their experience and their feelings of disconnection come from a privileged class position: the intellectual loser is a middle-class loser. And it is here that my conceptualisation of the loser object maps on to certain absences in Burt's argument. Donald K. Hedrick observes that Burt 'tosses' out a discussion of class 'because it does not bear a simple one-to-one relation to the "loser" figure who cuts across classes', and yet, he notes, the subject 'cries out for class consideration' (2000: 391). For instance, when aligning Burt's criticism with that of Jack Halberstam, Jarred Wiehe proposes that 'the slacker, the loser, and the failure occupy a queer position as they reorient life directions away from successful and productive ways of living' (2015: 77). The intellectual loser, however, mourns the very thing that frustrates them. Their misanthropic worldview doesn't long for alternative social structures or attitudes; instead, they hope naively for validation of their discernment. After all, to do more would remove the privileged position that allows them to function as both beneficiary of unequal social orders and jaded outsider. It is this self-deprecating logic which thereby protects the considerable class capital of the intellectual loser, even as it conceals it. Indeed, in characterising their inability to 'fit' in with society less as a failure per se, but rather as a surfeit of reason, intellect, progressiveness and so on, the intellectual loser trope aligns with a broader myth of male genius unappreciated in its time. This myth is pernicious for various reasons, including an underlying assumption that genius goes uncelebrated in its own moment because of the cost of its perceived difficulty – be that the complexity of the works produced (ahead of their time) or, often, the men themselves (destructive) – and that the price must instead be paid by the moment, which finally recognises their greatness. And yet recent #MeToo revelations or even older historical discussions of the abuse perpetrated by 'genius' men are often accompanied by an apparent need to question how we as a society should now view their art. Can we forget the price of such difficult men so that we can continue to enjoy the fruits of their 'genius'; a price that has, in reality, already been paid, and not by us?

Making the intellectual loser the subject of comedy does ameliorate some of the more concerning aspects of this logic, however, because even though it requires the valorisation of their loserdom, it does also open it up to critique. This can occur both within the comic format and beyond it. For instance, *Upstart Crow* repeatedly punctures the claims for Shakespeare's uniqueness by showing the frequency with which Mitchell-Shakespeare adapts existing literature and is guided to write better versions of his own plays by his friends and family. That these often unwanted but ultimately helpful suggestions come from individuals who would otherwise be removed from artistic production – women and lower-class men – is precisely the point: the loser's privilege does not help them towards genius. There is a patronising beneficence, however, in the suggestion that the genius is an object built out of the disenfranchised voices that would otherwise be unworthy of humanist valuations of greatness. The invariably white, middle-class and cis-gendered men who get to enjoy the pose of intellectual loserdom thus inhabit failure as an ironic pose; content in the knowledge that – as *Upstart Crow* dramatises – success is inevitable.

The intellectual loser described above is an archetype that Mitchell has certainly used to differing extents and degrees of success throughout his career (as I will continue to demonstrate), and in this case it carries an affective power through which we can view and understand his Shakespeare. The intellectual loser not only operates through Mitchell's comic persona in *Upstart Crow*, however, but through an even more complex appropriative network associated with the series's writer and producer, Ben Elton. Finally, the chapter will demonstrate the composite nature of the intellectual loser variable object (and its particular iteration here, the Mitchell-Shakespeare object) by reflecting on *Upstart Crow*'s place within the sitcom genre, Elton's characterisation of the playwright (a further Elton-Shakespeare object to consider), and the sitcom's shaping of the reception of and affective responses to Shakespeare's legacy. In doing so, the chapter will consider Burt's assertion that 'most instances of Shakespeare in mass media do not have sufficient hermeneutic density to qualify as politically transgressive' (2002: 7). The intellectual loser's simultaneous claim on and disavowal of power will thus be used to illustrate the limitations of *Upstart Crow*'s political and social critique.

David Mitchell

In conversation with his leading actor for the *Guardian*, Ben Elton shared that it was Mitchell's voice in his head 'from the first moment [he] started writing *Crow*', admitting further that it was 'very hard to imagine anybody else playing the Shakespeare [Elton] imagined' (Elton and Mitchell 2018). That Elton articulates such a close connection between *Upstart Crow*'s star and the character he performs is unsurprising. Mitchell is in many ways the perfect avatar for the version of Shakespeare Elton has imagined. Over the past two decades that Mitchell has occupied the public eye, he has cultivated a star persona and, indeed, a comic persona that is based on pairing a high degree of intellect with frustration at a world that does not reward or acknowledge his intelligence. The figure of the intellectual loser, with its characteristic wry and sardonic tone, is common across Mitchell's roles, whether playing fictional characters or himself. The comedy series *Peep Show* (2003–15), for instance, contrasts Mitchell's Mark Corrigan, a would-be historian, wracked by social and sexual awkwardness, against his flatmate, Jeremy 'Jez' Usborne (Mitchell's frequent comedy partner, Robert Webb), a confident but naive, failed musician. Jez's tendency to make declamatory or glib statements about his sexual appetites or the apparent rigours of being an artist are repeatedly met by Mark's withering cynicism. A typical exchange between the two demonstrates Mark's willingness to wield his superior intellect to mock his friend:

Jez: Look Mark, I'm a musician in case you'd forgotten. Yeah? I answer to a higher law. The law of 'if it feels good, do it'.
Mark: Oh, that's a great law, isn't it? What's that, Gaddafi's law?
Jez: It's the musician's law. Colonel Gaddafi could not lay down a bass hook, Mark. That should be clear even to you! (S3E5)

Mark's response to Jez is derisive but ultimately meaningless. He attempts to mock Jez's pursuit of the law of 'if it feels good, do it' by highlighting the dangers of unfettered personal freedom and, in doing so, his and the intellectual loser's preference for rigidly obeyed social strictures. His illustration of this through the allusion to Colonel Gaddafi is undercut by Jez's almost literal response to his intellectual ironising, however.

But lest it seem that Mark's intelligence is in any way preferable, such exchanges in *Peep Show* are tinged by the programme's characteristic nihilism. They are ultimately, and invariably, pathetic because neither Mark nor Jez are sites of serious investment or desire for the audience: both are profoundly mediocre men who fail to excel in anything, let alone the chosen markers of their identity such as Jez's 'coolness' or Mark's intelligence. Mark is certainly smarter than his friend, but his intelligence is always expressed through dogmatic put-downs or in association with pursuits such as live action role playing (LARPing) or an interest in the history of warfare – hobbies that are not necessarily dull but become tedious under Mark's extreme scrutiny. And this is a crucial aspect of the intellectual loser. Their intellect fails to eclipse their loser status and, in most cases, provides the terms for their failure. Jez's vapid question, 'What was it Shakespeare said?' is met with the pedantic answer, 'He said a lot of things' (S6E3); Mark's intelligence is obvious but never enviable.

In what is a repeated source of both comedy and melancholic reflection for the intellectual loser object, Mitchell's characters display forms of knowledge that serve no purpose. This aspect of the trope is defined relationally by the people who surround the loser. In comparison to those who he deems 'losers', Mark Corrigan doesn't know as much as he thinks, and tellingly, what he does know never helps. The final sketch of *That Mitchell and Webb Look* (2006–10), meanwhile, features John Watson (Webb) visiting his aged friend, Sherlock Holmes (Mitchell) in the care home where he now lives due to advanced dementia. The 'Old Holmes' sketch (S4E6) has a characteristically mordant tone, shifting rapidly between amusement at the behaviour of the clearly ill Holmes and profound melancholy; in a rare moment of lucidity, for instance, Holmes stares at Watson and utters, anguished: 'I can't get the fog to clear.' Even one of the greatest detectives in fiction is not spared intellectual loserdom, and this point is underlined in the sketch by Holmes's momentary recognition of his diminishment as well as Watson's clear distress. Holmes, who the sketch tells us has 'forgotten more about detective work than [Lestrade and Watson] will ever know', has thus tragically forgotten himself; and years later, Mitchell's Shakespeare will similarly protest his genius to family and friends who are convinced that he is an unfunny, 'fartsome try-hard' (S1E3). It is worth noting that already we see here the difficulty of applying the intellectual loser object to Shakespeare's legacy. While Holmes's reduced state can be readily imagined – indeed, the film *Mr Holmes* (dir. Bill Condon, 2015) did this exact thing – Shakespeare's greater posthumous celebrity is never at risk in quite the same way.

The intellectual loser is a sufficiently variable object to be nevertheless applied in different contexts, and key to further understanding the quality of Mitchell's loserdom is to see how it is consolidated – and indeed, defined – through the performance of a (parodic) class capital. The pairing of intellectual and social ineffectualness is certainly evident in Mitchell's characters, but perhaps most visible in the performed version of himself seen on panel shows, podcasts, YouTube videos as well as in his writing.[3] This happens in part because such formats require and cultivate an exaggerated version of participants' comic personas. The result in Mitchell's case has been to aggregate the core parts of his comic appeal and then deploy them in an ironic and deeply knowing performance of himself. Key features of Mitchell's misanthropic comic persona thus include an attention to detail that borders on the pedantic, a concern with upholding arbitrary social rules and other types of etiquette, and a disregard for mainstream cultural tastes and youth culture. These are qualities that echo the uselessness of Mark Corrigan's intelligence and exaggerate the perceived cost of being both the smartest man in the room but also – and relatedly – the most neurotic. As Julia Raeside (2016) writes, Mitchell's 'trademark' is 'neutered rage'; he is comically, ineffectually outraged by a world that seems devoid of logic and sense. Representative Mitchell-isms thus include the fabricated (but nevertheless representative) story on the panel show *Would I Lie To You?* (2007–)[4] that he was 'forced to abandon the purchase of a new armchair mid-transaction because he was so appalled by the shop assistant using the slang neologisms 'well jel' and 'amazeballs' (S6E8). *Would I Lie To You?* regularly engineers such comic encounters that highlight not only the pointlessness of Mitchell's intellect in the context of a comedy game show but the uselessness of his fussy middle-classness. This is done in large part through the programme's placement of Mitchell in opposition to the rival team captain and Lancashire-born comedian, Lee Mack, who provides a constant (and derisive) commentary on his southern, Cambridge-educated counterpart.[5] Mack rearticulates Mitchell's already parodic performance of fastidious middle-classness by performing an even more exaggerated form back at him. A moment when Mitchell distinguishes awkwardly between shoes used to play bowling and general leisure wear as 'normal life shoes', for instance, prompts Mack to deliver a skit in which the precocious young Mitchell summons his mother for his 'normal life shoes' (S8E4).

Mitchell-Shakespeare

That David Mitchell has enjoyed such success performing his variants on the intellectual loser speaks perhaps not only to his willingness to parody himself, but also to the tradition within which he works and the aforementioned variability of this object. How then does the Mitchell-Shakespeare object positioned at the heart of *Upstart Crow* build upon the same affective power of the intellectual loser? It provides a comic framework that operates by, first, recognising his character's advantage through his proximity to traditional sites of social capital (chiefly education and gender) and, second, subverting this superiority by showing its hollowness or lack of meaning. Unlike Burt's loser, who possesses cultural capital but seemingly does not use it (or, rather, does not realise their use of it), *Upstart Crow*'s framing of Shakespeare as intellectual loser exposes and ridicules the privilege that has elevated Shakespeare to his current mythical status. In Elton's (as opposed to Mitchell's) hands, the loser trope is thus activated to redistribute 'greatness' among the community of invisible women and lower-class men such as Bottom who helped him. Whatever talent Mitchell's Shakespeare has is indeed far from the spontaneous outpourings imagined in *Shakespeare in Love*, and instead requires dogged and often misguided efforts. The series takes pleasure in subverting the famed associations of some of Shakespeare's lines by showing them through a sceptical and often mocking eye. For example, Shakespeare's wife Anne (Liza Tarbuck) and daughter Susanna (Helen Monks) accurately predict that Juliet's yearning question 'Wherefore art thou Romeo?' (*Romeo and Juliet* II.i.75) will be misunderstood as 'Where are you, Romeo?' (S1E1) and Bottom, Shakespeare's manservant, provides frequent reminders that a good speech 'should be two lines, tops' (S2E4). *Upstart Crow* levels other criticisms at Shakespeare, too. Although the complaints of the likes of John Shakespeare and Bottom limit themselves to fairly low-lying fruit such as the convoluted syntax of his lines or, most commonly, the length of his plays, the female characters in the play often assert ideological or feminist critiques. And it is here that the series demonstrates some of its more interesting, if uneven, uses of the intellectual loser object to expose the misogynistic and racist structures that have supported Shakespeare's legacy. Gemma Whelan's fiercely intellectual Kate variously questions the ability of drugged individuals to give consent (S2E1), Shakespeare's sanitisation of violence against women (S2E2) and his depiction of race (S3E1), and she repeatedly punctures his claims to have invented a word or phrase by identifying its classical source. In the episode 'Sigh No More' (S3E4), meanwhile, Anne and William nearly lose their young son to the army after he is inspired to enlist by *Henry V*. Anne cautions her husband against 'xenophobic' fantasies where 'fake history masquer[ades] as truth' and peddles 'simplistic and manipulative distortions in place of complex, properly researched argument' (S3E4).

If Mitchell's own intellectual loserdom frequently skewers the futility of his concern with social niceties, *Upstart Crow* also complicates the relationship between Shakespeare and contemporary middle-class identity by depicting, over the course of three series, his efforts to become part of an intellectual and artistic elite. Far from the 'morally uplifting master of English letters' whose ubiquity means that his reputation 'no longer [. . .] depends on his specific achievements as a dramatist' (Dobson 1992: 214), this Shakespeare is unable to attain genteel respectability. His rival, Greene, takes every measure in his fictional position as Master of the Revels to prevent the lowly Shakespeare from attaining middle-class status; something that only begins to shift at the end of the second series when John Shakespeare gains a family coat of arms. As Shakespeare complains, talented individuals like him are unable to see success because a 'gaggle of snootish pamperloins from just two universities [Oxford and Cambridge] snaffle all the influence, jobs and cash' (S2E1). As he notes, this England – like the present day – is a place where 'spurious, unearned social status will polish even the most stinksome turdington' (S2E1). Of course, the pleasing irony of this aspect of *Upstart Crow* lies in the programme's refusal to grant Shakespeare the middle-class status that is so intrinsic to his contemporary legacy; a tension only heightened by the clear difference between the middle-class loserdom of Mitchell-Shakespeare and his bucolic Stratford family, who are clearly befuddled by the intellectual cuckoo in their midst.[6]

Shakespeare's friendship with Christopher 'Kit' Marlowe (Tim Downie) places his later association with cultural sophistication under scrutiny, moreover. Shakespeare laments Kit's cool and confident manner, wishing he shared the Cambridge-educated spy's sense of entitlement. It is in these moments of self-doubt and self-examination that Mitchell's Shakespeare – who begrudgingly gives Marlowe his most exciting plays, *Doctor Faustus* and *Tamburlaine* – most recalls Mitchell's loserdom via *Peep Show*'s Mark Corrigan. The two figures are locked into resentful relationships with more charismatic men who exploit their kindness, and yet they maintain these friendships in the desperate hope that their friends' *élan* will some day pass on. Shakespeare, at least, has Anne to remind him that such glamour is unsustainable: 'you're a fartsome baldy-boots, doll', she comforts her husband, 'own it' (S2E1).

But while Shakespeare's failure to achieve the glamour and artistic success he longs for through his friendship with Kit is a source of amusement for his family, there are occasions in *Upstart Crow* when his inability to translate his intellect to their level is played for poignant effect.[7] When the Shakespeares' son, Hamnet, dies of the plague, William is unable to accept his wife's thanks to God for having been 'gracious' in sparing their other two children. Shocked by the suggestion that Shakespeare does not believe, Anne challenges him: 'You're the clever one. You always know the answers!' (S3E6). Shakespeare's intelligence – here demonstrated in his questioning of a Christian God – provides no comfort for his family. Shakespeare's apparent agnosticism is but one example of how *Upstart Crow*'s Mitchell-Shakespeare object works by filtering the playwright as we know him through Mitchell's avowedly sceptical persona. Like Mitchell, Shakespeare is uncertain of the existence of an afterlife.[8] When Susanna presses her father on his beliefs and whether he thinks their family will meet Hamnet again, Shakespeare comments that they will see Hamnet in her, in Judith and Anne and in 'every thought', but not in heaven (S3E6). But, the playwright concedes, his wife is 'right about most things' (S3E6), and it is evident from Mitchell's anguished performance that it gives Shakespeare no pleasure to question the continuance of Hamnet's soul. Mitchell, too, has stated that although he is 'not convinced' of a God or an afterlife, he 'wants there to be something [after death . . .]; I like that thought' (Anonymous 2014a).

I have picked out this example in particular because, as will no doubt already be apparent, Mitchell-Shakespeare's failures are those already associated with the Mitchell intellectual loser. What is more, I propose that it is precisely the Mitchell-ness of his Shakespeare's failures that allows *Upstart Crow* to sustain contradictory values by invoking an expected Shakespearean celebrity, success, skill or virtuosity only in order to provide its opposite – failure, awkwardness, embarrassment – for comedic effect. Of course, Shakespeare's failure to share the beliefs of his wife is of a very different nature in this episode than *Upstart Crow*'s usual comic incongruity – the only cost of which is normally the blow it gives to Shakespeare's pride – but it is all the more striking for that. Shakespeare's concession that his wife is normally 'right' is even seemingly confirmed by the episode's title, 'Go On and I Will Follow', which, in its quotation of Adam's faithful service to his master Orlando in *As You Like It*, suggests that the Shakespeares will share in their son's afterlife. The dynamic between the always correct Anne and her failing husband underlines the unacknowledged basis of *Upstart Crow*'s comedy, moreover. As I've already indicated, Elton frames Shakespeare as an intellectual loser in order to acknowledge the community of people who will have invariably shaped his works, from providing critiques of his plays to – perhaps most importantly – allowing him to work in London free from immediate family obligations. *Upstart Crow* pays this community a debt of gratitude by showing their intrinsic connection to Shakespeare's output and, even, to the continued perception of his plays. The intellectual loser ultimately betrays its reliance on the simultaneous exertion and withholding of capital, however; because, if Shakespeare complains repeatedly that only upper-class 'folderols' like Greene or Marlowe are free to make mistakes without penalty, Mitchell-Shakespeare is failure's greatest beneficiary. Mitchell has made a living from performing losers (including himself) whose knowledge is unappreciated and mocked, and *Upstart Crow*'s Shakespeare continues to make a name for himself, even as each episode shows the extent of his reliance on his family and friends for inspiration.

Elton-Shakespeare

The series is not wholly invested in subverting Shakespeare's pre-eminent cultural authority, therefore, and evidence of this can be connected to *Upstart Crow*'s two major generic influences: the literary biopic and the sitcom. And it is at this point that I want to shift from focusing on the Mitchell-Shakespeare object to the Elton-Shakespeare object, and to consider some of the consequences of Elton's production of *Upstart Crow*. This is not to say that Mitchell has no influence on these topics; rather, that in order to pursue the complex and erratic network of meaning that *Upstart Crow* occupies and its subsequent dramatic and comic effects, one must disaggregate its parts. This is necessary because the Elton-Shakespeare object functions beneath the surface that the Mitchell intellectual loser object works over, and as a result, its influence is less visible by comparison, but no less significant. Elton's appropriative power must be traced instead through the script; the generic influences that *Upstart Crow* takes and adapts and then considers in terms of the programme's relationship to the history it depicts.

Writing on *Shakespeare in Love* (dir. John Madden, 1999) as an example of the literary biopic, Andrew Bennett argues that the film's success lay in anachronistically fusing a 'late twentieth-century sense of Shakespeare with a Shakespearian one' (2005: 2). The biopic is highly self-conscious, Bennett continues, with *Shakespeare in Love* imagining a Shakespeare 'as interested in the nature of his own name, and of his own identity [. . .], as we are' (2005: 2). Hila Shachar, too, rejects a necessarily conservative or nostalgic relationship between the biopic and the past it seeks to represent. Shachar argues instead that, far from dead as per Roland Barthes's suggestion, the author has been 'systematically resurrected' through a screen tradition that sees Romantic notions of authorship sit 'side-by-side with their interrogative postmodernist and intersectional strategies of deconstruction, and indeed, this romanticised figure is often the impetus for such deconstruction' (Shachar 2019: 17). *Upstart Crow* certainly shares this self-reflexiveness and occupies it as one of its major comic registers through a regular and prolonged wink to a future longed for by Mitchell's playwright; a future in which he is not questioned or ridiculed, but respected.

The complex temporal position that *Upstart Crow* occupies is also very much a result of its sitcom influences. The sitcom certainly shares a similar self-conscious sensibility with the literary biopic, but it moves the genre's artificiality beyond even the trite image of *Shakespeare in Love*'s protagonist crafting his signature. The high level of attention to detail evident in some of *Upstart Crow*'s period references is cast against a (literal) backdrop that is as hollow as the simple, static sets used for filming. In case this sounds as though it is a denigration of the sitcom, it is not; indeed, the sitcom lends *Upstart Crow* many interesting qualities (more of which later), but a commitment to verisimilitude is not among them. The majority of the series is filmed on two small sets: the Shakespeares' home in Stratford-upon-Avon and Shakespeare's London apartment. The rare occasions when the characters move 'outside' these locations are still visibly indoor sets, with similarly enclosed spaces based around a central feature such as a clearing in the wood or a front door, and unconvincing special effects such as dry ice. This is done because, as D'Arcen observes of the unsuccessful first series of *Blackadder*, which was filmed on location, comedy benefits from physical proximity to its audience. The sweeping vistas of Alnwick Castle in *Blackadder* only provided 'mixe[d] generic codes' and 'reinforce[d] or even increase[d] the historical distance between the past and present of the viewing audience' (D'Arcen 2014: 151). The later studio-based series were effective in comparison because they allowed the audience to more easily occupy the same 'space' as the characters. *Blackadder*'s lesson has clearly been applied to *Upstart Crow*, because the generic associations of the sitcom allow it to manoeuvre for comedic effect between the past represented by the characters and their cultural reference points, beliefs and politics; the present moment of the audience watching; and, in between, Shakespeare – a man 'ahead of [his] time' ('A Christmas Crow'). As with *Blackadder* at its funniest, *Upstart Crow* thus articulates its historical moment in order to comment on the present through the conventions of the sitcom. It is a curious quality of the series then, that in failing – or rather, not trying – to be wholly historically 'authentic', it more convincingly shows the parallels between the early modern and now, than if it had invested in more lavish set design and costumes or less anachronistic dialogue or plots.

Not all aspects of *Upstart Crow*'s sitcom lineage allow it to explore effectively the tensions between past and present, however; nor, as I will continue to explore, do they help the programme to succeed in its intended reframing of Shakespeare as intellectual loser rather than vaunted cultural icon. I opened this chapter by noting the importance of audiences being 'present' for comedy to function. The sitcom has a distinct relationship with its viewers, though. Brett Mills writes that unlike stand-up comedy, for instance, the 'sitcom never offers an onscreen space for audiences to disagree with comic content or critique the ideologies the comedy espouses' (2009: 17). Mills continues, 'television sitcom audiences never get to heckle and so sitcom can be seen as a form which, while attempting to adopt the audience interaction vital for comic success, does so in a manner which robs the audience of the voice it has in other comic arenas' (2009: 17). The laughter tracks that accompany many sitcoms indeed gesture towards an original moment of live performance and the replication of a potentially genuine audience reaction. The 'canned' quality of this laughter and its fairly uniform sound, however, signals the flattening of the first audience response by the time of broadcast or, in some cases, its potential manipulation. It would not be an oversimplification to assert also that the audiences who attend recordings of live shows are more inclined to be favourable or to perform their favour overtly, and that the strict monitoring and coaching of the audience by the production team would have a similar effect of guaranteeing a positive rather than critical reaction.

When combined with *Upstart Crow*'s efforts towards biography, the removed quality of the sitcom further complicates the programme's larger ambitions to imagine Shakespeare as an intellectual loser. This is because the position that Elton-Shakespeare assumes circumvents critique. In using the past to satirise contemporary issues, Elton neutralises the present, because whatever the intellectual loser's foibles are, they are not altogether a failure of intellect but a failure to utilise it meaningfully or in a way that is appreciated. He thereby represents Shakespeare, the intellectual loser, as an ineffectual vessel for a version of contemporary politics and culture that is fixed, irrefutable, obvious. The issue, of course, being that Elton's politics are neither as progressive nor his cultural tastes as 'hip' (Hedrick 2000: 392) as he might think. As mentioned previously, Kate functions in *Upstart Crow* to provide an ironic commentary on Shakespeare and the early modern period that reflects contemporary, progressive attitudes; or as Shakespeare puts it, a 'joyless, socio-political agenda' (S3E1). The series utilises this contrast between the earnest, thoughtful Kate and the loserish but largely 'common-sense' Elton-Shakespeare in most episodes at least once, and to such an extent that this trope is also subverted for comedic effect. Kate's assessment that *A Midsummer Night's Dream* is a bit 'wishy-washy' for her because it has so many fairies in it, for instance, is met with Shakespeare's surprise that Kate – 'of all people' – should make such a complaint (S3E1). Shakespeare continues gleefully, with a performative sense of moral capital, that 'NSFEP [Nymph, Sprite, Fairy, Elf and Pixie] characters are appallingly misrepresented in mainstream culture'. The abstraction of an important topic for comic effect is in itself not concerning, and is, perhaps, even laudable because the joke provides a mainstream yet low-stakes space through which to discuss the representation of minorities in the media. The conceptual correspondence in the joke between the acronym LGBTQIA (Lesbian, Gay, Bisexual, Trans, Queer, Intersex, Asexual) and *Upstart Crow*'s fairy-world equivalent, NSFEP, diminishes the original's significance, however. Equally concerning is that the joke serves to objectify LGTBQIA people into the same non-human category as the NSFEPs and, of course, affiliates queerness with the derogatory term 'fairy'.

This type of comedy, which can also be seen in Shakespeare's characterisation of *Twelfth Night* as the first 'non-gender specific trans comedy' ('A Christmas Carol'), fundamentally misses the point. *Upstart Crow* assumes the moral tenor of the present moment by acknowledging important contemporary issues such as antisemitism, trans rights or freedom of speech. But if the inclusion of these (often anachronistic) topics seems to suggest their importance and the need to discuss them on a large mainstream platform, the series also frames them as obvious matters, on which we – a progressive audience – agree. They are thus invoked only to be, moments later, waved away with a benign sense of amusement or – as with NSFEP – rendered absurd by exaggerated analogy. And yet Elton, like Shakespeare, could do with probing more deeply into the implications of his assumptions, because not only are such topics not *fait accompli* but they are represented in ways that belittle the continued need for activism. At the end of the Christmas special, 'A Christmas Crow', for example, Shakespeare wishes 'good will to all men' – Anne: 'and women!' – and those 'like my Viola, who aren't sure'. Given his earlier framing of *Twelfth Night* as a 'trans[gender]' play, Shakespeare's later description of Viola as someone who is not sure of their identity represents a grave and transphobic characterisation of transness as a failure to know oneself, rather than having a gender identity that does not correspond to your biological sex. The failure of these (presumably) well-intentioned throwaway jokes demonstrates an unanticipated complication to *Upstart Crow*'s use of the intellectual loser trope: its ability to expose the privilege that empowers 'genius' cuts both ways. Shakespeare's mythical status is stripped bare for comedy, but also revealed is the disingenuousness of a comic loserdom – Elton's and Mitchell's – founded on and powered by the effacement of the various kinds of educational, social or gender-based privilege enjoyed by both men.

Despite the potential inappropriateness of this, the imperative that Elton use Elton-Shakespeare to speak to contemporary issues, just as he did in *The Young Ones* or *Blackadder*, can be felt, even if his skewering of Thatcherite Britain was more pointed than the tired jokes about freedom of expression he writes in *Upstart Crow*. This potential for satire is built into the structure of the series itself. The final scene of each episode sees Shakespeare sit with Anne in front of the fire at home in Stratford. Their conversations range in tone and content depending on the episode that precedes them, and indeed, the extent of Anne's encouragement of her husband. Consistent across them, though, is their ironic reflection on Shakespeare's authorship and his place in a future world.[9] For instance, in the first episode of series two, Anne and William are inspired by meeting the con artist General Otello and discuss the prospect of black actors on stage. Shakespeare imagines that such a sight is 'a few centuries off' still and predicts a likely future where black performers' roles will be limited to 'a strong supporting character, perhaps' (S2E1). 'An irascible chief of the watch or a wise old judge', Shakespeare muses; 'Possibly the villain or the hero's best mate' (S2E1). Shakespeare's comic reflections mock the ludicrousness of race affecting stage casting practices. This is a benign enough aim. Through Shakespeare, Elton seeks to articulate how narrow the field is for black performers who will be typecast in supporting roles. But while *Upstart Crow*'s Shakespeare critiques the limited prospects for black performers, his dominance in the cultural canon and subsequent influence upon the nature of that canon has perhaps shaped this future. And lest we take Elton-Shakespeare's comments as a dismissal of racist beliefs *and* an ironic reference to a thriving contemporary tradition of black Shakespeareans, Jami Rogers (2016) notes that recent increases in racial diversity on stage have only led to the replication of the 'stereotypes BAME performers have been decrying in television practices' – precisely the stereotypes that Mitchell-Shakespeare names.

We cannot necessarily lay the blame for this at the actual Shakespeare's door, nor necessarily at Michell-Shakespeare's. Although it should be noted that critiques of middle-class privilege articulated by the privately educated, Cambridge graduate Mitchell do not land with as much weight, or indeed self-consciousness, as perhaps intended (a similar thing could be said of Elton, whose sole man of reason in an ocean of madness trope is a staple of the comedy he promotes). Elton-Shakespeare is in a way culpable, however, because he is not – and doesn't pretend to be – the historical Shakespeare. Elton-Shakespeare is embedded in a past that has been extensively (and lovingly) researched by the series's producers and then imagined through Elton's scripted dialogue. But in aspiring to construct Shakespeare's past at the same time as deconstructing the present moment in a mode typical of the literary biopic, Elton-Shakespeare is given authority over not only his history, but ours too. Dennis Bingham writes that in the biopic, 'private behaviours and actions and public events as they might have been in the person's time are formed together and interpreted dramatically' (2010: 10). *Upstart Crow* certainly engages gamely with this retrospective creative process, so that the writing of *Othello* is inspired by the meeting with General Otello and Shakespeare becomes an unlikely prophet of contemporary racial inequality, despite the play's complex attitude to race.

The Intellectual Loser

I want to turn this chapter towards its end by proposing that the reason for the aforementioned complications in *Upstart Crow*'s use of both the biopic and sitcom formats lies, in large part, in its appropriation of the intellectual loser as a variable object. As fans of Elton's work may have already observed, the sense of being misplaced or out of step with a world that seems conservative and ineffectual appears repeatedly in his oeuvre, whether expressed as part of left-wing satires such as *The Young Ones* or *Blackadder* or as the context for the musical *We Will Rock You*. It has appeared more recently in another depiction of Shakespeare authored by Elton: *All is True* (dir. Kenneth Branagh, 2018). Starring Kenneth Branagh as Shakespeare, *All is True* is a speculative biopic on Shakespeare's return to Stratford-upon-Avon near the end of his life, after the fire that destroyed the Globe Theatre in 1613. Defeated by the loss of the Globe, haunted still by the childhood death of his son, Hamnet, and estranged from Anne and his daughters by his failure to grieve with them, Shakespeare is ill at ease at home. In many ways, *All is True* thus presents a 'straight' version of *Upstart Crow*; this Shakespeare, too, is a loser. As Isaac Butler (2018) writes of the film,

> This is a Shakespeare befitting our present moment, one in which we are trying to renegotiate our relationship to powerful men, the work they produce, and their misdeeds. Shakespeare's wrongs aren't in the same league as a Harvey Weinstein or a Bill Cosby, of course. The Shakespeare of *All Is True* is merely a crap husband and father.

What Butler describes as the crapness of Shakespeare as husband and father in the film is significant, as it connects the tonally distinct Elton-Shakespeare objects together: they share an interest in a portrait of the Bard that is flawed, but in recognisably mundane ways. The absent commuter father; the inattentive husband flirting with the attention of other men (Mills 2009); issues no doubt recognisable to most of us, even if they inspire in one text melancholy and the other, comedy.

The pleasures of *Upstart Crow* lie, therefore, not only in its comic use of anachronism but in what it shares with *All is True*: a time-honoured part of celebrity mythology which is its pretence of peering beneath the glossy veneer, seeing the star at home, understanding what 'makes' them. But of course, both Elton-Shakespeare objects do this through fictional encounters, loosely drawn from a mixture of historical facts about Shakespeare's life and dramatic motifs drawn from his own creations. Indeed, citing Michael Bristol's argument that the 'real' Shakespeare only exists 'as the imaginary projection of an important tradition of social desire' (1999: 490), Andrew Bennett writes that 'if authors don't exist [. . .], we have to invent them' (2005: 35). What, then, can we say about the social desires that formed the Elton-Shakespeare object, and its subsequent performance and reification of symbolic meaning through Mitchell-Shakespeare and the intellectual loser? Bingham writes that the biopic – like the tabloid – 'transforms a public figure into a character' (2010: 10). The 'function' of the subject becomes to 'give the spectator a story' (Bingham 2010: 10). *Upstart Crow* is by no means unusual in this regard. The TV show *Will* (2017), for instance, imagines an even earlier period in Shakespeare's history and dramatises the young playwright's first season in London before he became a shareholding member of the Chamberlain's Men. Even more than Mitchell-Shakespeare, this Shakespeare fails to realise the genius ascribed to him. He is, the extremely youthful Laurie Davidson confesses, only good at writing 'flatulent dogs and mooning lovers' (S1E2). And yet it is striking that *Will*, like the later *Upstart Crow*, is similarly incapable of keeping to its basic premise of depicting a Shakespeare who fails to be, well, *Shakespeare*. Will has an early success in wrangling the company's star, Will Kemp (William Houston), under control, even though the actor correctly warns the green Shakespeare that his 'job is to write parts that make [Kemp] shine' rather than the other way around. Moreover, '*Will*'s constant anticipation of the playwright's later success appears in clashes over delivery with Richard Burbage (Mattias Inwood), arguments about pay with James Burbage (Colm Meaney) and scenes real and imagined where the playwright steps on stage to receive adulation from his audience' (Blackwell 2018: 32).

That this happens in both biopics speaks perhaps to the extent of Shakespeare's fame – it is inexorable – but perhaps also to a perceived inviolable quality to his celebrity. After all, even parodic versions of Shakespeareanism seen in television comedies such as *Frasier*, *Vicious* and *Extras* are played by the likes of Derek Jacobi, Ian McKellen and Patrick Stewart. Failing at Shakespeare or failing at being Shakespeare, it seems, requires skill. And this brings me to my final point that connects Mitchell, Elton, Shakespeare and *Upstart Crow*: the distinctly classed, self-deprecating logic of the intellectual loser trope illustrates both the uniqueness of this variable object when compared with similar 'loser' archetypes (the stoner of American film comedy, for instance), but also its potential limitations. In spite of his efforts to play characters whose intelligence is unremarkable or prone to fail them in the face of 'common sense', David Mitchell is something of a British public intellectual and is vaunted by his fans for his critical reasoning. *Would I Lie to You?* scripts opportunities to show the unproductiveness of Mitchell's pedantry, but this joke relies on our ability to recognise his evident intelligence and then to take pleasure in its apparent meaninglessness. The programme's comedy also relies on the audience's recognition that Mitchell's fussy middle-classness would otherwise yield more social capital than Mack's performative northern working-classness. It is funny chiefly because it withholds an expected dynamic.

Framing this variable object as an intellectual *loser* indeed obscures the powerful and complex class manoeuvres that can nonetheless be performed when claiming even failed middle-class capital. The aforementioned (probably fictional) example of Mitchell's outrage at a shop assistant using the words 'well jel' and 'amazeballs' is illustrative. The star is not befuddled by a world that makes no sense; he chooses instead to remove his patronage because of class (and presumably age-based) snobbery. Stephen Fry, the former host of the general knowledge quiz show, *QI* (2003–), inadvertently gestured towards this tension when describing the 'logically ruthless' world Mitchell occupies (Series 'M', E3). As one can no doubt easily imagine, Mitchell performs well on shows such as *QI* that share his delight in esoteric forms of knowledge. In one episode Mitchell is even granted his own fanfare as Fry's 'teacher's pet' for his ability to correctly answer a series of questions on the differences between Russian and French cuisine. Mitchell is abashed by the acclaim, noting wryly that he doesn't feel 'cool' because of it, but he is also clearly pleased, and in the world of *QI* at least, such precise and arcane knowledge is powerful currency. The implied distinction between the trivia discussed in the programme – the 'quite interesting' of its acronym – and that which has real world application or use is palpable. Mitchell's 'ruthless' logic, too, exists in a world where it exceeds what is already useful, but it continues to signal his dedication to further education and betterment. This is, importantly, a luxury afforded by Mitchell's middle-class capital, and yet it is minimised precisely by the same capital which, in a self-apologising manoeuvre, the star then parodies. Indeed, self-deprecation requires the possession of cultural or social capital and is a strategy for the 'natural[isation]' of particular class interests (Bourdieu 1984), as it calls for that paradoxically restrained wielding of huge amounts of symbolic power. The performance of intellectual loserdom thus becomes a gesture that simultaneously claims and disavows power.

The dual processes that shore up Mitchell's intellectual loserdom act concurrently, and yet their visibility depends on the context in which the variable object is applied. This is, indeed, perhaps the difficulty of a comic framework that is based on subversion: the thing being ridiculed must already exist as a possibility in the audience's mind. There is thus some comedy in pitting Mitchell against Mack on *Would I Lie to You?*, or Mitchell-Shakespeare against his uneducated servant, Bottom. But when this framework is invoked in other media contexts (the star's columns, books or 'soap box' video series, for instance) without its counterbalance, all that remains is – if self-deprecatingly or ironically delivered – Mitchell's apparent intelligence. To wit, in observing the ruthlessness of the star's logic, Fry praises the power of Mitchell's discernment.

Lastly, a related issue occurs with the Elton-Shakespeare intellectual loser. *All is True* reifies a particular Englishness as essential to William Shakespeare. This type may be more vulnerable or mundane than is currently allowed by his mythological status, but its entanglement with the middle-class capital of the intellectual loser charted throughout this chapter valorises a particular kind of middle-class masculinity. As with Mitchell – and indeed Elton himself – this is a disingenuous attribution to someone who wields economic, social and cultural capital in a fairly conventional manner.[10] Similarly, in *Upstart Crow* Elton utilises self-deprecation through the script, the small, familiar sitcom setting, and through Mitchell's star persona in order to make Shakespeare relatable and grounded. Describing the playwright in promotional materials as an 'early commuter', Elton indeed mobilises Shakespeare as part of a critique against privilege and the trapping of power in the hands of the few. He notes the importance of remembering that the 'man whose sublime genius and ferocious work ethic gave us the greatest body of work in all literature was the son of a dodgy glove maker and the 16th century equivalent of a State School kid' (Elton 2016).[11] And he partly succeeds in this. *Upstart Crow*'s deployment of sitcom tropes, settings and characters locates Shakespeare and his concerns in a recognisable, (mostly) accessible and, importantly, mainstream cultural context. Shakespeare himself remains remote, however. He may occupy a sitcom world, but this iteration still hopes that future generations will 'trust' in his genius and assume they are unintelligent for missing his meaning (S2E5); he hopes that there will always be 'time for obscure blank verse', because otherwise, Shakespeare exclaims, 'my life is a lie!' (S2E2).

Notes

1. A similar thing can also be seen in films such as *Shakespeare in Love* (dir. John Madden, 1999) or *Bill* (dir. Richard Bracewell, 2015). It should be noted that the latter film has a television heritage, as it stars and was written by the former principal performers of the children's comedy series *Horrible Histories* (2009–14), which also featured a number of sketches about Shakespeare.
2. See Blackwell 2017 for examples of this phenomenon and how it relates to the implied prestige of possessing a 'Shakespearean' identity.
3. Mitchell contributes regular comment articles to the *Observer* and the *Guardian* and has authored *Back Story: A Memoir* (2012), *Thinking About It Only Makes It Worse* (2014) and *Dishonesty is the Second-Best Policy: And Other Rules to Live By* (2019). Mitchell's misanthropic worldview and fondness for ironic understatement translates easily to the written word, and an indication of how recognisable his tone is can be seen in its replication in even the copy surrounding his publications. Faber & Faber's synopsis for *Thinking About It . . .*, for instance, summarises Mitchell's commiseration on the 'state of things in our not entirely glorious nation' and a press release for *Dishonesty . . .* concludes Mitchell's biography with the sly note that the star has been 'in two films, neither of which made a profit' (Smith 2019).

4. Given that *Would I Lie To You?* is currently in its thirteenth series, one must also assume that the majority of the preposterous stories shared by Mitchell and Mack are scripted, and are thus useful examples of the programme's broad caricature of their comic personas.
5. It is important to note that the class divide between southern Mitchell and northern Mack which the programme utilises for so much of its team captains' scripted comedy is purposely exaggerated, and the reality of their class backgrounds is far more complex. This is acknowledged by the stars themselves; indeed, as I have already indicated, there is a highly self-conscious register to the deployment of both Mitchell's and Mack's comic personas. For example, when satirising the perception of individuals from the north of England as impoverished, Mack commented to one guest, comic Jon Richardson, 'You're from the North. I bet you've just got an imaginary flannel [as opposed to a real one].' To which Richardson, from the same county of Lancashire as Mack, retorted, 'You said that like you're not from the North.' Mack answered, 'I'm not. I've completely converted now' (S6E7).
6. Harry Enfield, Liza Tarbuck and Helen Monks, who play John, Anne and Susanna Shakespeare respectively, all adopt broad Warwickshire accents. Mitchell, however, speaks with his usual accent, and Paula Wilcox's Mary Arden speaks with a more clipped, received pronunciation than the rest of her family. Shakespeare is, of course, mocked throughout *Upstart Crow* for his pretensions, but Mary, too, receives criticism for reinforcing an otherwise invisible class distinction between her and the family she married 'beneath' herself to join. As Anne chides her mother-in-law, 'You think you're so posh, Mary Arden. Like you aren't sewn into your winter knickers like everybody else' (S1E1). Importantly, the series does not ridicule social climbing in and of itself. The (often offensively) plain-speaking John Shakespeare desires to become a gentleman and succeeds. Shakespeare, too, is largely supported by the audience in his ambitions to outwit Greene, who stands as his chief obstacle to betterment. Rather, *Upstart Crow* targets Shakespeare and Mary for their efforts to obscure their humble contexts.
7. There are obvious parallels between the comparatively sombre tone of this episode and similarly melancholy aspects of Mitchell's previous work, including the aforementioned 'Old Holmes' sketch, as well as the final scene in *Blackadder Goes Forth* (1989), written by Elton and Richard Curtis.
8. Mitchell has shared the reasons for his agnosticism on many occasions, including in his autobiography, *Back Story*. In it, he acknowledges and agrees with the public perception of his 'rational and analytical approach to the world' (Mitchell 2012: 157). He debunks the idea that atheism is an inevitable conclusion from this, however. Instead, Mitchell argues that atheism involves a series of irrational decisions, including the need to 'draw a conclusion' and to perform a 'leap of faith, albeit a nihilistic one' (2012: 157). Like Shakespeare,

Mitchell thus doubts the existence of God, but is willing – and indeed hopeful – to be proved wrong.

9. The only exception to this is the final episode of series three, 'Go On and I Will Follow', in which the Shakespeares' youngest son Hamnet dies. This episode alone concludes with the couple sitting in silence, as Shakespeare narrates in voiceover Constance's lines from *King John*:

> Grief fills the room up of my absent child,
> Lies in his bed, walks up and down with me,
> Puts on his pretty looks, repeats his words,
> Remembers me of all his gracious parts
> Stuffs out his vacant garments with his form;
> Then, have I reason to be fond of grief? (II.iv.93–8)

10. The intellectual loser variable object is primarily a gendered one. There are exceptions, however, including the recent comedy series *Fleabag* (2016–19), written by and starring Phoebe Waller-Bridge. And it is perhaps telling (but unsurprising) that the aforementioned vulnerability of this comic framework to complication becomes even more apparent when it intersects with the performance of femininity. Ellen E. Jones, for instance, writes that despite *Fleabag*'s efforts to make the titular character relatable – 'she's literally turning to us and winking knowingly every few minutes' – the programme is just 'for posh girls. It just is' (Jones 2019).
11. Elton dedicates the entirety of the second episode of series three to parodying the theory that Shakespeare was not the author of his own plays.

Bibliography

Anonymous (2014a), 'David Mitchell: *Back Story* Interview', <https://www.youtube.com/watch?v=KGO_kwiyLw4> [accessed 8 January 2020].

Anonymous (2014b), '*Thinking About It Only Makes It Worse* by David Mitchell', <https://www.faber.co.uk/9781783350568-thinking-about-it-only-makes-it-worse.html> [accessed 2 January 2020].

Bennett, A. (2005), *The Author*, Abingdon: Routledge.

Bingham, D. (2010), *Whose Lives Are They Anyway? The Biopic as Contemporary Film Genre*, New Brunswick, NJ: Rutgers University Press.

Blackwell, A. (2017), '"How do I act so well?" The British "Shakespearean" Actor and Cultural Cachet', in C. Kennedy-Karpat and E. Sandberg (eds), *Adaptation, Awards Culture and the Value of Prestige*, Basingstoke: Palgrave, pp. 211–29.

Blackwell, A. (2018), *Shakespearean Celebrity in the Digital Age*, Basingstoke: Palgrave.

Bourdieu, P. (1984), *Distinction: A Social Critique of the Judgement of Taste*, trans. Richard Nice, Cambridge, MA: Harvard University Press.

Bristol, M. D. (1999), 'Shakespeare: The Myth', in D. S. Kastan (ed.), *A Companion to Shakespeare*, Oxford: Blackwell, pp. 487–502, doi:10.1111/b.9780631218784.1999.00030.x [accessed 17 July 2020].

Burt, R. (1998), *Unspeakable ShaXXXspeares: Queer Theory and American Kiddie Culture*, Basingstoke: Palgrave.

Burt, R. (2002), *Shakespeare After Mass Media*, Basingstoke: Palgrave.

Butler, I. (2018), '*All is True* is a Shakespeare Biopic for the #MeToo Generation', *Slate*, 21 December, <https://slate.com/culture/2018/12/all-is-true-shakespeare-movie-accuracy-kenneth-branagh-hamnet.html> [accessed 8 April 2020].

D'Arcen, L. (2014), 'You Had to be There: Anachronism and the Limits of Laughing at the Middle Ages', *postmedieval: a journal of medieval cultural studies*, 5, pp. 140–53.

Desmet, C. (2017), 'Alien Shakespeares 2.0', *Actes des congrès de la Société française Shakespeare*, 35, DOI: https://doi.org/10.4000/shakespeare.3877 [accessed 8 January 2020].

Dobson, M. (1992), *The Making of the National Poet*, New York: Oxford University Press.

Elton, B. (2016), 'Only Snobbish Elitist Britain Could Say that Shakespeare Didn't Write his own Plays', *Radio Times*, 9 May, <https://www.radiotimes.com/news/2016-05-09/ben-elton-only-snobbish-elitist-britain-could-say-that-shakespeare-didnt-write-his-own-plays/> [accessed 9 January 2020].

Elton, B., and D. Mitchell (2018), '"Shakespeare was an overworked commuter": David Mitchell and Ben Elton Quiz Each Other', *Guardian*, 26 August, <https://www.theguardian.com/tv-and-radio/2018/aug/26/upstart-crow-ben-elton-david-mitchell-talk-comedy> [accessed 12 December 2019].

Hatfull, R. (2019), '*Upstart Crow* Season Three (Review)', *Shakespeare Bulletin*, 37:2, 300–3.

Hedrick, D. K. (2000), 'Review', *Shakespeare Quarterly*, 51:3, 390–3.

Jones, E. E. (2019), '*Fleabag* is a Work of Undeniable Genius. But it is for Posh Girls', *Guardian*, 20 April, <https://www.theguardian.com/tv-and-radio/2019/apr/20/fleabag-posh-girl-television> [accessed 8 April 2020].

Jones, K. W. (2001), *Accent on Privilege: English Identities and Anglophilia in the U.S.*, Philadelphia: Temple University Press.

Mills, B. (2009), *Sitcom*, Edinburgh: Edinburgh University Press.

Mitchell, D. (2012), *Back Story*, London: HarperCollins.

Raeside, J. (2016), '*Upstart Crow* Review: Ben Elton finds the Comedy in Shakespeare's History', *Guardian*, 10 May, <https://www.theguardian.com/tv-and-radio/2016/may/10/upstart-crow-review-ben-elton-comedy-shakespeare> [accessed 13 December 2019].

Rogers, A., and A. Thorpe (2014), 'Interview with the RSC's Hannah Miller, Head of Casting, and Kevin Fitzmaurice, Producer', *Contemporary Theatre Review*, 24:4, 486–93.

Rogers, J. (2016), 'Is the Door Really Open for Black Actors to Star in Shakespeare?', *The Stage*, 6 October, <https://www.thestage.co.uk/features/2016/door-really-open-black-actors-star-shakespeare/> [accessed 12 December 2019].

Shachar, H. (2019), *Screening the Author: The Literary Biopic*, Basingstoke: Palgrave.

Shakespeare, W. (2012), *Romeo and Juliet*, ed. R. Weis, London: Bloomsbury.

Shakespeare, W. (2016), *Hamlet*, ed. A. Thompson and N. Taylor, London: Bloomsbury.

Shakespeare, W. (2018), *King John*, ed. J. J. M. Tobin and Jesse M. Lander, London: Bloomsbury.

Smith, J. (2019), 'Faber Announces New Book by Comedian David Mitchell', 7 February, <https://www.faber.co.uk/blog/faber-announces-new-book-by-comedian-david-mitchell/> [accessed 2 January 2020].

Wiehe, J. (2015), 'Queer Slackers in Billy Morrisette's *Scotland, PA*', *Shakespeare Bulletin*, 35:4, 575–97.

7

Prosthetic Properties: The Materiality of Race and Gender in *The Hollow Crown: The Wars of the Roses*

Emily MacLeod

All of Shakespeare's history plays have an iconic object at their centre, the foremost symbol of kingship, the crown. The emphasis on significant objects in the title of the BBC's *The Hollow Crown: The Wars of the Roses* (2016) foreshadows the extreme focus that these adaptations give to material things. Andrew Sofer in *The Stage Life of Props* classifies one use of theatrical props as a kind of 'visual shorthand', which is easily applied to the use of objects in screen adaptations of Shakespeare (Sofer 2003: 20). Props give the audience information about character and status in *The Wars of the Roses*. The audience identifies the pious King Henry VI with his rosary beads and the feckless King Edward IV with a cup of wine. This reliance on objects to signify and perform meaning, however, is most present in the portrayal of two female characters in *Henry VI* – Joan of Arc and Margaret of Anjou. Objects are used to stand in for whole speeches and scenes with these characters, particularly in the case of Joan, whose role is drastically cut. While Margaret wields some props that are present in the Shakespeare text, most notably her bloody napkin, Joan is associated with an object added specifically for the film adaptation: a Virgin Mary statue. The objects adhere visually to their owners as a kind of prosthesis that not only enlivens the body to which it is attached, but also takes on a 'life' of its own. They evoke gendered and racialised histories of violence and the commodification of female bodies. The choreography of these objects and the blatant colour scheme pull them into the realm of lively matter, as they work alongside the bodies of women in a kind of assemblage that punctures myths of 'colour blindness' in Shakespeare performance.[1]

Multiracial casting in Shakespeare's comedies and tragedies both on stage and in film is much more common than in productions of the history plays.

British Equity, the union for performers and theatre workers, criticised director Trevor Nunn in 2015 for arguing that 'historical verisimilitude' justified his choice to have an all-white cast for his production of *The Wars of the Roses* at the Rose Theatre Kingston (qtd in Owen 2015). Sophie Okonedo, who plays Queen Margaret in *The Hollow Crown*, was the first actress of colour to be cast in the role in any major production of *Henry VI* on stage or in film. Apart from playing Cressida at the National Theatre in 1991, Okonedo did not have much experience with Shakespeare on stage or screen.[2] Her 'non-traditional' casting in a practically all-white Shakespeare history play, therefore, appears to fit into the 'framework' that, Brandi Wilkins Catanese writes, 'endorses a hierarchy in which colour-blind casting gives black actors access to great art that would otherwise remain out of reach' (2011: 64). When asked about his casting decision, director Dominic Cooke called Okonedo simply the 'best person in th[e] country to play th[e] part' (qtd in Debnath 2016). This language of casting based on a 'meritocratic model' is often used in support of 'colour-blind' casting, as Ayanna Thompson observes in *Colorblind Shakespeare* (2006: 6). In the same interview, Cooke also cites this tradition of casting in theatre, and refers to Shakespeare's retelling of history as a 'myth' about 'who we are as a society', which should, he implies, reflect the racial diversity of the world today (Debnath 2016). In both series of *The Hollow Crown*, however, the directors use what L. Monique Pittman calls 'on-location naturalism', similar to the style of Kenneth Branagh's *Henry V*, which is his only Shakespeare film to feature an all-white cast (Pittman 2015). Cooke attempts to recreate the medieval settings of the original plays and strives for authenticity of design and setting. This 'naturalism' is challenged, however, by the 'colour-blind' casting employed in both series, as Pittman examines in her article on the casting of *The Hollow Crown* adaptation of *Henry V* (Pittman 2016).

The realistic production design does not support Cooke's 'mythic' vision, and Okonedo is the only principal actor of colour in an overwhelmingly white cast that does not actually reflect modern society. Thus Cooke's stated reasoning of wanting to reflect modern England in the racial make-up of his cast is not borne out in the film. We must assume therefore that this casting is, as Cooke suggests, meant to be 'colour-blind' and that Okonedo's race is not supposed to signify in our interpretation of the production. But, as Thompson (2008) observes, it is important to 'assess how a [Shakespeare] production renders the semiotic value and meaning of [the] actor's race'. Catanese likewise emphasises how the 'interpretive competencies' of the spectators 'challenge the performing body's efforts to speak for itself' in situations of purportedly 'colour-blind' casting (2011: 18). The audience, therefore, cannot ignore how the objects associated with Margaret in the editing of the film continually highlight the actress's racial difference from the all-white principal cast, despite the director's claims to a merit-based 'colour-blind' casting process. Just as material things (costumes, props, actors' bodies) worked on the early modern stage to highlight the performance of gender and racial difference, objects in this film (such as Joan's statue and Margaret's handkerchief) join with actors' bodies to foreground both their racial and gender identities. The dynamic theatrical histories of these objects, particularly of the handkerchief, provide the audience with a visual shorthand that connects the narrative to other stories of racial and gendered violence and injustice.

Props, Assemblage and Prosthesis

Through repeated close-ups of objects and editing techniques such as montage, the camera in *The Wars of the Roses* ascribes great significance to the relationship between women's bodies and things. Therefore, objects on film, like stage properties, illustrate what Jane Bennett calls 'the curious ability of inanimate things to animate, to act, to produce effects dramatic and subtle' (2010: 6). Bennett uses the language of performance, of producing dramatic acts, to show how props and stage objects are prime material for discussions of object-oriented ontologies. Marlis Schweitzer and Joanne Zerdy similarly suggest 'that objects and things powerfully script, choreograph, direct, push, pull, and otherwise animate their human collaborators' (2014: 6). Stage properties are also, to use Robin Bernstein's term, 'scriptive things', objects that attain 'agency' through their 'constant engagement' with humans (2011: 12). These things can behave unpredictably in performance and create meanings that theatre-makers might not necessarily have intended. Bernstein, in her work specifically on objects with racist histories and iconography, refers to this engagement between people and things as a kind of 'dance' that 'constructs race' (2009: 69). In *The Wars of the Roses*, the feminised and racialised stage properties perform as 'scriptive things' with vital materiality, as the camera forces them to 'dance' with the female characters in order to both support and undermine the bodies with which they interact.

Just like a handkerchief or a goblet, an actor's body can also be considered as an 'object' of/in performance. Sofer, in his analysis of the semiotics of stage performance, notes that 'it is hard to draw a firm distinction between subjects and objects on stage, since subject and object alike function as volatile theatrical signs' (2003: 6). To view an actor's body as an object recalls the language that Frantz Fanon uses in describing his experience as a Black man in a white supremacist society ('an object among other objects') (2008: 89). Chapters in this volume by Kim and Pittman, Corredera, Denslow and Bailey explore the significant tensions in the past between critical race theory and posthuman, object-oriented studies. Katherine Behar in her introduction to *Object-Oriented Feminism* also raises these concerns, noting how 'object-oriented thinking stands to evolve feminist and postcolonial practices to reconsider how the very processes of objectification work' (2016: 8). *The Wars of the Roses*, despite Cooke's claims of 'colour blindness', brings together the bodies of actors and props into dynamic and agentic assemblages that create significant energy. I wish to explore how the 'objectification' of these human/non-humans works to dispel myths of colour blindness and bring issues of race in/as performance to the fore. Bennett's theory of assemblage (modelled after Deleuze and Guattari) helps to elucidate the ways in which material things and actors in this Shakespeare adaptation invoke the power and force of racial histories and meanings. An assemblage, or 'a confederation of human and non-human elements', affects our 'understanding' of what constitutes agency. How, Bennett asks, might that 'understanding . . . alter established notions of moral responsibility and political accountability?' (2010: 6). Like Kim, I am also interested in Alexander G. Weheliye's use of the term 'racialising assemblage', where 'bodies, forces, velocities, intensities, institutions, interests, ideologies, and desires' are brought together to construct race (Weheliye 2014: 12). Here, in *The Wars of the Roses*, the props of the female characters, along with the bodies of the actors, form a kind of 'racialising assemblage' that is forceful and dynamic.

This connection between actors and objects participating in 'racialising assemblages' goes back all the way to Shakespeare's own theatrical practices. On the early modern stage, material things served as markers of human difference, as an all-white male company used costumes, cosmetics and props to identify characters who were female and/or foreign. Valerie Wayne notes how 'the female body was itself absent from the English Renaissance stage', necessitating stage properties to 'register that absence and materialise women's exclusion' (2002: 300). Early modern performance scholars Will Fisher and Ian Smith use the word 'prosthesis' to refer to these kinds of material identifiers. Objects such as wigs or beards, Fisher writes, when attached to the actor's body, 'shape or materialise' the gender of that body (2006: 31). Ian Smith refers to the use of prosthetic devices such as paint and black cloth in the performance of blackness onstage. Smith suggests that these methods construct a 'wholly material and insubstantial' identity for the racially othered character, who is 'stripped of subjectivity' and defined by this materiality (2003: 34, 38). The actor's body, along with this material prosthesis, creates a specific kind of 'power' that Bennett ascribes to these kinds of 'heterogeneous assemblages' (2010: 23). Unlike David Mitchell and Sharon Snyder's disability studies' definition of prosthesis as that which endeavours to make a body 'fit in' or 'de-emphasise difference' (Mitchell and Snyder 2000: 3), racial prosthesis works to intentionally mark the body connected with it as 'other', and even as inhuman or demonic. Smith justifies his use of the term because these materials served 'literally' as 'additions to the bodies of white actors to compensate for parts of the body that are missing – black arms, hands, legs, faces, necks, hair' (2003: 42). The addition of these objects in *The Wars of the Roses* to the bodies of the actors does not always 'compensate' for 'missing' parts (such as eliminated scenes or text), but rather works to highlight that which the film-makers want to leave untheorised, namely the racial identity of the actors. To apply Smith's theory here, blackness becomes an object, whereas the underlying whiteness of the actors resists this kind of classification. Behar also describes white supremacy's orientation 'around . . . transparent whiteness' (Behar 2016: 11), which in this case works to produce dynamic racialising assemblages of bodies and prosthetic objects, akin to those presented on the early modern stage.

Shakespeare's stage used material signifiers to supply the absence of actual women or people of colour, but on film objects attach themselves to the gendered and racialised bodies of these actors to highlight their racial difference through the camera's gaze. Directors and editors create an intimate relationship between audience and image in a medium such as television, because they orient the audience's gaze towards these prosthetic objects as crucial elements of their storytelling method. The camera shots dictate where the eye will focus, unlike the relative freedom of watching the action onstage. Roberta Sassatelli points out that in our digital age with streaming services, viewers have even more control over their watching experience: 'you can freeze frames, you can repeat sequences . . . you can go to the essence of the film as a framed reality made of frames' (2011: 143). The audience therefore has a very different relationship with the objects being framed on screen than they have with props and bodies on the stage. The focus on prosthetic devices and scriptive things in *The Wars of the Roses* draws our attention to the female characters and orients our gaze towards Joan's whiteness and Margaret as a woman of colour in a fictionalised white medieval England. The way the camera frames Okonedo's body in relation to objects such as the golden candlesticks and goblets, the handkerchief and the chess pieces in these three films makes her race become visible semiotically through assemblage. Other cinematic elements, such as colour, costumes and editing, likewise emphasise the whiteness of Joan of Arc, deliberately set up against Margaret in this adaptation.

Joan and Margaret

In *1 Henry VI*, the object that adheres most to Joan is her sword, which establishes her role in the masculine world of the battlefield. In *The Wars of the Roses*, Joan (Laura Morgan) is almost immediately associated instead with a white statue of the Virgin Mary, a much more feminine symbol, that she sees in a vision. Joan's presence in the adaptation is relegated to only a few scenes. Instead of establishing her character through text and action, as in the scene where she meets the Dauphin and beats him in a physical fight or the scene where she begs for aid from demonic spirits, *The Wars of the Roses* uses objects to show her piety and her contact with mystical, potentially supernatural elements. Joan's religious faith here is not articulated through her speeches to the Dauphin about her vision of the Holy Mother, but through a flashback in which we see a white statue crying blood and calling out to her. The bloody tear, which drops on to a white sheet, and the disembodied voice animate the statue and make it an unexpectedly lively piece of matter. While images of bleeding male bodies on the battlefield are omnipresent, the image of blood trickling from a female form on to a white sheet has a whole host of other connotations – menstruation, the consummation of marriage, childbirth – all unassociated with the virgin Joan. The whiteness of the statue as well as the bloody tear that stains the white cloth recall the words that Joan speaks to the Dauphin in *1 Henry VI* (but which are not spoken in the film): 'And, whereas I was black and swart before, / With those clear rays which she infused on me / That beauty am I bless'd with which you see' (I.ii.85–7). In the film, the speech where she originally speaks these lines is shortened and adapted into an address that she gives to her troops, not just the Dauphin. Her whiteness, however, is still foregrounded when, during her speech, a black soldier in her ranks is shown as she references her former 'base vocation' (I.ii.81). The editing of the film thus aligns her former 'black and swart' state with the soldier, in contrast to her present status as a white and beautiful woman blessed by the Virgin. Both Joan's whiteness and her virginity, highlighted by her orientation to this white statue, stained cloth and the black soldier, compound to centre her as a fixture of pure white womanhood.

While Joan transgresses gender norms by fighting as a soldier, this adaptation moves her capture from the battlefield to her bedroom. There

York scoops her up and carries her like a reluctant bride, clad in a white nightgown, over the threshold. The feminisation of Joan in these final moments works to preserve her as a kind of damsel-in-distress, fitting an image of whiteness that contrasts sharply with Margaret. York's act of lifting Joan up is subtly echoed in the next shot, when a soldier lifts a golden candlestick from a table to place it on a pile of goods. The candlestick is part of the spoils of the battle that the English have just won, with Joan and Margaret now added to the pile.

This adaptation follows a performance and scholarly tradition of directly comparing both Margaret and Joan as unruly Frenchwomen. In Michael Boyd's *Histories* cycle for the RSC (2000 and 2006), the same actress played both characters – she emerged as Margaret like a phoenix from the flames of Joan's execution. In *The Wars of the Roses*, the introduction of Margaret is intercut with the capture of Joan for a similar pairing effect. Before he encounters Margaret, Somerset (Ben Miles) cautiously moves through a dark hallway in the midst of the siege. As his shadow exits one frame, we see a dagger enter the shot. That dagger, and the white sleeve of the arm holding it, signals the first appearance of Margaret of Anjou.[3] Somerset neatly fends off her blade, pulling her from her hiding place into full view. He is enamoured with her beauty, and promises to make her queen of England by marrying her to King Henry. One of Margaret's first lines is a rejection of this offer. She says, 'To be a queen in bondage is more vile / Than is a slave in base servility' (*1H6* V.iii.112–13). By invoking the imagery of bondage and slavery, Okonedo's race becomes strikingly visible in this scene of capture. Thompson argues that 'colour-blind' casting cannot wipe racism from an audience's memory, that it can 'creep up to the surface . . . in spite of the colourblind approach' (2006: 10). In this case, a loaded word such as 'slave' acts almost as agentic matter in itself to produce energetic and racist tensions. This series of images from both Joan and Margaret's captures shows exactly how objects, like language, can cause race to 'creep up', serving as what Roland Barthes would call a 'punctum' that 'rises from the scene', 'shot like an arrow to pierce' the viewer (Barthes 1981: 26).

As Margaret's father Reignier sits at the table, under guard, Somerset proposes his plan to wed Margaret to King Henry. Somerset sits facing Reignier, leaving Margaret to stand at the head of the table between them. She becomes another object to be haggled over, as is made clear through the editing that links her with the golden goblets and candlesticks that the soldier in the foreground is shifting from one pile to another. She is also linked in the text to an object of great value: Somerset calls her a 'diamond' that he will 'set safe' in England (*1H6* V.iii.174). This description could refer to feminine purity and virginity, but diamonds are also associated with foreignness later in the series when King Henry refers to his crown as having 'diamonds and Indian stones' (*3H6* III.i.63). Margaret's position between the seated men also puts her in line with a broken pot lying on the table and a scroll of paper, the remnants of a defeated household.

In the 1983 BBC production, the performance of Julia Foster, the white actress playing Margaret, is markedly different. In this scene she smiles; she is coy and flirtatious. She looks between her father and the English lord with interest and energy. In *The Wars of the Roses*, Okonedo's eyes throughout this scene are downcast, and she is silent. The image of a woman of colour being haggled over as an object of sale is disturbing, and it is made even more so by her lack of expression. Margaret's body, on display in her white gown, is both motionless and emotionless. Okonedo plays a character visually and thematically attached to these scriptive, prosthetic things that reconfigure the scene as one charged with the violence of the commodification of black bodies throughout history. The staging and choreography of these objects alongside her stillness magnifies what Soyica Diggs Colbert has called the 'hypervisibility' of blackness in performance, which creates a 'shadowed black body', 'reducing black people to materiality – walking archives' (2011: 4). Colbert attributes this 'production of blackness' to 'uninhibited looking' at black bodies throughout history from the auction block to the minstrel show (2011: 7). The camera connects our 'looking' at Okonedo with the objects surrounding her, emphasising her status as an object as well. The choreography of these objects, the goblets and candlesticks placed among the spoils of war, links them prosthetically to the black, female body that they are deliberately placed beside. The camera orients our eyes to them, and makes the audience draw a connection between objects and bodies on display, highlighting both racial and gender identities.

Colour-Coded Assemblages

Unlike Joan, Margaret's role in this adaptation is left relatively intact, given that she is a key player in the main arc of the English civil wars that dominate the second two parts of *Henry VI*. Also, unlike Joan, Margaret in *The Wars of the Roses* is shown as sexually deviant and excessive, based on the portrayal of her affair with Somerset. The coding of whiteness with Christianity and purity and blackness with death, destruction and immorality here points to the most basic of medieval colour associations. In the second part of *The Wars of the Roses*, Margaret and her army disrupt the York family's domestic space in a very similar scene to that of the defeat of the French in the first part. A sinister musical score accompanies this action, which is intercut with images of soldiers fighting and white women screaming. Unlike the white nightgown that she wore on her first appearance, Margaret is now dressed in black, the shade that Smith states was semiotically associated with devils and hell on the early modern stage (2003: 41). Next she approaches a tapestry with a white rose, the ensign of York, and sets it alight. Destroying the white textile symbol of her enemy's house serves as a foreshadowing of her use of another white textile object in the next scene, when she dips a handkerchief in the blood of York's son and stuffs it in York's mouth. Two significant props in this scene, the bloody napkin and the paper crown, are adapted here to foreground Margaret's increased power and her 'shadowed black body', as well as the religious imagery of whiteness formerly associated with Joan.

Margaret receives this napkin or handkerchief in this adaptation as a present from Somerset, who becomes her lover before his death at the hands of the Yorkists. Embroidered with the red rose of Lancaster, the cloth first appears in a scene of illicit affection between them. Fisher notes the significance of the handkerchief as a sign of affection between men and women, the most famous dramatic example being the one in *Othello*. Unlike the white statue linked to Joan, which shows her virginity, Margaret's use of the handkerchief symbolises her sexual appetite, as well as working as a kind of racial prosthesis. That the word 'hand' is part of the word 'handkerchief' attaches the cloth linguistically to the body, just as one's 'hand' serves as a metonym for marriage (Fisher 2006: 33). Ian Smith's theory that the handkerchief used in *Othello* was made of black cloth, an extension of the racially cross-dressed actor's textile prosthesis, provides a new way to read the use of Margaret's handkerchief here (Smith 2013). If the handkerchief as love token can stand in for the skin of the giver, then the whiteness of the handkerchief links it to the whiteness of Somerset's skin, and brings visceral meaning to Margaret being aided by the 'hand' of her dead lover in her act of revenge against their greatest enemy, York. Associating Margaret, played by an actress of colour, with a handkerchief similar to the one used in productions of *Othello* (though spotted with red roses, rather than strawberries) functions much like the goblets and other spoils of war in the first scene to make her racial difference more visible.

In many ways, the handkerchief acts here as a palimpsest, or what Jonathan Gil Harris calls 'polychronic matter' in which 'different historical "moments" ... of religion, race, and sexuality are repeatedly made to' interact (2010: 170). The handkerchief here can be interpreted as a racialised and sexualised object, but the blatant Christian imagery used in the film 'folds in' religious meanings that set up the binary of 'Margaret as black devil' and 'the Yorks as white sacrifice'. Through the actors' skin colour, their emblem of the white rose and their costumes, *The Wars of the Roses* establishes the York family as representative of whiteness. This whiteness is comparable to Joan's, which is ironic given that they are enemies at the beginning of the film. This assemblage of white emblems here works as a device to showcase Christian piety and virtue, while blackness is linked to figures of devils and hell. Textually, there are ten different lines in Shakespeare's plays where the words 'black' and 'devil' appear together, and nine lines that link the words 'black' and 'hell'. In Shakespeare's original text, Margaret mocks York by placing a paper crown on his head. This adaptation uses a crown of thorns instead, not only a reference to the roses of the title, but also the traditional depiction of Christ's crucifixion. The body of York's son lies with his arms outstretched in a position that evokes Christ on the cross. The alignment of the Yorks here with white Christianity contrasts with Margaret's black hood and the fire from the castle in the background. She is textually 'othered' as well: York calls her an 'Amazonian trull' and refers to her face as 'vizard-like, unchanging' (*3H6* I.iv.114, 116). Whether or not the reference to her vizard or mask is an early modern theatrical reference to the boy player's make-up as well as a comment on Margaret's lack of pity, it reminds us of other material prostheses used in the performance of blackness, materials that 'masked' interiority as well as signifying otherness and inhuman behaviour.

The assemblage of Margaret's body and the handkerchief creates an explosively energetic force that drums up racial, sexual and religious tensions and associations. A similar white cloth appears in two medieval mystery plays, where a woman uses a handkerchief to clean the face of Jesus, which transforms the cloth into a sacred relic (Sofer 2000: 131–2). Margaret wipes York's face with her handkerchief, casting him as Jesus in a corrupted recreation of this scene, where blood, not sweat, is imprinted on the fabric. While a handkerchief's normal use is to soak up excess moisture, such as sweat or tears, Margaret dabs it at the still-bleeding neck of York's son Rutland. This transgressive use of the white cloth, now stained with blood, makes it an even more charged and powerful object. She further mocks York by wiping his eyes with this symbol of his deceased enemy Somerset, and stuffing it in his mouth to gag him. By placing such an emphasis on this stage property that has accumulated racialised as well as religious meanings over time, we see Margaret become the monstrous woman who is later punished by the murder of her own son. This monstrosity gains even more racialised imagery in her appearances later in *Richard III*, where she is associated both materially and dramatically with darkness, death and haunting.

This black and white imagery continues to be employed to mark bodily difference and evil intent in the opening scene of *Richard III*, where Richard's non-normative body is put on grotesque display. The whiteness of Benedict Cumberbatch's body, distorted by CGI effects, contrasts with the dark lighting around him. This contrast is also reflected in the black and white chess pieces in the game he plays against himself. His face in some shots is almost completely in shadow – tying blackness and darkness of visage with the dark deeds that he is plotting. The black and white chess pieces serve as a visual motif throughout the film, and Richard is often seen at the board, plotting his political strategy. Their design is reminiscent of the Lewis chessmen, a medieval chess set that historically had red pieces opposing white ones, which would have aligned chromatically with the red and white roses of York and Lancaster (McLain 2010). These black and white pieces instead pick up on the imagery of his father's death and serve as symbols of the racial difference between the victorious Yorks and the defeated Queen Margaret. At the end of the film, after Richmond's final speech, there is a shot of a dark room, where we see a single chess piece, lying on its side. Because of the lighting, it is hard to tell if the piece is white or black, though it looks to me like a white piece in shadow, similar to Richard's body in the first scene. While this object could represent Richard, who Margaret herself calls 'hell's black intelligencer', the camera next shows Margaret, who is surrounded by dead soldiers on the battlefield (*Richard III* IV.iv.73). Even though she has seen Richard defeated, she is not victorious. Instead she stands in the midst of the fallen bodies, like pawns, that mark the end of England's brutal civil war. As the camera zooms up and out to reveal more and more corpses on the field, the frame loses sight of her, drowning her in a sea of death. Her punishment for the pain that she has inflicted is not to die, but to survive and see the destruction. She is once again placed in an assemblage of agentic matter, both animate and inanimate.

Conclusion

In these films, the fallen chess piece, the golden candlesticks, the white statue and the bloody handkerchief rise through the screen to puncture the myth of 'colour-blind' Shakespeare performance promoted by Cooke. They point instead to the ways in which scriptive things throughout the film act as a racial prosthesis, marking Margaret's difference, and centring whiteness as the norm. Just as prosthetic objects and material things were used to represent racial difference on the early modern stage, objects work to foreground racial difference (both blackness and whiteness) on film through their assemblage with the bodies of actors. They become prosthetic through their association with bodies, which is made explicit because the camera orients our gaze to see the bodies in relation to objects, and at times as objects themselves. Objects can be racialised not just through colour but through their proximity to racialised bodies. These props fight against 'colour blindness' because of their social lives, and are indelibly linked to histories of racism and racial differentiation, just as bodies of colour have been objectified and commodified for material gain. Here, objects work prosthetically to animate racial (and violent, racist) histories of the body. Instead of refusing to acknowledge the racial ramifications of this casting by calling it 'colour-blind', we must address how Okonedo's race, when put in a basically all-white production, can be read semiotically through the use of specific props and costumes that reproduce visual and cultural codes of difference. If Cooke wanted to represent modern society by casting multiracially, as he suggests in his interview, he could have cast more actors of colour, thereby expanding the ways in which racial difference can signify within the narrative. Instead, by casting the role of the foreign queen Margaret with the only actress of colour, Cooke shows, intentionally or not, how much an actor's race can matter, and *become* matter.

The Hollow Crown: The Wars of the Roses foregrounds the display of racialised female bodies through their interactions with objects. The camera, through the frequent use of close-ups and montage, gives these props power, not only to act as symbols but to perform as assemblages themselves in tandem with the human actors. Margo Hendricks, in an essay on race and gesture in Shakespeare film adaptations, writes that 'the performed body is a body to be read and, ideologically, made meaning of in relation to cultural intersections with Shakespeare's play-texts. How we read that body is very much determined by its movements, gestures, and its appearance – make-up, costume, and, of course, the actor's body' (2006: 193–4). I would add to this list that objects, whether literally connected to that body or made to 'dance' with it by the camera through montage and editing, serve a similar function in animating the way that the audience perceives racial difference. The importance of attention to objects and their lively, agentic and prosthetic qualities must be considered when adapting these stories for twenty-first-century audiences.

Notes

1. For more on 'colour blindness' in theatre performance, see Thompson (ed.) 2006, Catanese 2011 and Pao 2010.
2. She was best-known for her Oscar-nominated performance in *Hotel Rwanda* and her Tony-winning role in *A Raisin in the Sun* opposite Denzel Washington. Both of these dramas centred her identity as a black woman in stories rife with racial tensions. In 2019, three years after *The Wars of the Roses*, she received an Olivier Award nomination for her performance as Cleopatra at the National Theatre.
3. In this adaptation, Somerset, not Suffolk, captures and seduces Margaret.

Bibliography

Barthes, R. (1981), *Camera Lucida: Reflections on Photography*, trans. R. Howard, New York: Hill and Wang.
Behar, K. (2016), *Object-Oriented Feminism*, Minneapolis: University of Minnesota Press.
Bennett, J. (2010), *Vibrant Matter: A Political Ecology of Things*, Durham, NC: Duke University Press.
Bernstein, R. (2009), 'Dances with Things: Material Culture and the Performance of Race', *Social Text 101*, 27:4, 67–94.
Bernstein, R. (2011), *Racial Innocence: Performing American Childhood from Slavery to Civil Rights*, New York: New York University Press.
Catanese, B. W. (2011), *The Problem of the Color[blind]: Racial Transgression and the Politics of Black Performance*, Ann Arbor: University of Michigan Press.
Colbert, S. D. (2011), *The African American Theatrical Body: Reception, Performance, and the Stage*, Cambridge: Cambridge University Press.
Debnath, N. (2016), 'Sophie Okonedo was the "Best Actress" to Play White Shakespeare Role in *The Hollow Crown*', *Sunday Express*, 6 May, <https://www.express.co.uk/showbiz/tv-radio/667894/Sophie-Okonedo-Undercover-The-Hollow-Crown-Benedict-Cumberbatch-Dominic-Cooke> [accessed 3 August 2019].
Fanon, F. (2008 [1952]), *Black Skin, White Masks*, trans. R. Philcox, New York: Grove Press.
Fisher, W. (2006), *Materializing Gender in Early Modern English Literature and Culture*, Cambridge: Cambridge University Press.
Harris, J. G. (2010), *Untimely Matter in the Time of Shakespeare*, Philadelphia: University of Pennsylvania Press.
Hendricks, M. (2006), 'Gestures of Performance: Rethinking Race in Contemporary Shakespeare', in A. Thompson (ed.), *Colorblind Shakespeare: New Perspectives on Race and Performance*, New York: Routledge, pp. 187–204.
McClain, D. L. (2010), 'Reopening History of Storied Norse Chessman', *New York Times*, 8 September, <https://www.nytimes.com/2010/09/09/arts/09lewis.html> [accessed 1 August 2019].

Mitchell, D., and S. Snyder (2000), *Narrative Prosthesis: Disability and the Dependencies of Discourse*, Ann Arbor: University of Michigan Press.

Owen, J. (2015), 'Trevor Nunn Defends All-white Shakespeare Histories', *The Independent*, 15 August, <https://www.independent.co.uk/arts-entertainment/theatre-dance/news/trevor-nunn-defends-all-white-shakespeare-histories-10457512.html> [accessed 3 September 2020].

Pao, A. (2010), *No Safe Spaces: Re-casting Race, Ethnicity, and Nationality in American Theatre*, Ann Arbor: University of Michigan Press.

Pittman, L. M. (2015), 'Shakespeare and the Cultural Olympiad: Contesting Gender and the British Nation in the BBC's *The Hollow Crown*', *Borrowers and Lenders: The Journal of Shakespeare and Appropriation*, 9:2, <http://www.borrowers.uga.edu/1580/show> [accessed 18 August 2020].

Pittman, L. M. (2017), 'Color-Conscious Casting and Multicultural Britain in the BBC *Henry V* (2012): Historicizing Adaptation in an Age of Digital Placelessness', *Adaptation*, 10:2, 176–91.

Sassatelli, R. (2011), 'Interview with Laura Mulvey: Gender, Gaze and Technology in Film, Culture', *Theory, Culture & Society*, 28:5, 123–43.

Schweitzer, M., and J. Zerdy (2014), *Performing Objects and Theatrical Things*, Basingstoke: Palgrave Macmillan.

Smith, I. (2003), 'White Skin, Black Masks: Racial Cross-Dressing on the Early Modern Stage', *Renaissance Drama*, 32, 33–67.

Smith, I. (2013), 'Othello's Black Handkerchief', *Shakespeare Quarterly*, 64:1, 1–25.

Sofer, A. (2000), 'Absorbing Interests: Kyd's Bloody Handkerchief as Palimpsest', *Comparative Drama*, 34:2, 127–53.

Sofer, A. (2003), *The Stage Life of Props*, Ann Arbor: University of Michigan Press.

Thompson, A. (2006), 'Practicing a Theory/Theorizing a Practice: An Introduction to Shakespearean Colorblind Casting', in A. Thompson (ed.), *Colorblind Shakespeare: New Perspectives on Race and Performance*, New York: Routledge, pp. 27–46.

Thompson, A. (2008), 'To Notice or Not to Notice: Shakespeare, Black Actors, and Performance Reviews', *Borrowers and Lenders: The Journal of Shakespeare and Appropriation*, 4:1, <http://www.borrowers.uga.edu/782039/show> [accessed 18 August 2020].

Thompson, A. (ed.) (2006), *Colorblind Shakespeare: New Perspectives on Race and Performance*, New York: Routledge.

Wayne, V. (2002), 'The Woman's Parts of Cymbeline', in J. G. Harris and N. Korda (eds), *Staged Properties in Early Modern English Drama*, Cambridge: Cambridge University Press, pp. 288–310.

Weheliye, A. G. (2014), *Habeas Viscus: Racialising Assemblages, Biopolitics, and Black Feminist Theories of the Human*, Durham, NC: Duke University Press.

PART III
HUMAN OBJECTS

8

'Intermission!': Reading Race in the Objects of *Key & Peele*'s 'Othello Tis My Shite'

Shanelle E. Kim

The *Key & Peele* sketch 'Othello Tis My Shite' (2013) begins with an interruption. A herald announces 'Intermission!' outside the Globe Theatre in London; the vignette imagines two black men, Lashawnia (Keegan-Michael Key) and Martinsia (Jordan Peele), reacting to a performance of *Othello* during the breaks after each half of the play. Hilarity ensues as they rave over the first half of the play, only to seethe with rage at the Moor's fate in the second. '[T]is about time Shakespeare doth scriven the play that places a brother amongst the firmaments', the character Martinsia declares excitedly to his companion ('Othello Tis My Shite', 00:32–34). Martinsia's expression of excitement, however, references not *Othello*, but another Shakespeare text. Perhaps Shakespeare's best-known use of the word 'firmament' is in what is commonly referred to as Hamlet's 'What a piece of work is man' speech. In it, Hamlet describes the heavens as 'this brave o'erhanging firmament' (II.ii.266). He goes on to marvel at the capacities of humankind: 'how like an angel in apprehension; how like a god' (II.ii.272).[1] In comparing human faculties to the divine, Hamlet associates humanity with the 'firmament', that is, '[h]eaven, as the place where God dwells' (*OED*). What makes humankind *human* is its union with the divine as a godly creation. Martinsia's reference to this speech in his expression of delight, however, suggests that prior to *Othello*, 'brothers' – black individuals – have been excluded from the human community, whose being derives from the 'firmaments'. After all, the early modern cultural imagination characterised the devil as a figure with 'skin like a Niger' (Reginald Scot in Loomba and Burton 2007: 114). Humanity is determined by its proximity to the firmament; the black individual, however, is closer to the devil – and therefore must be excluded from human being. As Matthieu Chapman argues, 'If Christian symbolism aligns blackness with death and positions whiteness as the opposite of blackness, then we can read whiteness as coinciding with notions of life' (2017: 60). There is no 'brother amongst the firmaments'; the Great Chain of Being is the cultural through line – the colour line – in the binaries dividing white from black, life from death, God from the devil, human from non-human.[2] The intermission between the first and second halves of *Othello* reveals the gap between the depiction of the black individual as a brother in the 'vast human family of human beings' and his literal and ontological death (Du Bois 1995: 21).

Martinsia's line demonstrates how 'Othello Tis My Shite' uses references not only for comedic effect, but also to reposition early modern objects in relation to the ontological colour line. The humorous allusions throughout the sketch require familiarity with the Shakespeare *oeuvre* and early modern English culture as well as with works from the black popular culture canon (such as the 1971 film *Shaft*) and the Harlem Renaissance. These references bring a variety of objects into the same orbit, inviting further investigation into how these objects shift ontologically when they appear together. Martinsia's allusion to Hamlet's speech brings the earlier tragedy into *Othello*'s orbit, prompting a comparison between how the Danish prince and the Moor of Venice have been positioned with respect to the firmament – and to humanity. 'What a piece of work is man', Hamlet marvels (II.ii.269), 'how like a god . . . the paragon of animals' (II.ii.272–3). 'O, the more angel she', Emilia cries when she discovers Desdemona dead by Othello's hand, 'and you the blacker devil!' (V.ii.134–5). The sketch brings to the surface the disparity between Hamlet's wonder at (and boredom with) humanity's near-divine faculties and Emilia's comparison of Othello with the devil. Chapman writes, 'the Early Modern English, to define their own humanity, positioned black Africans as beings that existed outside the ontology of the human' (2017: 17). In order for Hamlet and Desdemona to retain their white human ontology, they must be like gods and angels – and Othello must become blacker, less human and more like the devil. Martinsia's comment that it is 'about time Shakespeare doth scriven the play that places a brother amongst the firmaments' situates the two plays together in order to expose the binary dividing black and white as the very same one that distinguishes heaven from earth, human from non-human.

The other references throughout the sketch function in a similar manner: they bring temporally and culturally asymmetrical objects together in shifting systems that reveal how Shakespearean objects become human tools for excluding black individuals from human ontology. In other words, the *Key & Peele* sketch references objects – texts, images – in order to expose how they turn black individuals into objects themselves, reinforcing what Stuart Hall describes as the 'rigid binary coding' of racialisation (1998: 290). In this chapter I examine several of the objects in the sketch. I ask what other objects they evoke, and what kinds of networks relate those objects. The sketch reveals each reference to be a single object engaged in two different systems: one system perpetuates the division between white subject and black object, while the other collapses such distinctions and reasserts blackness as a human ontology. Frantz Fanon argues, 'The black man has no ontological resistance in the eyes of the white man' (2008: 90). His words spotlight inherent problems in object-oriented ontology (OOO) from a critical race studies perspective. However, I suggest that 'Othello Tis My Shite' offers Shakespeare appropriation as a mode for converging the two in order to expose and confront the objects undergirding the cultural structures that deny black subjectivity.

Currently very little scholarship engages both OOO and critical race studies, and understandably so, for object theorists often couch their concepts in language that strikes discordantly to a race-conscious ear.[3] For example, OOO's insistence on dissolving the boundaries between human and thing – a foundational principle of the field – neglects a history in which humans *were* things. In *Vibrant Matter*, Jane Bennett imagines that a turn to objects will reveal the 'extent to which human being and thinghood overlap, the extent to which the us and the it slip-slide into each other. One moral of the story is that we are also nonhuman and that things, too, are vital players in the world' (2010: 4). Levi Bryant enlarges on the overlap between human and thing; he argues that 'there is only one type of being: objects. As a consequence, humans are not excluded, but are rather objects *among* the various types of objects that exist or populate the world, each with their own specific powers and capacities' (2011: 20). For a large community of human beings, however, the slippage between selfhood and thinghood was already a painful reality: slavery facilitated the transmutation of black human into commodified object. Frank B. Wilderson contends that 'the Slave is not a laborer but an anti-Human' (2010: 11). For Wilderson, the slave is evidence of a clear distinction between human and non-human: the slave *is* the thing. Saidiya Hartman, however, argues that the slave occupies the liminal space between humanity and thinghood. She writes that the slave lives a 'bifurcated existence as both an object of property and a person (whether understood as a legal subject formally endowed with limited rights and protections, a submissive, culpable or criminal agent, or one possessing restricted capacities for self-fashioning)' (Hartman 1997: 5). The slave exists in the overlap between human and object that both Bennett and

Bryant describe. While Wilderson describes the total exclusion of the black self from the human community, Hartman suspends the black individual in the liminal space between person and thing. For both critical race scholars, however, the close association between black human and object becomes clear. Bringing their writings into conversation with Bennett and Bryant, then, reveals that OOO's impulse to collapse the distinctions between thing- and personhood overlooks – even elides – the traumatic effects of objectifying individuals. In elevating objects in order to unseat the human from the top of the ontological hierarchy, OOO scholars neglect to account for how the imbrication of thing- and personhood has suppressed black humanity rather than extending ontology to the object.[4] For the lived experience of the black individual, the oscillation between person and thing has resulted not in the extended agency of the object, but rather in a severe limitation on human powers and capacities. Perhaps the lack of dialogue between OOO and critical race studies results from the fact that OOO is predominantly *white* and, as such, offers theories from a white perspective unburdened by and inattentive to the racial trauma of slavery.

Slavery and its conversion of the person into property, however, is not the only mechanism that causes the black individual to vacillate between thing- and personhood. Even before England's complete immersion in the transatlantic slave trade, the early modern period struggled with the problem of ontologically classifying the black individual. Imtiaz Habib's seminal investigation into the early modern archives evidences this difficulty, as the prohibition of slavery, Elizabeth I's order for the banishment of black persons, and Britain's entry into the slave trade all participate in an ongoing eradication of the black individual's existence as a subject. Habib argues that the early modern period develops a negation of black subjectivity, resulting in the black person as 'seen but denied, known but unacknowledged, and more present than before but just as invisible' (2008: 65). Habib's scholarship reveals the spots in the early modern archive where black English individuals become visible, as well as where they disappear. He writes, 'To deal with the beginnings of black people in early modern England is therefore to deal with absences, with the non-visibility of a presence whose communitarian processing has to write the grammar of its sight in order to reveal the objects of its view' (2008: 19). The black person, then, is simultaneously visible and absent from view in the early modern English archive.

Objects, too, are simultaneously absent and present. Ian Bogost explains, 'If we take seriously the idea that all objects recede interminably into themselves, then human perception becomes just one among many ways that objects might relate' (2012: 9). Just as Habib argues that black English individuals become invisible in and through the historical record, Bogost contends that objects must be understood as partially hidden from human view. However, while the absent presence of objects frees them from the dominance of human perception, this same absent presence works to exclude black individuals from humanity. I juxtapose Habib and Bogost in order to suggest that OOO scholars frame objects in terms that are similar to the treatment of black individuals in the historical archive. And by doing so, they reinforce the similarities between black person and object without granting black people the expanded powers of the object that OOO purports to allow. In order to interact with critical race studies, OOO scholars need to acknowledge that the current 'human' in their person-and-thing formulations is white – and therefore free from a traumatic history of thingification – and change the terms in which they frame such interactions. Resisting a default to a white human allows a reassertion of visibility and viability for black individuals.

'Othello Tis My Shite' sets its scene in an early modern England where two black men visibly interact with various objects that participate in a system that would deny human ontology to black individuals. The sketch resists the negation of black subjectivity on several fronts. First, they are visible as members of the human community in early modern England. The sketch thus brings into view the population of black people that the early modern English record obscures, according to Habib's research. Furthermore, the sketch portrays two free black people; their rich costumes suggest that Lashawnia and Martinsia are not servants or (illegal) slaves but rather black English people of better means than their white companions in the sketch. Their focal centrality as well as the juxtaposition between their luxurious dress and the duller costumes of those around them visually inverts the traditional contrast between white and black individuals in early modern English portraiture. Kim F. Hall's examination of black subjects in Renaissance paintings reveals that they were often depicted as attendants, serving to emphasise the whiteness of English aristocrats, and also as 'meta-objects, symbols for the accumulation of profitable foreign goods during this era' (Hall 1995: 212). Rather than depict black subjects as luxury objects that reify whiteness and fuel the appetite for accumulation, the sketch represents Lashawnia and Martinsia as consumers, not commodities, in the early modern English market. They attend the theatre; they wear rich clothes; they purchase and eat the goods sold outside the playhouse.

Finally, the sketch uses references to expose early modern objects as units in man-made systems that transubstantiate black humans into objects.

Bennett describes objects as coming together in 'assemblages', which are 'ad hoc groupings of diverse elements, of vibrant materials of all sorts' (2010: 23). I read how the *Key & Peele* sketch reveals early modern objects – Shakespearean texts and adaptations, Renaissance paintings, other elements of culture – as units in what Alexander Weheliye terms a 'racializing assemblage', which 'construes race not as a biological or cultural classification but as a set of sociopolitical processes that discipline humanity into full humans, not-quite-humans, and nonhumans' (Weheliye 2014: 4).[5] Using Weheliye's configuration of the racialising assemblage becomes critical for understanding the references in the *Key & Peele* sketch as objects in racialising assemblages that objectify black individuals.

Furthermore, the term 'assemblage' in both Weheliye's and Bennett's concepts directs attention to the human hand that is doing the assembling. I am not suggesting that Shakespearean objects are always units in a racialising assemblage that excludes the black individual from the human community. Rather, I argue that they have been appropriated for that purpose. Reading the reference-objects in 'Othello Tis My Shite' as Shakespeare appropriations in racialising assemblages allows us to seize them from those very systems and craft new networks that assert black ontology as human. It is for this reason that I continue to use Bennett's 'assemblage' as a term to describe the shifting aggregations of objects in the sketch.[6] The term is also useful for its political implications – that is, 'assemblage' as the verbal cousin of the word 'assembly', the 'gathering of persons' (*OED*). Bennett uses 'assemblage' in order to distance object relations from human perception and instead imbue them with their own vital force as 'ad hoc groupings of diverse elements' (2010: 23). Yet even as she attempts to detach objects from the human perspective, the term 'assemblage' is, in fact, grounded in the human. Assemblages of human beings appropriate Shakespearean objects such as *Othello* and the broadside into a racialising assemblage that operates according to and upholds the white–black/human–non-human binary. In and of themselves, Shakespearean objects do not have their own vital force in denying black ontology; it is human beings who employ them to that end. Even as the sketch exposes how Shakespearean objects can be tools for negating black human ontology, it also demonstrates how they can be wrested from that function and reappropriated into new networks that assert black subjectivity.

As a material object referencing an artistic object that appears and then disappears from the screen, the broadside advertising the performance of Shakespeare's *Othello* at the beginning of the sketch provides an example of how a reference functions as an object. The sketch begins with a shot of a large sheet declaring 'ptic*Othello: A Tragedy in Five Acts*' pasted on a wooden board before panning out and away to Lashawnia and Martinsia (00:16–00:23). According to Bryant, objects need not be tangible in order to possess what he refers to as 'onticology': 'In addition to natural beings, onticology also counts technologies, symbolic entities, fictional entities, groups, nations, works of art, possible beings, artificial entities, and many other entities besides as belonging to the domain of real being' (Bryant 2011: 41). According to this rubric, Shakespeare's *Othello* – detached from any particular material form – is just as 'real' as the physical broadside announcing the play. And just because the broadside is visible in the sketch does not mean that it has a material form. After all, it is a digital image mediated through the screen rather than a physical object that the viewer can experience 'in real life'.[7] However, Christy Desmet argues that according to the principles of OOO, a digital object is just as 'real' as a physical one. Applying Bogost's theories to an interactive digital application of *Macbeth*, Desmet homes in on an image of Lady Macbeth's tub in the application as an example. 'A pixelated tub', she writes, 'exists on the same terms as the most of solid objects of film sets or immersive theatre experiences' (Desmet 2017: 16). According to Desmet's application of Bogost's theories, the broadside as it appears in the sketch, its reference to the Shakespeare text, the unseen performance of *Othello* that it advertises and the play itself (detached from performance and print) all exist just as much as the prop poster used in filming, an actual early modern broadside for *Othello* and any performance of the play.

It is helpful to think of the references in 'Othello Tis My Shite' as 'real' objects according to Bogost's and Desmet's phenomenologies because doing so rightfully accords them the force they have in material reality. It becomes necessary at this juncture to bring up a potential site of tension between OOO and critical race studies. Taken to extremes, many OOO theorists – including Bogost, Desmet and Bryant – suggest that the lived experience is no more 'real' than a fictional or imaginary one. If the pixels that make up a digital application exist equally with human bodies (which, according to OOO, are also objects), does that mean that a digital, fictional or imaginary world is just as real as the natural one? And does assigning equal regard across many realities diminish the lived experience? Such questions gain significant weight when considering a potential exchange between OOO and critical race studies. While some race theorists consider the possibility of non-material realities, many argue for the primacy of the lived experience of the natural body. Hortense Spillers spotlights the black body as the site where the American grammar of race brutally imprints its 'hieroglyphics of the flesh' (1987: 67). Race consciousness, then, requires recognition of the intangibilities that result in violence on the flesh. She writes, 'We might concede, at the very least, that sticks and bricks *might* break our bones, but words will most certainly *kill*' (Spillers 1987: 68). For Spillers, words are just as – more, even – material in effect as sticks and stones in doing violence against the black body. And if words are as real as sticks and stones, then so are references, playtexts, images and the infinite number of other objects, both material and intangible, that have been appropriated as tools for carving hieroglyphics into black flesh. Integrating Spillers's theories with Bogost's and Desmet's alien phenomenologies in my examination of the sketch's objects allows an avowal of the cultural force and potential violence that intangible 'words' can possess as units in a racialising assemblage. However, Spillers's observations also indicate that critical race studies cannot fully embrace OOO theories, for race-conscious thinking means acknowledging that retaining the relative value of the human body is imperative.

With this in view, the broadside's reference to – and announcement of – the performance of Shakespeare's *Othello* becomes a confrontation of the text as an object (or Spiller's 'words') used to deny the black subject's humanity through objectification. That objectification occurs through the translation of the black body into commodity. In the sketch the broadside appears as an advertisement for an object (the performance) among other merchandise; the camera zooms out and pans away from the board to reveal various fruits, vegetables and other consumables available for purchase outside the playhouse. Paying to watch *Othello*, the sketch implies, is akin to purchasing food; it is an act of participation in a consumptive economy that traffics in the binary that transmutes the black individual into an object. Chapman asserts that early modern dramas 'staged numerous unnamed, silent black characters that, although no longer devils, still presented blackness as the abject of humanity' (2017: 47). While Othello is neither unnamed nor silent (and indeed, Chapman goes on to argue that the play positions him as ontologically equal to Iago and the other Venetians),[8] the sketch suggests that the early modern performance of Shakespeare's text deals in blackness as the non-human. Othello may have a name, and he may speak, but in the early modern playhouse, Othello was a white man.[9] Black Othello is therefore an invisible, unnamed, silent, non-human character on the English stage. The image on the broadside brings to light the fact that black Othello does not exist in the early modern theatre. In fact, the image does not have anything to do with *Othello* at all, but is rather an altered image of a nineteenth-century print portraying the Holy Roman Emperor Henry IV's walk along the road to Canossa, with a black man's face superimposed on top.[10] The image reveals a gap where Othello should be – there is no brother among the firmaments for the early modern performance of Shakespeare's play but rather a black absence. The visual composition of the image also reveals the early modern *Othello* as reinforcing the exclusion of the Moor from the human community: the outline of a wall separates Henry IV/Othello from the other individuals in the image. The diagonal contour suggests that *Othello* reinforces the colour line, keeping a brother out of the firmaments, as illustrated by the small community of the subjects in the upper left-hand corner. The individual elements of the broadside – its function as an advertisement, its location in the market, the image and its own various details – relate to reveal a racialising assemblage that commercialises the exclusion of the black individual.

The superimposition of a black man's face over Henry IV's, however, also enacts in miniature the transposal of the broadside at the end of the sketch. Towards the end, the camera pans over another broadside – this time for *Shafte: A Play in Five Acts*, which Shakespeare writes after Lashawnia and Martinsia threaten him for killing Othello in the second half of the play (03:06–12). The sketch uses a single object – the broadside – to refer first to Shakespeare's *Othello* and then to the 1971 blaxploitation film *Shaft*, starring Richard Roundtree. The broadsides at the beginning and the end are nearly identical (both posters use the same image, only changing the man's face in the foreground) in a pattern that recurs throughout the sketch: the sketch uses a single object first to refer to an early modern (usually Shakespearean) object that contributes to a denial of black subjectivity. That object changes, however, in connection to the black human bodies in the sketch, which exposes the Shakespearean object as being used as a tool in an ontologically oppressive structure while simultaneously engendering resistance by having two black individuals reappropriate that object.

The broadside reveals the mechanism by which the other references function in the rest of the sketch. It not only suggests a juxtaposition between *Othello* and *Shaft* in relation to black ontology, but also reveals the broadside form as a unit in two competing systems. A single object acts as a reference for an infinite number of other objects, each of which is a unit in an infinite variety of systems. Here, a reference (the broadside as it appears in the sketch) alludes to one unit, which is either a Shakespearean text or adaptation, or another object from early modern culture – in this case, Shakespeare's *Othello* – as used in a racialising assemblage. However, the object refers to a second unit (here, the film *Shaft*) which is either an allusion to Shakespeare in a non-adaptive text or another object of popular culture, in a system that asserts black humanity. The reference-objects throughout 'Othello Tis My Shite' require double vision to see how each object participates in both systems. In so doing, the sketch reveals how Shakespearean objects have been used to objectify black individuals while also suggesting that those same objects can be read as resistant to this denial of black ontology.

Detaching objects from human use becomes particularly tricky when reading things such as clothing, which form a dialectical constitutive relationship with the human body. As Ann Rosalind Jones and Peter Stallybrass contend in their seminal work on costumes in the early modern playhouse, 'clothes have a life of their own; they both *are* material presences and they *absorb* other material and immaterial presences' (2000: 204). This mutually constitutive dynamic intensifies when there is a *black* body underneath the clothing; the fabric absorbs race, which attaches the *immaterial* cultural racialisations to the material of black skin. In 'Othello Tis My Shite', Lashawnia wears a red velvet doublet and pants, red tights, a ruff around his neck and a feathered beret. The ensemble evokes the 1579 portrait by an unknown artist of Sir Francis Drake, who stands erect, his right hand splayed over a globe on the table.[11] He, too, wears a red-breasted doublet and red pants, red tights, and a ruff on his neck, and he has a large beret in his hand. To read the objects (the doublet, the ruff, the beret) of Lashawnia's costume according to a conventional object studies reading – that is, without considering the body within – would be to assemble them into one network (within the sketch) that resembles another historical assemblage (within the painting). Yet accounting for the actor's black body shifts the relationship between these two assemblages – and here I use Bennett's term – for costumes make apparent the human labour that goes into bringing together the individual units into a larger object.

The 1579 painting of Drake becomes particularly evocative because of the explorer's associations with conquest and proto-colonialism; the luxuries he wears are inseparable from the globe that he claims with his right hand and the sword hanging at his side. Rich red fabric, lace and black velvet represent both the non-white bodies that will be enslaved to produce them as well as the imbalance of trade that led to English anxieties, which in turn produced the imperialism that would replace the limits of their own economy.[12] To transpose these objects of luxury on to Lashawnia's black body creates a intermedial, transhistorical *chiaroscuro* between dark and light bodies inhabiting similar clothing. On Drake, these luxuries promise the vast benefits of expanding England's borders by exploiting non-English bodies and commodifying them as objects to trade – both directly and indirectly – for other goods. On Lashawnia, these materials expose the painful history of that enterprise while offering a potential for resistance by imagining a world where a black body can participate in a market of objects as consumer and not commodity.

I am not suggesting that the human agents behind the sketch's costumes deliberately drew on this specific portrait of Drake for inspiration. Instead, the 1579 image presents objects that were and would continue to be recognisable as the fabricated elements of luxury in the early modern period. And the sight of those materials attached to Lashawnia's person exposes the dark underbelly of the market, which created the desire for such goods as well as the black body itself as a commodified object. In her study comparing the parallels between representations of apes and Africans in the early modern period, Kim F. Hall writes that 'both functioned as highly symbolic commodities in the early modern period. They became domesticated amusements, pets in wealthy households that emphasized the luxury and wealth of the owners. They are also increasingly juxtaposed in visual representation' (in Macdonald 1997: 125).[13] Portraits such as this one reinscribed the dependence of white luxury on objectifying the black body as both coveted commodity and exchangeable product.[14] To read only the objects that make up the costumes in the sketch and the painting would be to overlook the human labour that went into their production as well as both the colonialism and race-resistance of their human use. Together, these units of luxury – white lace, red silk, black velvet – assemble into a network that reconfigures depending on the body at its centre.

If the visual similarities between the sartorial assemblages affixed to the bodies of Sir Francis Drake in 1579 and Lashawnia in 2013 expose the Renaissance luxury market that commodified black bodies, Martinsia's costume reflects the inescapability of such hierarchies.[15] In stark contrast to his companion's bright red ensemble, Martinsia wears a black velvet doublet with gold accents and matching pants with yellow tights. These yellow stockings reference, of course, *Twelfth Night*'s Malvolio, who is punished for his class ambitions – that is, for his desire to become a consumer of the luxury objects procured through England's proto-imperial trading practices. Tricked into believing that his mistress loves him, Malvolio imagines himself living in the lap of luxury after their marriage: 'Calling my officers about me, in my branched velvet gown, having come from a daybed where I have left Olivia sleeping' (II.v.46–8). Pairing the yellow stockings with the velvet doublet and pants suggests that Martinsia is Malvolio, a servant who has succeeded in becoming the master, wearing a black velvet gown. Yet on Martinsia, the yellow tights draw attention to how, like Malvolio, black individuals have been punished for attempts at social advancement. Throughout Malvolio's narration of his daydreams, Fabian and Sir Toby interject with scoffing asides. 'Bolts and shackles', Sir Toby protests when Malvolio suggests that the two will become kinsmen (II.v.55). Indeed, bolts and shackles have precluded black individuals' participation in the luxury market as anything other than commodities.

While the combination of black and yellow references *Twelfth Night*, the black velvet doublet also evokes *Hamlet* and the ontological death of the black human. The visual reference to a long tradition of dressing the Danish prince in mourning alludes to a play that begins with grief over a loss. The sketch further reinforces its allusions to *Hamlet* later on, when Martinsia demands how the Bard could make the Moor 'shuffle off this mortal coil', citing a line from the play's familiar 'To be or not to be' soliloquy (02:20–22; *Hamlet* III.i.66). The quote homes in on *Hamlet* as a tragedy about mourning and death. This triangulation between costume, quotation and black body creates a network of referential objects that interrogates the ontology of black bodies – as well as the *Shakespearean* network's role in that process.

For the purposes of visual comparison, I have chosen to compare Martinsia's costume with Laurence Olivier's mourning ensemble as Hamlet in his 1948 film adaptation of the play. I have selected Olivier's film for its familiarity – J. Lawrence Guntner calls it 'probably the most influential Shakespeare film and Hamlet portrayal of the twentieth century' (in Jackson 2007: 121) – as well as its cultural capital. Kenneth S. Rothwell argues that the Shakespearean auteur 'at mid-century reclaimed the British role as guardian of its national poet' (2004: 47). The juxtaposition between Olivier's Hamlet and Peele's Martinsia again serves as a reminder that to detach the human body from its material objects in the context of race is to distort the scale down the ever-shifting network(s) of Shakespearean appropriations. The visible contrast between a white and a black body clothed in the dark objects of mourning visualises the enduring question of who gets to speak Shakespeare, and how. The similarity in costuming prompts a comparison between a white, classically trained actor speaking Shakespeare's lines in a 'faithful' film adaptation of a tragedy, and a black comedian parroting familiar passages for laughs in an irreverent, ephemeral sketch that throws Shakespearean references into a jumbled network with other artistic objects.[16] The sight of Martinsia in Hamlet's mourning costume draws on the familiar only to make it strange: it asks, can a black man wear, and be, Hamlet? The sketch challenges our assumptions of what the 'Shakespearean' looks like and sounds like, as well as our ideas of what constitutes the right environment for speaking Shakespeare. And in putting forth a black man who dresses and talks like Hamlet when speaking of the Moor, the sketch produces a photonegative challenge to Olivier in blackface in his own film adaptation of *Othello* (1965). If Olivier can be both Hamlet and Othello, the sketch argues, so can a black man.

In this case, the physical environment in which the human body and its prosthetic Shakespearean object appears matters as well. While both Olivier's film and the *Key & Peele* sketch produce a fictional 'dreamscape rather than a representation of a social reality anchored in a specific time and space' (Crowl 2014: 57), they differ in their vision for the setting of that fantasy. The Elsinore of Olivier's *Hamlet*, as Samuel Crowl observes, is 'empty: the film has no "extras" except for the audience of the play scene and the final duel and even then they are kept to a minimum' (2014: 58). By contrast, the fictional Elizabethan world in 'Othello Tis My Shite' is thickly peopled: a milieu of individuals in Elizabethan dress constantly bustle around Lashawnia and Martinsia, often carrying their own Shakespearean objects.[17] The juxtaposition between the unpopulated Elsinore of Olivier's film and the highly peopled fantasy London of the *Key & Peele* sketch points up two different perceptions of how to make Shakespeare. The narrow, deep focus on Hamlet's interior thoughts and his literal isolation in the film coincides with the image of Olivier as the auteur, which Harry Keyishian defines as the concept that 'identifies the individual vision of particularly strong directors as the most important element shaping their productions' (in Jackson 2007: 73). Olivier's *Hamlet* evinces a Romantic view of author and auteur: both Olivier and Shakespeare share a singularity of genius that manifests in the turnings of the mind. This paradigm lauds the very best exemplars of human exceptionalism, reinforcing a structure that elevates the white, male voice and vision of Shakespeare and his adaptors. The film's overall fidelity, moreover, upholds an ideal for Shakespearean appropriations as singularly committed to a single play, creating a hierarchy that positions Shakespeare's text above all else.

The two protagonists and the busy multitude in 'Othello Tis My Shite', however, challenge the Romantic author/auteur paradigm; here, speaking and making Shakespeare is collaborative. Diana E. Henderson argues that approaching Shakespeare and appropriations of his work collaboratively 'focuses attention on the connections among individuals, allowing artists credit and responsibility, but at the same time refusing to separate them from their social location and the work of others' (2006: 8). Unlike the absent population of Olivier's film – denuding it of explicitly political aspects – the *Key & Peele* sketch produces a social location even as it depicts a fictional version of early modern London.[18] Shakespeares, the sketch suggests, cannot be separated from their social dimensions; whenever 'Shakespeare' enters an environment, both Shakespearean object and that context exert pressure on each other. And this is a collaborative making in which the collective that makes the new Shakespeare might not look or sound anything like the 'original', and in fact could threaten the Shakespearean object's place at the top of the hierarchy.

The evocation of *Hamlet* in the sketch not only challenges a top-down structure in Shakespearean appropriation, however; it also incites interrogations of how the Shakespearean contributes to the death of black subjectivity. Martinsia's costume and his anger over the loss of Othello's 'mortal coil' evinces a sense of mourning for the Moor. As befitting the tragic form, both Hamlet and Othello die at the end of their respective plays, yet only one is mourned. Upon arriving to find Hamlet dead, Fortinbras orders his men to honour the Danish prince for his death: '[A]nd for his passage / The soldiers' music and the rite of war / Speak loudly for him' (V.ii.382–4). By contrast, *Othello* closes with an indictment of Iago; no soldier's music speaks loudly for the Moor, even though there is more evidence for his military success than there is for Hamlet's martial prowess. Instead, Othello himself reminds his companions, 'I have done the state some service, and they know't', and he pleads with them, 'Speak of me as I am' (V.ii.349, 352). A black death is not mourned, but expected. Chapman argues that the Elizabethan period saw the death of black ontology: 'Once the black body began to appear in society and on the stage, the connection between conceptual blackness and social death became grounded in the black body' (2017: 73). In ending with grief for one body and not the other, Shakespeare's texts contribute to this social death.

Furthermore, when mapped onto Martinsia's black body, this network of Shakespearean objects – costume, quotation, text, adaptation – suggests that mourning Hamlet comes at the cost of Othello. Anne Cheng argues that discourses of grief and melancholy rely on erasing the Other. She writes, 'By taking in the other-made-ghostly, the melancholic subject fortifies him- or herself and grows rich in impoverishment. The history of the ego is thus the history of its losses' (Cheng 2001: 8). In producing a black body dressed in Hamlet's mourning and quoting Hamlet's grieved lines while reacting to *Othello*, the sketch exposes a paradigm that mourns white death at the cost of black ontology, and then reappropriates white mourning for that very loss.[19] The sketch demonstrates not only how early modern luxury objects result in the commodification of the black body as a thing, but that such a process results in an unmourned loss that erases black ontology altogether. The sight of Martinsia dressed in the Danish prince's mourning answers *Hamlet*'s initial question of 'Who's there?' with the all-too-real spectre of the ungrieved Other erased in the production of the Shakespearean objects that uphold white mourning at the cost of black subjective death.

Besides the literal deaths of tragic form, the sketch indicts comedy, too, for its exclusion of the black subject from the human community. At the beginning of the sketch, Lashawnia and Martinsia celebrate that 'things are looking up for the people of the darker hue' by clasping hands and dancing as they sing, 'Hey, nonny, nonny' (01:12–15). The line recalls the penultimate scene of *As You Like It*. In that scene, Touchstone and Audrey look forward to their soon-to-be marriage and two pageboys offer a song of celebration:

And therefore take the present time,
With a hey, and a ho, and a hey-nonny-no,
For love is crownèd with the prime,
In springtime, the only pretty ring time,
When birds do sing, hey ding a ding, ding.
Sweet lovers love the spring. (V.iii.34–9)

Denying black subjects their human ontology entails the loss of the rituals that are a part of communal living – death and mourning is one of those rites; marriage and celebration is another. In the sketch Lashawnia and Martinsia enact a ritual that never appears in *Othello*: they celebrate his marriage to Desdemona. Iago degrades their union as mere sexual copulation between two animals: 'an old black ram / Is tupping your white ewe'; 'your daughter and the Moor are now making the beast with two backs' (I.i.90–1, 116–17). Iago dehumanises Othello by using an animal metaphor that reduces him to lascivious sexual functions; by extension, Desdemona, too, loses her humanity in joining herself to the Moor. And Brabantio mourns the marriage as a loss of his daughter: 'It is too true an evil. Gone she is' (I.i.162). By saying his daughter is 'gone', Brabantio implies that Othello's non-ontology is a black hole that swallows up Desdemona's human subjectivity through their association. According to the Venetians, the marriage between Othello and Desdemona is not to be celebrated, but grieved as a loss, for his black inhumanity subsumes her white ontology.

As Lashawnia and Martinsia dance while singing a song that celebrates love in another play, then, they introduce a contrast between a comedy that extols heterosexual white-on-white love and a tragedy that mourns an interracial heterosexual union. Just as the ungrieved loss of Othello bolsters the mourning of Hamlet, the sketch suggests that reviling interracial love reinforces the celebration of *white* love and its contribution to racial blood purity.[20] The dance mounts a resistance to the fears of miscegenation engendered by the social death of the black subject: Desdemona and Othello's marriage, it argues, deserves just as much celebration as white '[s]weet lovers [who] love the spring' (*As You Like It* V.iv.39). Their union is not a loss of human ontology, but proof of their existence as social subjects; Lashawnia and Martinsia's coordinated, culturally circumscribed movements challenge the uncontrollable, bestial thrusts in Iago's animalistic metaphors. The 'Hey nonny nonny' dance imparts a legitimate social life – and, therefore, human ontology – to Desdemona and Othello's union by celebrating it like any other marriage.

By depicting two black men celebrating an interracial marriage by appropriating white rituals, the sketch also uses those same means to assert humanity through black homosocial activity. Hartman writes that for black slaves in America, resistance to dehumanisation was 'waged in everyday practices . . . in which the assertion of needs, desires, and counterclaims could be collectively aired, thereby granting property a social life and an arena or shared identification with other slaves' (1997: 69). The shared dance and song grants Lashawnia and Martinsia a social life and insists on their humanity, reappropriating the Elizabethan world that erases their ontology into an arena for shared identification.

The dance also reclaims space for black human subjects in the Elizabethan world by evoking *Key & Peele* itself as it references the song from *As You Like It*. The sketch borrows its format from the show's popular 'valets' sketches, which depict two black men excitedly discussing some cultural object or icon while humorously getting some details wrong, exaggerating their reactions and physical movements to absurd proportions. The sketch visually reinforces its connection to the 'valets' sketches with Lashawnia's red velvet doublet, as the valets usually wear red velvet waistcoats. By referencing the valets, the sketch casts Lashawnia and Martinsia not just as two black men, but as *many* black men made visible at all layers of early modern England's social fabric. They are wealthy black men publicly participating in the luxury market, but they are also the black men of the lower classes gathering in the playhouses and the streets: the pages, the servants, the valets – personal attendants to gentlemen (*OED*). By drawing together the valets sketches and *As You Like It*, 'Othello Tis My Shite' offers up the possibility that the two pages *could* have been two black men celebrating in the streets like the two valets, in some other early modern England that did not deny black subjects their humanity. And the relationships between Shakespeare's text, the valets sketches, and Lashawnia and Martinsia's dance visually reminds us that there *were* black people in Renaissance England. The sketch's 'Hey nonny nonny' dance imagines an alternative existence for Elizabethan black lives, one that celebrates human community rather than reiterating a record that 'consisted of the terrible things said about them or done to them' (Hartman 2008: 13). Just as black slaves in America waged resistance through everyday practices, the sketch suggests that black Elizabethan subjects also danced, celebrated and reappropriated white communal rituals in defiance of a legal discourse that denied them complete ontology.

'Hey, nonny, nonny' further uncovers the tension between negation and resistance by referencing yet another artistic object: Langston Hughes's poem 'Shakespeare in Harlem' also appropriates the song from *As You Like It*. The poem and its accompanying image links the absent presence of the black subject to Shakespeare:

> Hey ninny neigh!
> And a hey nonny noe!
> Where, oh, where
> Did my sweet mama go?
>
> Hey ninny neigh
> With a tra-la-la-la!
> They say your sweet mama
> Went home to her ma. (Hughes 1942: 111)

The first stanza evokes the pages' song and its celebration of romantic union, only to reappropriate them to speak of a romantic separation – there are no sweet lovers in the springtime, but rather a 'sweet mama' whose whereabouts are unknown. The celebration of presence becomes a lament for an absence; Hughes's poem creates an assonance between 'noe', 'oh' and 'go', translating the amorous 'ohs' in the pages' song into expressions of woe. As with the Hamlet costume, the poem evokes an air of mourning for a missing black subject – in this case, the 'sweet mama'. The first stanza also introduces a question at its close, contrasting with the steady declaratives of the *As You Like It* song and its own bold exclamations in the first two lines. The 'Where, oh where / Did my sweet mama go?' separates the 'lover and his lass' that appears in the first line of the pages' song (*As You Like It* V.iii.16). The following stanza proposes an answer to where the speaker's 'sweet mama' has gone, but it frames it with the tenuous 'they say', making her whereabouts uncertain. Hughes's poem transforms the certainties of the pages' song into the black subject's slippage between absence-presence.

Yet even as it points up the uncertainty of black ontological existence, the assemblage of the sketch, the pages' song and Hughes's poem offers up the possibility of resisting the negation of black subjectivity. The image accompanying the poem depicts a Harlem community in white lines set against a black background, inverting the traditional pattern of black lines on white paper. The photonegative drawing challenges racial discourses that assume 'that blackness is an aberration and whiteness the original' (Hall 1995: 13). The image suggests the converse; its juxtaposition with the poem – black lettering on white paper – challenges the assumption that Shakespeare is the original and Hughes is the derivative. 'Othello Tis My Shite' enacts a similar resistance as Lashawnia and Martinsia speak Shakespearean lines 'before' they appear in print under his authorship. The sketch imagines that black subjects could have been the origin for early modern fashions, for poetic phrases such as 'this mortal coil', or for popular songs such as 'hey nonny nonny'. In so doing it posits black subjects as makers of artistic objects in direct opposition to negations of black ontology. And by drawing on artistic objects across time, culture and media, 'Othello Tis My Shite' reveals the flexibility of racial discourse to deny black subjectivity across such bounds and then offers other objects to challenge that denial.

I entitled this chapter 'Intermission!' not only because the break between the first and second halves of the play serves as the setting for 'Othello Tis My Shite', but also because intermissions are the space for a different kind of assemblage. Returning to Bennett's description of the assemblage brings to the surface their potential: 'Assemblages are not governed by any central head . . . Each member and proto-member of the assemblage has a certain vital force, but there is also an effectivity proper to the grouping as such: an agency of the assemblage' (2010: 24). Though she writes about the groupings of objects, Bennett's words take on another valence in the context of the intermissions during performances, which prompt *human* assemblages. Audience members gather in 'ad hoc groupings of diverse elements' to discuss, to celebrate, to reproach, bringing new objects of the performance into view (Bennett 2010: 23). 'Othello Tis My Shite' reminds us of the power in the human assemblage that comes into being during the many intermissions in this ongoing performance of race studies in Shakespeare.

After their revels and laments, Lashawnia and Martinsia track down and take hold of the Bard, forcing him to write another play, *Shafte*, one that truly sets a brother among the firmaments. In so doing, they catalyse the creation of a new world similar to the one Ta-Nehisi Coates imagines in a letter to his son about police brutality against black bodies: 'Somewhere out there beyond the firmament, past the asteroid belt, there were other worlds where children did not regularly fear for their bodies' (2015: 20). Lashawnia and Martinsia make black life visible and viable at all levels of early modern English society and celebrate their existence. They literally appropriate Shakespeare and then set him to the task of creating an object that resists the reduction of black individuals to objects.

This act of seizure is what the sketch does with its references writ large: 'Othello Tis My Shite' takes hold of the Shakespearean objects that have been appropriated into racialising assemblages and then reappropriates them to assert black human subjectivity. As Peter Erickson writes, 'Allusions are transformative' (2007: 8). The sketch illustrates how audience members, viewers, readers, makers and scholars of Shakespeare can and do change his objects as they gather during intermission. Alexa Huang and Elizabeth Rivlin write that when it comes to Shakespeare, 'Not only those who act but those who watch and hear are charged with ethical responsibilities; it is the audience who, upon exiting the theater and its presentation of make-believe action, must use their interpretive experience to make choices in the world' (2014: 7). The intermission is the space where that interpretation becomes ethical appropriation. Reading Shakespearean objects race-consciously means not only revealing the racialising assembling lurking behind each thing, but also appropriating – as in, 'assign[ing] to a special purpose or use' (*OED*) – them into new networks that diversify our understanding of the human. And as Lashawnia and Martinsia demonstrate, that endeavour must be a collaborative effort.

Notes

1. Further reinforcing its ties to *Hamlet* is Martinsia's all-black ensemble, which looks very similar to Hamlet's mourning costume in Laurence Olivier's 1948 film adaptation of the play (an association I explore later on in this chapter).
2. Sujit Sivasundaram writes that the Great Chain of Being was 'inherently contradictory in positing relations between man and the rest of creation, while at the same time placing man in a superior category close to the deity' (2015: 159). He emphasises how the concept served to perpetuate a divide between races, which is analogous to the distinction between human and

animal. Sivasundaram examines this connection in order to argue for interdisciplinary scholarship drawing from the sciences, animal studies and postcolonial studies. The relationship between the latter two fields is especially fraught, for reasons similar to the difficulty of interfacing critical race studies and object-oriented ontology, which I describe later in this chapter.

3. Posthumanism more broadly has often proved a helpful lens for critical race theorists to consider the decentralisation of the white humanist subject. Critical race posthumanist Sylvia Wynter seeks to extend subjectivity beyond the arbitrary human boundaries of race and gender. However, as Anthony Bogues writes, Wynter still considers diversifying 'human' to be of the utmost importance; he argues that she sees a 'hidden human that needs to be brought to the fore out of bondage' (2006: 325). Jason Hill similarly champions posthumanism as a mode for combating racialisation, which he links to blood: 'glorification of blood identity is strongly problematic because it shuts people outside the domain of the ethical, and, a fortiori, the human community' (2009: 3). Zakiyyah Iman Jackson summarises the perspective of critical race posthumanists such as Wynter and Hill: 'The hope was not that black people would gain admittance into the fraternity of Man – the aim was to displace the order of Man altogether. Thus, what they aspired to achieve was not the extension of *liberal* humanism to those enslaved and colonized, but rather a transformation within humanism' (2013: 672). Jackson's words indicate the powerful potential of posthumanism for critical race studies; yet certain forms of the posthuman are more compatible with critical race theory than others. Perhaps one reason for this is that race-conscious posthumanists consider the human to be paramount; as Alexander Weheliye writes, 'we might do well to conceive humanity as a relational ontological totality, however fractured this totality might be. Not doing so will extend the conflation of one genre of the human: western Man with a real object (extrahumanly instituted and based completely in physiology)' (2014: 32).

4. Louis Chude-Sokei examines the role of technological advancement in the objectification of the black subject, noting in particular the discourses that compared black people to machines while also using those developments as 'objective proof of cultural superiority' (2016: 82). His analysis reveals not only the transmutation of the black subject into the thing but also how the black body becomes an object appropriated as a tool to aid this process.

5. Weheliye argues that 'race becomes pinioned to human physiology, exposing how the politicization of the biological always already represents a racializing assemblage' (2014: 12). Barbara Hodgdon notes that performance of Shakespeare brings this process to light: 'Layered onto the body, "blackness" . . . may be constructed – and viewed – as a performance' (1998: 44). Both Weheliye's and Hodgdon's assertions reveal the urgency of separating bodies from objects in view of racialising processes.

6. I use 'assemblage' as opposed to 'networks', or Christy Desmet's and Ian Bogost's favoured term 'systems', because it upholds the sense of human gathering, though I find Bogost's 'unit' to be helpful in considering how the object relates to other objects in the same group (Desmet 2017: 1). Desmet uses Bogost's units and systems because she is working with digital objects; however, I am focusing on Lashawnia and Martinsia as two black people. Networks, units and systems, however, might be useful terms for considering how objects might relate in configurations that resist Stuart Hall's 'rigid binary coding' in its technological connotations (Hall 1998: 290).
7. Lisa Nakamura argues that a Shakespearean object in an Internet video makes it as alien as everything else that appears on the web; *Othello* and 'Othello Tis My Shite' are on the same pixelated plane. At least in theory, the Internet flattens objects into networks without a hierarchical topography by rendering everything into copy; she writes, 'in a virtual environment like the Internet where *everything* is a copy, so to speak, and nothing has an aura since all cyberimages exist as pure pixelated information, the desire to search for an original is thwarted from the very beginning' (Nakamura 2002: 6). Her description of the Internet as a space that collapses chronological order – which in turn upholds a hierarchy – underscores why, in theory, appropriating Shakespeare on the Web might evacuate his texts of power as originals by rendering them into copies of objects. However, Nakamura also warns against idealising the Internet as a utopia for dismantling the hierarchies of the material world: 'Women and people of color are both subjects and objects of interactivity; they participate in digital racial formation via acts of technological appropriation, yet are subjected to it as well' (2008: 16). The Internet allows users the potential to reshape racial formations, but it can also grant them the power to reinforce racialising assemblages.
8. Chapman argues that *Othello* 'reveals the anxiety over the Moor's status as ontologically equal to the English' (2017: 123). This anxiety fuels the attempt to deny that ontological status in early modern English drama.
9. Dympna Callaghan's examination of the early modern staging of *Othello* reveals how stage properties are also objects employed 'to *produce* racial difference *and to control it nevertheless*' (2000: 92).
10. After a disagreement with the emperor over lay investiture, Pope Gregory VII excommunicated Henry IV, who made the journey to Canossa where the pope was staying in order to do penance and beg absolution (Blumenthal 1988: 125).
11. *Sir Francis Drake*, c. 1581, oil on panel, 1813 mm x 1130 mm, National Portrait Gallery, London, available at <https://npg.org.uk/collections/search/portrait/mw01932/Sir-Francis-Drake> [accessed 1 September 2019].
12. Jonathan Gil Harris writes that early modern England understood its dependence on foreign trade for economic health, while at the same time 'England assumed its national identity in relation both to readily demonizable "forraine"

bodies (other nations, their citizens, their goods), which potentially damaged its economic health, and to universal "rules" of transnational commerce, which sustained it' (2004: 8). Anxieties about the English economy's relation to markets arose when it came to the cloth industry; Roze Hentschell writes, 'As foreign fabrics are imported into England and worn on the English body, they are perceived of as disrupting the domestic wool cloth industry. This calls into question the cultural capital of English cloth, thereby creating a crisis of national identity' (2008: 103).

13. Scholars have examined the theoretical frictions between the fields of animal and race studies, especially in light of studies such as Hall's, which reveal the dehumanisation of black subjects through bestialising language. Jinthana Haritaworn writes, 'To quote an anonymous grad student, the turn to animal studies at times reflects a desire for an "Other that doesn't talk back"' (2015: 212). For arguments in favour of imbricating postcolonial and animal studies, see Sujit Sivasundaram.

14. Simon Gikandi argues that the aesthetic of modernity – part of which is the luxury market – was built on slavery: 'Slaves occupy an important part in the explanatory structures of modernity from natural history to the aesthetic. But they exist in this framework as proof of their incapacity for modern identity. They are, in effect, constituted as unmodern subjects or simply objects of modern trade' (2011: 36). While Gikandi examines the eighteenth century onwards, his description applies to early modern commodification of the black body as well.

15. Martinsia's black clothing also serves as a visual reminder that black cloth was often used to represent black bodies on the medieval and early modern stage. Ian Smith's seminal scholarship on this tradition in relation to the handkerchief in Othello demonstrates that such textiles 'conveyed a body less subtle from the point of view of verisimilitude, but more ideologically expressive in the representation of the black body in its stark materiality and tangible objecthood' (Smith 2013: 10). Black fabric and other stage technologies for representing black bodies objectified blackness in the early modern period. The image of Jordan Peele, a black man dressed in black textiles that evoke this tradition, resists that very objectification.

16. As I note later on, Key's and Peele's body movements and the humour in this sketch reference the popular 'valets' sketches on their show, but the hyperbolic movements and exaggerated speech patterns played for comic effect might also suggest blackface minstrelsy traditions. Robert Hornback's work on blackface traces a longer and broader history of the tradition reaching back to the medieval period and extending across the Atlantic. As 'Othello Tis My Shite' is set in early modern England and the other 'valets' sketches are presumably set in the United States, reading them as a reappropriation of comic blackface would be fruitful for considering the transnational and transhistorical reiterations of racist blackface.

17. These include mugs, pamphlets, pipes and shopping carts full of produce, all of which contribute to creating a vision of an active market economy in the sketch.
18. Crowl suggests that the film's focus on the internal in fact makes it politically contingent, citing Anthony Dawon's scholarship contextualising the film within post-Second World War anxieties in both Britain and America (Crowl 2014: 61).
19. In his analysis of the play, Jacques Lacan writes, 'The work of mourning is first of all performed to satisfy the disorder that is produced by the inadequacy of signifying elements to cope with the hole that has been created in existence, for it is the system of signifiers in their totality which is impeached by the least instance of mourning' (1977: 38). The sketch suggests that that hole in existence is blackness, which is to be mourned.
20. Jean E. Feerick writes that in the early modern period, race was 'a way of "speaking the body" quite distinct from modern paradigms first and foremost because it defined the body primarily through the qualities of its *blood*' (2010: 9).

Bibliography

Bennett, J. (2010), *Vibrant Matter: A Political Ecology of Things*, Durham, NC: Duke University Press.

Blumenthal, U. (1988), *The Investiture Controversy: Church and Monarchy from the Ninth to the Twelfth Century*, Philadelphia: University of Pennsylvania Press.

Bogost, I. (2012), *Alien Phenomenology, or What It's Like to Be a Thing*, Minneapolis: University of Minnesota Press.

Bogues, A. (2006), 'The Human, Knowledge and the Word: Reflecting on Sylvia Wynter', in A. Bogues (ed.), *After Man, Towards the Human: Critical Essays on Sylvia Wynter*, Kingston, Jamaica: Ian Randle, pp. 315–38.

Bryant, L. (2011), *The Democracy of Objects*, Ann Arbor: Open Humanities Press.

Callaghan, D. (2000), *Shakespeare Without Women: Representing Gender and Race on the Renaissance Stage* New York: Routledge.

Chapman, M. (2017), *Anti-Black Racism in Early Modern English Drama: The Other 'Other'*, New York: Routledge.

Cheng, A. A. (2001), *The Melancholy of Race: Psychoanalysis, Assimilation, and Hidden Grief*, Oxford: Oxford University Press.

Chude-Sokei, L. (2016), *The Sound of Culture: Diaspora and Black Technopoetics*, Middletown, CT: Wesleyan University Press.

Coates, T.-N. (2015), *Between the World and Me*, New York: Penguin Random House.

Crowl, S. (2014), *Screen Adaptations: Shakespeare's Hamlet: The Relationship between Text and Film*, New York: Bloomsbury.

Desmet, C. (2017), 'Alien Shakespeares 2.0', *Actes des congrès de la Société française Shakespeare*, 35, https://doi.org/10.4000/shakespeare.3877 [accessed 11 September 2020].

Du Bois, W. E. B (1995), *W. E. B. Du Bois: A Reader*, ed. David Levering Lewis, New York: Henry Holt.

Erickson, P. (2007), *Citing Shakespeare: The Reinterpretation of Race in Contemporary Literature and Art*, New York: Palgrave Macmillan.

Fanon, F. (2008 [1952]), *Black Skin, White Masks*, trans. Richard Philcox, New York: Grove Press.

Feerick, J. E. (2010), *Strangers in Blood: Relocating Race in the Renaissance*, Toronto: University of Toronto Press.

Gikandi, S. (2011), *Slavery and the Culture of Taste*, Princeton: Princeton University Press.

Habib, I. (2008), *Black Lives in the English Archives, 1500–1677: Imprints of the Invisible*, Burlington, VT: Ashgate.

Hall, K. F. (1995), *Things of Darkness: Economies of Race and Gender in Early Modern England*, Ithaca: Cornell University Press.

Hall, S. (1998), 'Subjects in History: Making Diasporic Identities', in W. Lubiano (ed.), *The House That Race Built, Original Essays by Toni Morrison, Angela Y. Davis, Cornel West, and Others on Black Americans and Politics in America Today*, New York: Vintage, pp. 289–99.

Haritaworn, J. (2015), 'Decolonizing the Non/Human', *GLQ: A Journal of Lesbian and Gay Studies*, 21:2, 210–13.

Harris, J. G. (2004), *Sick Economies: Drama, Mercantilism, and Disease in Shakespeare's England*, Philadelphia: University of Pennsylvania Press.

Hartman, S. (1997), *Scenes of Subjection: Terror, Slavery, and Self-Making in Nineteenth-Century America*, Oxford: Oxford University Press.

Hartman, S. (2007), *Lose Your Mother: A Journey Along the Atlantic Slave Route*, New York: Farrar, Straus and Giroux.

Henderson, D. (2006), *Collaborations with the Past: Reshaping Shakespeare Across Time and Media*, Ithaca: Cornell University Press.

Hentschell, R. (2008), *The Culture of Cloth in Early Modern England: Textual Constructions of a National Identity*, New York: Routledge.

Hill, J. (2009), *Beyond Blood Identities: Posthumanity in the Twenty-First Century*, Lanham, MD: Lexington Books.

Hodgdon, B. (1998), *The Shakespeare Trade: Performances and Appropriations*, Philadelphia: University of Pennsylvania Press.

Hornback, R. (2018), *Racism and Early Blackface Comic Traditions: From the Old World to the New*, New York: Palgrave Macmillan.

Huang, A., and E. Rivlin (eds) (2014), *Shakespeare and the Ethics of Appropriation*, New York: Palgrave Macmillan.

Hughes, L. (1942), *Shakespeare in Harlem*, New York: A.A. Knopf.

Jackson, R. (ed.) (2007), *The Cambridge Companion to Shakespeare on Film*, Cambridge: Cambridge University Press.

Jackson, Z. I. (2013), 'Animal: New Directions in the Theorization of Race and Posthumanism', *Feminist Studies*, 39:3, 669–85.

Jones, A. R., and P. Stallybrass (2000), *Renaissance Clothing and the Materials of Memory*, Cambridge: Cambridge University Press.

Lacan, J. (1977), 'Desire and the Interpretation of Desire in *Hamlet*', *Yale French Studies*, 55/56, 11–52.

Loomba, A., and J. Burton (eds) (2007), *Race in Early Modern England: A Documentary Companion*, New York: Palgrave Macmillan.

Macdonald, J. (ed.) (1997), *Race, Ethnicity, and Power in the Renaissance*, Teaneck, NJ: Fairleigh Dickinson University Press.

Nakamura, L. (2002), *Cybertypes: Race, Ethnicity, and Identity on the Internet*, New York: Routledge.

Nakamura, L. (2008), *Digitizing Race: Visual Cultures of the Internet*, Minneapolis: University of Minnesota Press.

Rothwell, K. (2004), *A History of Shakespeare on Screen: A Century of Film and Television*, Cambridge: Cambridge University Press.

Shakespeare, W. (2007), *Othello: Texts and Contexts*, ed. Kim F. Hall, New York: Bedford/St. Martin's.

Shakespeare, W. (2015), *As You Like It*, ed. B. Mowat, P. Werstine, Folger Shakespeare Library, <https://folgerdigitaltexts.org/html/AYL.html> [accessed 17 July 2020].

Shakespeare, W. (2016), *Hamlet: Revised Edition*, ed. A. Thompson and N. Taylor, New York: Bloomsbury.

Shakespeare, W. (2015), *Twelfth Night*, ed. B. Mowat, Folger Shakespeare Library, <https://folgerdigitaltexts.org/html/TN.html> [accessed 17 July 2020].

Sivasundaram, S. (2015), 'Imperial Transgressions: The Animal and Human in the Idea of Race', *Comparative Studies of South Asia, Africa, and the Middle East*, 35:1, 156–72.

Smith, I. (2013), 'Othello's Black Handkerchief', *Shakespeare Quarterly*, 64:1, 1–25.

Spillers, H. J. (1987), 'Mama's Baby, Papa's Maybe: An American Grammar Book', *Diacritics*, 17:2, 65–81.

Weheliye, A. G. (2014), *Habeas Viscus: Racializing Assemblages, Biopolitics, and Black Feminist Theories of the Human*, Durham, NC: Duke University Press.

Wilderson, F. B. (2010), *Red, White, & Black: Cinema and the Structure of U. S. Antagonisms*, Durham, NC: Duke University Press.

9

Sight Unseen: Visualising Variability through Ontological Representations in *Macbeth*

Valerie Clayman Pye and Cara Gargano

All hail, Macbeth, hail to thee

(*Macbeth* I.iii.48)

The proclamation is heard in our mind's eye, in our audience's ear; it is seen – on the page, perhaps, or embodied on stage. What is *Macbeth*? Is it the network of words on the page, the bound material we reach for in an effort to produce the object? Is it the thing we see performed? Is it an encapsulation of over four hundred years of established associations of what *Macbeth* could (or should) be? Is it an amalgamation of all of these things, or none of them; something yet to be discovered? While performance studies asks us to consider each performance as its own discrete entity in time and space, we suggest that our understanding is enriched by seeing these discrete performances as part of a quantum temporal/spatial network that underpins the play. In this chapter, we propose that *Macbeth* functions as a hyperobject, 'massively distributed in time and space relative to humans' that simultaneously '[occupies] a high-dimensional phase space that results in their being invisible to humans for stretches of time' (Morton 2013: 1). The hyperobject that we know as *Macbeth*, therefore, contains all permutations of playscript and performance across both time and space.

Timothy Morton notes the relationship between object-oriented ontology and quantum phenomena: 'OOO is deeply congruent with the most profound, accurate, and testable theory of physical reality available'. Morton states, 'Actually it would be better to say it the other way around: quantum theory works because it's object-oriented' (2013: 41). Like hyperobjects, quantum phenomena are 'irreducibly undecidable, both wave-like and particle-like' (Morton 2011: 180). Morton also notes that 'quantum theory is performative' (2011: 181); performance folds, compresses or elongates time. When we perform or witness performance, we become part of the play's quantum potential, a contributor to its endless capacity for meaning. This means that a hyperobject's potentiality, when put into a performance matrix, allows us to engage in a dense, four-century old, global, transmedial network. *Macbeth*, as a network, is its own tiny ontology, in Ian Bogost's sense, rejecting a separation between real and fictional and allowing both to exist simultaneously. Moreover, because this potentiality is absorbed into the whole object, on stage we are able to recognise the power of what remains invisible at a particular moment in the network. In performance, *Macbeth* is therefore defined by the paradox of accommodating both present/absent object identification and assemblages that are simultaneously random and patterned. *Macbeth*'s networks exist in a state where they are both seen and unseen. While we can argue that, to a certain extent, all of Shakespeare's plays can be defined by similar networks of absent/present assemblages, we focus on *Macbeth* because of the specific relationship and friction between what is visible and invisible both onstage and in the world of the fiction.

As a playscript, *Macbeth* is present, fixed on the page, a representation of the absent performance. As a performance *Macbeth* is present on stage in real time, although its text, its author and previous performances hover over it as present but unseen ghosts. Each of these forms of presence relies on a spectrum of absence that exists within each respective network. Quantum potential can only be understood in an alternative (multiple) dimensional time/space where several possibilities exist simultaneously. The interplay between the playscript and performance modalities creates a tension of variability between what is, what is not, and what could be: a tension that negotiates an incalculable number of possible manifestations, both materially and immaterially. Furthermore, while the text is a fixed pattern on the page, each individual performance is its own tiny ontology, organised through a rehearsal process that draws order from *Macbeth*'s quantum potential and is then subject to the variability of the rehearsal process and subsequent variabilities of its changing audiences. In this way, each individual production, made up of individual performances, also functions as its own tiny ontology, as a network that is also absorbed into *Macbeth*'s overall quantum potential. We use tiny ontology in Ian Bogost's sense, not as 'small' but as 'a dense mass of everything', which is both visible and invisible yet still present (Bogost 2012: 21–2). This 'dense mass' is the network of potentiality that characterises the hyperobject *Macbeth*;

a hyperobject whose potential is only realised when the performance (an intricate pattern of codified behaviours), the text (a pattern of semiotic meaning) and time (in both the actual and the theatrical sense) interact. When we experience performance, as artists or audience, we participate in a selected visualisation of particular patterns, patterns that are part of a larger whole object, which lurks just out of sight.

As Timothy Morton explains, 'quantum theory views phenomena as quanta, as discrete "units"' (2011: 179). Both plays and performances are made up of their own phenomenological units. 'The disaggregation of a Shakespearean text into "units" – semantic segments, words, lines or even morphemes – is the condition of existence for digital texts' writes Christy Desmet (2017: 5). Drawing from Bogost's theory of Alien Shakespeare, Desmet teases out the ways Bogost is inspired by Bruno Latour's actor-network theory, which identifies that a network is peopled by 'actants' both human and non-human. Bogost identifies how individual 'units' both exist independently and also relate to each other (Bogost 2012: 3). In performance, *Macbeth* also depends on actor-network theory; it is also animated by human and non-human 'actants'. As a result, the play *Macbeth* lives in a state of quantum potential, whereby it – as a hyperobject – is made temporarily whole by the elements of the dense mass that each performance network organises and makes visible. Even as a given production of *Macbeth* manifests its own tiny ontology, that tiny ontology can only exist as part of a larger whole because 'Shakespeare' is also *its* own complex network, made up of a number of interrelated components (as is, arguably, a production by a theatre company). Simply stated, *Macbeth*'s quantum potential (the possibility of multiple results) collapses into a single manifestation when it is observed and, for a moment, a particular network is made visible: this is what we call the theatrical experience. Each observation of this manifestation formulates its own particular tiny ontology, one that navigates its way through a particular trajectory of time and space. In this way, *Macbeth* exists on a spectrum of possible manifestations, each one with its own distinct tiny ontology, one that is made visible during a given performance of the play. As a variable object, the choices that are established within the rehearsal studio help to consolidate what is made visible to the audience, but as the reading of *Macbeth* demonstrates later, what is selected to remain invisible still threatens to emerge, as the audience's gaze and experience cannot be fully controlled.

Time also functions as an object on stage, and understanding its place in the larger performance network enables us to draw connections between performances. In our daily, non-theatrical lives, we assume an arrow of time, where there is an obvious, one-way directionality creating a cause/ effect continuum. Theatrical time more closely resembles Ilya Prigogine's theory of dissipative structures, more commonly known as chaos or complexity theory, where the arrow of time does not apply and there may be no privileged present based on a completed past and an open future. Moreover, at the end of *Order Out of Chaos*, Prigogine writes that 'time is a construction and therefore carries an ethical responsibility' (1984: 312). In performance, time is bent and appropriated in ways that enable actors and audience – much like a time machine – to transport and manipulate alternate, parallel universes. In the theatre, audiences and performers alike straddle the liminal space between present and absent time(s) to encompass 'this wide and universal theatre' (*As You Like It* II.vii.137). As time is manipulated, it creates temporal and actual fluctuations that act as a mechanism for pattern randomness. As time itself becomes its own ontology as part of the larger hyperobject of *Macbeth*, those temporally situated present/absent objects, such as Macbeth's dagger, become protagonists in their own right. This transformation suggests a fold in time/space that doubles back on itself, creating a portal between past, present and future.

As an object, the construct of fictional time is complicated by the performance ontology's capacity to distort how an audience reads time; time in a performance network creates a prismatic effect that commingles actual and fictional time. In this way time may function as the ultimate hyperobject in performance as it both collapses and expands the spectator experience. Spectators are witness to the actual 'two hours traffic of our stage' (*Romeo and Juliet* Prologue 12), as well as the virtual manipulation of time inherent in any theatrical endeavour. Audience members are put into the network that facilitates their connection with the Elizabethan stage, regardless of whether the production is one that engages with 'original practices' or not. In a sense, every performance can be considered an object that conflates time. It is a virtual reality 'headset' or rather 'mindset' that an audience 'dons' when entering the play space and where chronological time is suspended in favour of a compressed, imagined time. Thus, a live performance is a sort of 'fleshy' virtual reality, where past, present and future are collapsed into an hour, as we jump 'o'er times, / Turning th'accomplishments of many years / Into an hour-glass' (*Henry V* Prologue 29–31).

This notion of a 'fleshy' virtual reality points to a distinction between digital and live performance: 'the striking difference between researchers who work with flesh and those who work with computers is how nuanced the sense of the body's complexity is for those who are directly engaged with it' (Hayles 1999: 244). During performance, virtual and actual might be said to merge, as the actor's actual body both disappears and becomes the virtual absent/embodied body of the character, programmed by the code of the rehearsal process. Put simply, performance makes anything possible. In *How We Became Posthuman*, N. Katherine Hayles refers to the body as a 'congealed metaphor, a physical structure whose constraints and possibilities have been formed by an evolutionary history that intelligent machines do not share' and one that is that is 'resonant with cultural meanings' (1999: 284). During the rehearsal period, that evolutionary process is coupled with the material and virtual experience of the actors, including their relationship with the objects they encounter, in both their material and metaphoric existence, and this process is manifest when staging the play. The rehearsal room is a virtual/real space in which performance potential is explored, and although decisions about what will be presented onstage are codified, discarded potentialities remain present. These discarded potentialities and codified choices are further complicated by the insertions of each new audience, which infect/affect the performance network.

Theatrical time facilitates stage objects as variable objects with the potential both to manifest with multiple meanings and to function as theatrical protagonists. Andrew Sofer frames this virtual and material distinction in terms of stage objects to explain the unique duality of absence/presence onstage. Sofer points to the 'peculiarly theatrical phenomenon' of the 'power of stage objects to take on a life of their own in performance' (2003: 2). When we read a text, he suggests, we tend to neglect the material presence of an object, while on stage objects become both active and actant. In *Macbeth*, such objects are particularly slippery, oscillating between levels of presence and absence, materiality and virtuality. Unlike in the text, in the embodied world of the performance, subject and object become equal on stage because they both occupy material and virtual space, as they are both absent/present (their presence evoked by others) and present/absent (as Banquo's ghost is seen by Macbeth and the audience but not by the other characters on stage). When things assume affective agency they return us to Bogost's 'flat' ontology in which things, like humans, are also empowered. On stage, all objects –including actors – are hyperobjects with their own ontologies, and as such, *Macbeth* could equally be the story of the dagger as protagonist as it moves the action through the play in alternating manifestations of presence and absence, creating alternating situations of pattern and randomness.

Such an approach underlines the text's own position as a hyperobject, and print history bears out such an assumption. With scripted drama, it is common to consider the text as the starting point for what will come to fruition in a subsequent performance, and to assume a concentrated, stable meaning. The text is assumed to be fixed: it is published, established and set down on the page in a predetermined fashion; it is an object to be translated and activated. Of course, even a fixed text is ghosted by other related texts, both by those that serve as its inspiration and, if we acknowledge a playtext's quantum potential, by other possible versions. In this way, even if we accept a given edition as the 'original', we simultaneously agree to put aside those absent, yet interrelated, texts that surround the established text. When a text is selected for performance, whichever form of that text that is introduced is only one possible (present) text. In this way, when a practitioner reaches for the text *Macbeth*, they hold in their hands a randomised sequence of potential texts that could have been made manifest on the page. In the hands of theatre artists, the text is a hyperobject teeming with infinite potential.

Although we suspect that he was not specifically referencing time on a quantum level, when Ben Jonson so aptly wrote that Shakespeare was 'not for an age but for all time', he unwittingly alluded to the performance context that overrides the specificity of Shakespearean time and place in favour of something more enduring. In a dramatic text, the underlying vision for performance exists in a playscript in ways that remain absent in other genres. In print, even when we have a present 'text', our understanding of what constitutes a playtext such as *Macbeth* is wholly dependent on the absent presence of the actors: the live bodies on stage that activate the text in a sort of 'fleshy' virtual reality. The way in which a playtext is an incomplete manifestation of potential is further complicated by the material practices of the Elizabethan playing company; practices that included the compartmentalisation of the text into performance possibilities in the form of cue scripts, which exemplifies how the text was quite literally an object.

Macbeth was first published in the First Folio of 1623; the first time a collection of Shakespeare's plays appeared in print. Collated seven years after Shakespeare's death, there remains a good deal of distance between the author's hand (and the notion of an author's intention) and the orthography of this particular text on the page. The First Folio for *Macbeth* was set according to a prompt copy (Shakespeare 2015: 302), which for all the reasons stated above is both complete and incomplete. By its nature, a prompt copy contains elements of performance so that *Macbeth* once again is both present and absent; it sustains both its fixed pattern and its capacity for random potential. Original performance elements, then – the decisions made by actors that make visible the first network of meaning – become codified in text, rendering the performance a collapse of the distinction between person and object visible in print.

A text, then, becomes an attempt to fix the form of immeasurable potential manifestations, both for the laying down of future texts and for the building up of character(s) on the stage. And yet, character – that entity we recognise on the stage (or in our reader's imagination) – is the manifestation made by the setting of marks on the page; the symbols that, together, formulate characters who embody those said marks (Pye 2017: 86). This collapse puts the text's original performance history into its characters, which in print become material objects that are passed down through future performance networks. Although we may view the text as a present object, its very presence is predicated on and imbued with the absence of its embodiment, which attempts to fulfil its quantum potential, using character to collapse time between a production in 1606 and one in 2020. The text – which may be 'fixed' by Shakespeare (or, by a network that we recognise as 'Shakespeare') – is present, yet dependent on the network of absent code that enables a form of hyperpresence.

The text, *Macbeth*, present since roughly 1606 and concretised in the 1623 First Folio, takes on a hyperpresence as a result of its networked transformation by the absent disaggregation of units that form the networked code. Either as a reader or an audience member, the user cannot engage with the present *Macbeth* (or the present Macbeth, Thane of Glamis) without the absent/present network of meaning that underpins both performance and print: the commands, signs and symbols that surround and support that particular mode of engagement drive the ways in which an audience or readership decodes the network that becomes particularly visible at the given moment of experience. Just as the absent/present code presents the text to the user, the actor's presence depends upon its own coded network that presents the text to the audience. In this way, the performance network materialises the immaterial; it re-members what is from what is not, it creates something out of nothing – or 'some' thing out of 'no' thing. And yet we might go further. The 'no' thing that literary text supposedly represents is drawn from material objects in performance, which is how the quantum understanding of time works. Performance is an embodied system of semiotic code that signifies, activates and animates the text, and the text, reflecting this, reimagines this code, and projects the potentialities within this network on to diverse future performances. This semiotic web presents a cycle of reception and connection that draws lines between actors and audiences in its own present/absent form. In this sense, the transmission from performance to text to performance again oscillates between the random potential of the rehearsal room and the contained organisation of the printed text.

As its own digital network, the rehearsal process depends fully on this same pattern/randomness, whereby the orthographic pattern of text interfaces with the random nature of embodied performance. The quantum potential of the rehearsal process multiplies exponentially when an ensemble of performers assembles to embody the patterned text; each individual performer, as a future onstage hyperobject, brings with them their own embodied experience and tacit knowledge which influences and informs the formulation of the production 'pattern'. As the ensemble rehearse the play, they explore an immeasurable number of patterned choices to most effectively communicate and embody the story set forth by the play's text. Each of those choices is informed by the actors' past experiences, by the embodied and tacit experiences of both their individual lives and also their independent experiences in training and performance, which in turn is informed by the individual experiences and training of those with whom they have worked in the theatre. In this way, the rehearsal process serves as its own emerging network that makes visible the assemblage of experiences that aims to codify a performance, by establishing a repeatable trajectory across time and space – assembling a pattern out of the disparate networks of meaning available. Every rehearsal process drives towards establishing the performance pattern, sorting through an intricate web of embodied choices that makes visible the newly forged network from the larger hyperobject *Macbeth* and submitting this pattern to its audience as part of the theatrical experience.

The performance network offers incalculable possibilities for the text's existence. Each rehearsal process creates its own network for performance. Each performance relies upon a foundational code, which is established over the course of that process, so that rehearsal becomes a form of language making – or code writing – that becomes visible in performance. Once the pattern established through rehearsal is fixed and can be replicated, it is later subject to another continuum of randomness when this trajectory is presented before an audience. Each audience brings to the theatre its own experiences, which influence and affect the patterned presentation of performance. As the pattern/randomness interfaces with the distinction between actual time (the duration of performance in the physical theatre) and virtual time (the fictionalised world of the play, which both compresses and expands accordingly), the hyperobject playtext and hyperobject performance enter yet another process of randomisation, and the material traces left will contribute to future manifestations of *Macbeth*.

If performance is a network whereby the embedded code of performance enables audiences to read/experience the performance-body as an alternate body in space and time, we might imagine it as a digital construct in which the interface is the outward presentation, sustained by an organised, invisible code, a text that, like the performance script, does something active. We might argue, then, that the actor–audience agreement inherent in Shakespeare's text serves as a form of binary code that circulates through the particular performance network on which the performance interface depends. This allusion allows for the transformability of text in a performance context, and the variability that *Macbeth* has undergone as a performance text that moves through stages of organisation towards embodiment. As a result, every performance cannot help but accommodate elements of what is (actually) seen and what is (virtually) experienced, so that the performance encompasses a spectrum of actuality and virtuality that is particular to the performance paradigm of Shakespeare's theatre. Its dependence on language, a system of material and immaterial codes to create virtual reality in actual and quantum time, facilitates a collapse across time and links us, in the twentieth century, to the seventeenth-century audience, experiencing *Macbeth* with nothing but character and language to guide them – through the one-room, aural landscape of performance, where the shared light between the actor and the audience locates both audiences in the presence of each other, with the agreed-upon story shared between them. The hyperobject, therefore, suggests how performance, regardless of its setting and particular style, never fails to put us in agreement with Shakespeare.

The 'neutral' platform stage of Shakespeare's theatre, then, depends on the contract of agreement between participants. This agreement makes visible the particular network in play, as the regulated pattern of language is invited to expand and transform through the theatrical imagination. The prologue to *Henry V* famously evinces such an agreement: 'Think when we talk of horses that you see them' (line 26), the Chorus implores; 'let us . . . on your imaginary forces work' (lines 17–18). The theatrical 'work' executed on behalf of the audience offers theatregoers and theatre-makers governing principles for engaging with Shakespeare's texts in performance, and for deep and resonant readings of the texts as theatrical documents. The neutrality of the playing space pulls the performance out of recognisable time in its lack of recognisable reality; this gives the rare objects that do appear (either material or imagined) a hyper-importance in relation to time.

Even if a performance network makes visible a stable code written by the rehearsal process, that network is never fully 'fixed', as it is constantly subject to the vicissitudes of the audience-organism. The network retains its original code, but must adjust and process new data that disrupts the existing network. This potential variability, which is introduced by the live audience, is mitigated by the actor who functions as an embodied synapse of the code; one that attempts to keep the processing network functioning according to the established pattern. In this way, the actor attempts to retain the tiny ontology established, while simultaneously incorporating the audience's influence into the networked code.

As performance is an embodied manifestation of the semiotics of the text, the digital network of embodiment also serves as a means of appropriation, whereby each performance appropriates the playtext into an embodied exchange between text/actor/audience. As an actor prepares to embody a role, they engage in a form of corporeal interpretation and translation, so that an actor who plays Macbeth emerges from the tiny ontology of the rehearsal and production process affected and informed by the milieu that results from that particular pattern of bodies, ideas and burgeoning network, which would be entirely distinct from another Macbeth – and another *Macbeth* – that emerges from a different networked ontology. In this way, a rehearsal period not only cultivates its own language and writes its own code, which is distinct to that network, but that code – although subject to the random insertions of audience feedback – becomes a fixed network that is receptive and responsive to the organism of performance.

Each performance fixed network, then, is more than the sum of its parts, both human and non-human. As a hyperobject the performance takes on a life and meaning of its own that can never be exhausted, even after the performance ends. While each performance network is fixed through the coming together of these bodies, the participants in the process are unique, discrete units. The process becomes an aggregate of the individual discrete units to create a more complex, congealed, metaphoric body: the performance. The audience encounters this illusion of an external whole in and through performance. The audience organism (Cook 2010: 1) can either cohabitate with the congealed corporality (Hayles 1999) symbiotically, or the audience can affect and infect the performance network as if it were a virus.

How does *Macbeth* (as a performance text) – and the objects within it – exploit, examine and expand the elasticity of an experience of those characters and objects, an experience that depends upon the actor/audience agreement? How does this inherent agreement shape the relationship between character and object? How does the spectators' encounter with objects within this agreement differ from the non-theatrical experience of objects in daily life? We will consider this by scrutinising three objects of note: Macbeth's dagger(s), Banquo's ghost and Lady Macbeth's damned spots. From its opening, *Macbeth* is weird: a short-circuited network that ignites the potential for action that surges through the remainder of the play. This opening, a mere eleven lines in the First Folio, thrusts the audience into the midst of an existing event to which they are not privy. 'When shall we three meet again?' opens the play. The returning prompt, 'again', indicates that these three have already undertaken their meeting. This first example of presence/absence alerts us to how visible objects in *Macbeth* draw questions about what is not visible, alerting us to the enormous, organised and not-yet-organised structures of knowledge that constitute *Macbeth*.

In performances of *Macbeth*, then, time is interchangeable with other stage properties, which include objects, characters and settings. That time is at the forefront of the theatrical experience is evident when, as *Macbeth* opens, the First Witch asks: 'When shall we three meet again?' (I.i.1). The word is echoed by the Second Witch's response, 'When the hurly-burly's done / When the battle's lost or won.' This evokes time past, 'meeting again' referring to an earlier encounter, and time future, 'when the battle's lost and won' (I.i.3–4). However, time is instantly conflated with place as the First Witch asks 'Where the place?' (I.i.6) and the Third Witch: 'There to meet Macbeth' (I.i.7). Through these remarks, the audience is drawn into the chronotopic web of the action that will take place in this concrete space to 'make imaginary puissance' (*Henry V* Prologue 25) with the cast.

Act I, scene ii offers a second example of presence/absence as the Captain prepares us to encounter Macbeth. Here, *Macbeth*'s preoccupation with appearances draws our attention to the nature of the theatrical event, which is juxtaposed against spectral objects. The theatre, like *Macbeth*, presents a continual spectrum of visual variability. The Captain says, 'For brave Macbeth (well he deserves that name), / Disdaining Fortune, with his brandished steel, / Which smoked with bloody execution' (I.ii.16–18). Fittingly, the first time that the audience encounters Macbeth's dagger, the object's presence is central to the tale, but it is markedly absent. The tale presages both Macbeth's actual dagger and his imagined one in the minds of the audience. So that when, in II.i, Macbeth contends with the dagger of the mind, he is actually illustrating how the idea of quantum time works within the play itself: he has entered into a feedback loop that recalls the Captain's account. In his use of visible and invisible objects, Shakespeare primes us to remain attuned to those things that are and are not made material for the audience's sake, but materialise within the world of the fiction. If performance functions as a digital (as opposed to analogue/chronological) network, *Macbeth* reminds us of the presence of invisible things such as actors – who can function as both embodied fictional characters as well as invisible ghosts that haunt the performance network (Cook 2018) – audiences (that hyperlink across time) and props, which can function as 'time machines' (Sofer 2003).

'Is this a dagger which I see before me', Macbeth asks (II.i.33). There is no dagger before him, nor is there an (actual) dagger in the playhouse. The dagger-object exists only in the agreement between the storyteller and the story-experiencer; it is perpetually a 'dagger of the mind' (II.i.38). Repeatedly, Shakespeare asks us to think and, therefore, to see (Pye 2017: 13). So, too, does Macbeth, who tells us not only what to see, but how to see it: 'The handle toward my hand?' (II.i.34). In this distinction, we begin a series of repetitions, which also echo the feedback loop introduced by the dagger's presence. First, the double 'ha' – the handle toward my hand – and even the sound produced by words reverberates through the playhouse as a recalled form of 'how', an expulsion of air that rides an open vowel into existence, which then propels Macbeth into action with the next alliteration: the activated back-of-the-tongue 'K' sound. 'Come let me clutch thee' (II.i.34) – two guttural (velar) consonants manifested into actions: two verbs that launch Macbeth to (actually) reach for the (virtual) dagger. Macbeth's reaction to the invisible dagger activates the back of the actor's tongue, which creates a reflux-like effect that simultaneously evokes spitting. This repetition of sounds produces a psychological effect on both the actor and the audience, prompting an innate, visceral response in return. When exaggerated, this sound repetition creates the voiceless counterpart to what we associate with gagging and retching. (As we demonstrate later, these vocal sounds function as objects themselves.) Macbeth's monosyllabic response, 'I have thee not and yet I see thee still' (II.i.35) creates a temporal effect; one that slows the spectrum of time so that the audience – and Macbeth – may wrestle with the absence/presence of the object and the very presence/absence that results; it creates a reality that is predicated on absence.

If we centralise an object, the same way we centralise the character of Macbeth, we can see the play from the dagger's perspective and further understand how quantum time works on stage, as the dagger's history links past, present and future, and motivates, manipulates, enables and finally perpetrates the crisis. If objects have agency, then, the dagger reflects and creates Macbeth's desire for the crown in a feedback loop that heightens the power of the object over Macbeth. If his mind 'creates' the dagger, the dagger can appropriate the play; as Amy Cook would say, it is the 'object that takes the action' (2010: 31), both representing Macbeth's mental space and controlling it. As it gains power it becomes material, it doubles itself to become the two bloody daggers that do the deed and later infect the mental states of both Macbeth and his Lady. When Donaldbain notes that 'Where we are, / There's daggers in men's smiles' (II.iv.133), he suggests that daggers and their potential iterations begin to litter the stage both metaphorically and materially. In a lesser way, these potential iterations foreshadow the absent/present spots that Lady Macbeth will see on her hands: 'What, will these hands ne'er be clean?' (V.i.37). Like the dagger, the bloody spots both refer to Macbeth's murderous past and predict the Lady's future destruction.

As Macbeth wrangles with the presence of the absent dagger his language illustrates that he enters a new relationship with time – the end of his line hangs on a qualified connection to time: still; 'and yet I see thee still', he states (II.i.5), and speaks into existence the double entendre at the end of the verse line, the juxtaposition between still-ness and the continuous and constant active presence: still. Macbeth refers to this absent/present dagger familiarly once he commences action: the dagger has anthropomorphised into the familiar 'thee', but only before finding a need to rename the dagger: fatal vision (II.i.36). How apt, for an absent but very present apparition to be coined 'deadly sight', which leads Macbeth to test the limits of his sensibility: 'Art thou not, fatal vision, sensible / To feeling as to sight' (II.i.36–7). This launches Macbeth into a series of naming and renaming what is (and is not) before him, as the object morphs from the familiar 'thou' back to the objectified 'dagger' and, finally, to the realisation of a 'false creation' (II.i.37–8), as all things in the theatre are.

This negotiation between the actual and the virtual continues, as Macbeth renames the object once again; he returns first to the familiar 'thou' and then coins the absent/present an instrument. 'And such an instrument' folds time into a knotted web of possibility and inevitability (II.i.43). In this moment of transfiguration, the speech shifts, and moves towards a recurring alliteration of 'w'/'wh' sounds that indicate the inevitable deed foretold by the witches: *when*. We are transported with Macbeth back to the first word uttered in the play, 'When'. Of the twenty lines spanning II.iv.41–61, only three lack a form of the 'w'/'wh' repetition, which intensifies over the twenty lines from qualifiers to more highly saturated imagery. This sequence moves from 'which' (II.i.41), 'way', 'was' (II.i.42), 'was' (II.i.43), 'worth' (II.i.45), 'which' (II.i.47), 'which' (II.i.48), 'world' (II.i.49), 'wicked' (II.i.50), 'witchcraft' (II.i.51), 'withered' (II.i.52), 'wolf' (II.i.53), 'whose', 'watch', 'with' (II.i.54), 'with' (II.i.55), 'which', 'way', 'walk' (II.i.57), 'whereabout' (II.i.58), 'which', 'with', 'whiles' (II.i.60), and finally, 'words' (II.i.61): the very 'characters' upon which characters are built. Each component character that we see as a 'letter' and hear as a sound is its own unit that formulates the larger whole we recognise as words; each individual word comprises the larger fiction. In this way, these linguistic units contribute to the dense mass that makes up the tiny ontology of the hyperobject *Macbeth*. When spoken by an actor, these units also serve as portals that connect that actor across time to the network of performers who have spoken that text and have been absorbed into the assemblage of the network known as *Macbeth*.

The continually changing dagger remains linked inextricably to the evolution, suspension and manipulation of time, hinging on the qualification, 'yet'. Macbeth, in dialogue with the absent/present dagger, states, 'I see thee yet,' (II.i.40); the word 'yet' is a derivative of 'still' that has linguistically taken on an alternate temporal mode that suspends time. Macbeth continues, 'in form as palpable / As this which now I draw' (II.i.40–1). Here, Macbeth heightens the relationship between time and object by juxtaposing the distinctions between the absent/present dagger (which [he] sees before [him]) and the present/absent heretofore sheathed and therefore, absent [actual] dagger; between then and now: as [he] draw[s]. In conflating the two daggers, he simultaneously conflates the time between the envisioned and the actual objects and the imagined event that hangs between the two.

As Macbeth moves ('with Tarquin's ravishing strides') towards the inevitable, towards the time when the deed will be done, the text heightens to a rhyming couplet: 'Whiles I threat, he lives; / Words to the heat of deeds too cold breath give' (II.i.60–1). The rhyming couplet would have indicated an exit; indeed, the embodied speech transforms Macbeth. The speech traverses from vision to action: possibly an exit to execute the task. Macbeth is interrupted by the ringing of a bell, present from the first printing of the text, which states, 'A bell rings' (II.i.62). The bell, which jars Macbeth and disrupts the forward momentum, is a manifestation of the absent/present: a planned randomisation of a traditional pattern. The bell is rung; it is heard, though not necessarily seen. Its presence interrupts the actual onstage action. It requires Macbeth to restart his exit: 'I go, and it is done; the bell invites me' (II.i.63). Macbeth shares with his audience, who in the process transform from confidants to co-conspirators as Macbeth embroils them in the action (Pye 2017: 24–30).

Once the murder has occurred, Macbeth has transformed potential action into embodied action and moves Duncan from present to absent object. This transformative action should have freed Macbeth from his own imagination, but instead he becomes embroiled in a repetitive cycle of reckoning between perception and reality – as does every audience member in the theatre. 'Present fears / Are less than horrible imaginings, / My thought, whose murder yet is but fantastical, / Shakes so my single state of man / That function is smothered in surmise, / And nothing is, but what is not', Macbeth states (I.iii.139–44). Again, this juxtaposition of the absent/present and the present/absent (what is unseen, but inherently present, and what is materially present, but is rendered invisible) is precisely what the theatrical event depends upon. On stage, 'nothing is, but what is not' (I.iii.144); and like an Escher print, in the theatre the cyclical notion of embodied character is such that what *is* (embodied text on stage) is comprised of what *is not* (the actor's corporeal instrument, which exists continually as a discrete entity – on stage and off).

Macbeth must then meet with the progeny of his actions: Banquo's ghost. As a ghost, Banquo represents the paradox of objects/bodies/time/space: Banquo is both an embodied actor and a spectral presence, and he both represents a future pattern of action and links Macbeth inextricably to his past actions. 'Enter the Ghost of Banquo, and sits in Macbeth's place' (III.iv) states the stage direction, which breaks up what appears to be a (potential) shared Alexandrine line between the Macbeths. The indication in the Folio – whether written by Shakespeare or recorded stage business from the prompt book – demonstrates that there was a body on stage that represented (or re-presented) the murdered Banquo. In this way, the audience – who are complicit in Macbeth's actions – sees what he sees: presence/absence, while the other characters see only absence/presence: the response to the unseen Ghost. Although all this hinges on the potential inherent in the agreement between the players and the playgoers, it also depends on the pre-established patterns and sustained agreement between the performers themselves. The actors on stage agree to un-see the visible body, and the playgoers see manifestations of embodied presence according to the storytelling contract.

The final example in Act V, scene i, in which Lady Macbeth contends with the presence of her absent spots, depends on storytelling, once more eliciting performance's co-dependency on descriptive language that is, in Shakespeare, codified in the Folio and subsequent editions. Here again, the First Folio features a stage direction: 'Enter Lady, with a Taper'. 'Lo you, here she comes', states the Gentlewoman; 'This is her very guise, and upon my life, fast asleep. Observe her, stand close' (V.i.19–20). The modern edition sets a total of three full stops, where the Folio drives towards clarity with a series of colons, so that this series of statements moves directly towards discovery; its orthography serves as another hiccup in the pattern/random network. 'How came she by that light?' asks the Doctor (V.i.21). 'Why it stood by her: she ha's light by her continually, 'tis her command' (V.i.22–3). In these few short lines the Gentlewoman acknowledges the meta-theatricality of the performance network and points to audience agreement. The audience, contracted to acknowledge the 'guise' of each player who 'struts and frets [their] hour upon the stage' (V.v.24–5), now must agree to mis-take – or to intake – the 'manner' of coded behaviour within the embodied performance. Like Banquo's ghost, Lady Macbeth's spotted hands are objects that link past and present actions; her attempts to control this manifestation of the absent/present can be seen as an attempt to negate her past actions, to rewrite the code of the performance text and thereby reorganise the dense mass of the hyperobject. Lady Macbeth, however, actively points at the space-time continuum of the theatrical performance through her manipulation of time. Just as time is always simultaneously virtual as well as actual in the theatre, so is the case with Lady Macbeth's taper. Moreover, by keeping the taper continually lit, Lady Macbeth forcefully manipulates time into a perpetual daylight, whereby she may avoid the terrors of the dark. When we consider the ghost of the original performance conditions, which haunt the contemporary performance network, we see time fold in on itself once again: the midday performance conditions of the Elizabethan theatre were bathed in light. Through the audience contract, the absent dark must overcome the present light. The present audience must agree to the storytelling contract that rewrites the network code, which says it is dark, and thereby requires a taper – a taper which must be constantly illumined to stave off the absent/present dark.

Shortly after, Lady Macbeth begins a cycle of absence/presence, which escalates towards a climax with significant implications for the performance network. 'Yet here's a spot', she states. As she strives to cope with what she perceives to be the material manifestation of her actions, she is haunted by the ghost of her corporeal experience. The friction between the virtual and the actual occurrences overtakes multiple senses, from sight, to touch, to smell. In this, Lady Macbeth's wrangling with her experience of absence/presence is far more sophisticated than that of her husband, who must only reconcile the short-circuiting between feeling and sight. 'Here's the smell of the blood still' (V.i.50). Still. Like Macbeth's repeated 'still', Lady Macbeth's 'still' folds time back on itself to the moment when the deed was done.

'All the perfumes of Arabia will not sweeten this little hand', she continues (V.i.50–1), until the patterned sensory overload short-circuits the pattern, and all our Lady can state is, 'Oh, oh, oh' (V.i.52): a glitch in the system, overcome by the transfiguration of the code. Even as she fights to return to the pattern of normalcy with her domestic instructions, 'Wash your hands, put on your nightgown, look not so pale' (V.i.62–3), the 'whirligig of time' (*Twelfth Night* V.i.370) impedes her restoration. 'I tell you yet again, Banquo's buried; he cannot come out on's grave' (V.i.63–4). She wrangles with time's conflation as we have seen elsewhere, with both the witches' meeting and with Macbeth's absent/present dagger. The haunting power of Lady Macbeth's actions hovers over the 'present' time, which has folded and looped back on itself, a ghost in the machine. This manifests in another glitch, which leads Lady Macbeth to her fatal demise. 'To bed, to bed', begins her repetitive glitch (V.i.66), but unlike Macbeth's earlier receptions, Lady Macbeth's words trap her in the feedback loop of quantum time. Like a skipping record, the dialogue catches: 'come, come, come, come' she loops (V.i.66–7); 'give me your hand. What's done, cannot be undone' (V.i.67–8), she prophesies over what is and what is not, until she utters her final words, 'To bed, to bed, to bed' (V.i.68). The code cannot be reset. There is no hand to take. 'What's done, cannot be undone' (V.i.67–8).

Timothy Morton (2015) argues that 'an artwork cannot be reduced to its parts or materials, nor can it be reduced to its creator's life, nor to some other context however defined . . . Art is charisma, pouring out of anything whatsoever, whether we humans consider it to be alive or sentient or not.' As a hyperobject, *Macbeth* the play is then a metaphor for the vastness of the theatrical experience, even as Macbeth the character is analogous to the playgoer who is drawn into the action by the hyperobjects that rule the performance of the play.

These hyperobjects are situated within the performance network and contribute to the series of code which is comprised of both the playscript and the lived experience. In this way hyperobjects co-author the coded work of art even as they serve as time machines, drawing together performances across the 400-year history of Shakespeare production. In an apt analogy to the claims we have made about the quantum potential of the dense mass of a visible/invisible theatrical experience, Carlo Rovelli notes that 'the temporal structure of the world is different from the naïve image that we have of it' (2018: 199); the hypertextuality of *Macbeth* occupies many temporal positions simultaneously. The theatre is a privileged space for a more vast understanding of time and space and for interaction with objects that take on agency and become protagonists in their own right. In all theatre, what is done is undone and then redone in a subsequent performance. The text may exist physically but escapes the material world as it disseminates itself and comes into contact with minds, bodies, sets, lights, costumes, audiences, ideologies or oppressions, events; it takes on its own intrinsic reality that is not reality at all.

Bibliography

Bogost, I. (2012), *Alien Phenomenology, or What It's Like to Be a Thing*, Minneapolis: University of Minnesota Press.

Carlson, M. (1994), 'Invisible Presences – Performance Intertextuality', *Theatre Research International*, 19:2, 111–17, https://doi.org/10.1017/S0307883300019349 [accessed 29 April 2020].

Carlson, M. (2001), *The Haunted Stage: The Theatre as Memory Machine*, Ann Arbor: University of Michigan Press.

Cook, A. (2010), *Shakespearean Neuroplay: Reinvigorating the Study of Dramatic Texts and Performance through Cognitive Science*, New York: Palgrave.

Cook, A. (2018), *Building Character: The Art and Science of Casting*, Ann Arbor: University of Michigan Press.

Desmet, C. (2017), 'Alien Shakespeares 2.0', *Actes des congrès de la Société française Shakespeare*, 35, DOI: 10.4000/shakespeare.3877 [accessed 29 April 2020].

Hayles, N. K. (1999), *How We Became Posthuman: Virtual Bodies in Cybernetics, Literature, and Informatics*, Chicago: University of Chicago Press.

Morton, T. (2011), 'Here Comes Everything: The Promise of Object-Oriented Ontology', *Qui Parle*, 19:2, 163–90, www.jstor.org/stable/10.5250/quiparle.19.2.0163 [accessed 29 April 2020].

Morton, T. (2013), *Hyperobjects: Philosophy and Ecology after the End of the World*, Ann Arbor: University of Minnesota Press.

Morton. T. (2015), 'Charisma and Causality', *ArtReview*, 10 December, <https://artreview.com/november-2015-feature-timothy-morton-charisma-causality/> [accessed 23 January 2020].

Moston, D. (ed.) (1998), *Mr. William Shakespeares Comedies, Histories, & Tragedies: A Facsimile of the First Folio, 1623*, New York: Routledge.

Prigogine, I. (1984), *Order out of Chaos: Man's New Dialogue with Nature*, trans. I. Stengers, London: Heinemann.

Pye, V. C. (2017), *Unearthing Shakespeare: Embodied Performance and the Globe*, New York: Routledge.

Rovelli, C. (2018), *The Order of Time*, trans. E. Segre and S. Carnell, New York: Riverhead Books.

Shakespeare, W. (2008), *Twelfth Night*, ed. K. Elam, London: Bloomsbury.

Shakespeare, W. (2012), *Romeo and Juliet*, ed. R. Weis, London: Bloomsbury.

Shakespeare, W. (2015), *Macbeth*, ed. S. Clark and P. Mason, London: Bloomsbury.

Sofer, A. (2003), *The Stage Life of Props*, Ann Arbor: University of Michigan Press.

10

The Thing Itself: Performance and the Celebrity Text

Louise Geddes

Since the turn of the twentieth century, dramatic theatre[1] has relied on the invisibility of craft as a marker of quality, emphasising an internalised performance process that is predicated on the erasure of the scripted play. In spite of the necessary shift away from naturalistic theatre that new aesthetics, shrinking arts budgets and black-box theatres have facilitated, classical theatre, that is, stagings of scripts from the global dramatic canon, continues to encourage a fourth-wall performance aesthetic of its actors, even when the design, direction and text itself make apparent other possibilities. Since Stanislavsky's formulation of a technique based on experiential acting processes that positions the embodiment of authentic feeling (often framed as artistic 'truth') as the cornerstone of performance, conventional stagings of scripted drama have striven for a verisimilitude of naturalism, even when the play is famous and unavoidably recognisable as a repetition. Alastair Coomer, the National Theatre's head of casting, suggested that 'acting is often at its best when it is least noticeable' (Gardner 2018), and even the great theatrical innovator Peter Brook has lauded the invisibility of performance when he noted that when performing Hamlet, Adrian Lester is 'an actor that can be so at ease with this complex language that he can make you feel he is inventing it' (Croall 2018: 87).

    This concealment of craft is driven by the assumption that a famous play is a predictable thing and is to be decoded through performance. As objects to be interpreted, therefore, stagings are often seen as offering opportunities to transcend the materiality of the text and access something quintessentially and authentically human. Moreover, performance's emphasis on liveness is equally an attempt to repudiate classical theatre's dependence on human acts of repetition by denying the iterative nature of the famous text as it is passed down simultaneously through print and performance. For example, as audiences flock to see Adrian Lester in Brook's *Hamlet* because he is a famous actor, directed by a famous director, performing a famous role, they seek out something that is both immediately recognisable and entirely fresh, searching for new understanding and insights into an already well-known object. This chapter explores this contradictory impulse and it does so by reconceptualising the well-known object – that is, the play and all that it encompasses – as a celebrity whose materiality must be accounted for in theatrical staging, and examines the pressure that such celebrity, manifest as it is in an admiration of Great Roles, exerts on its actors.

As both Coomer's and Brook's observations of acting indicate, stagings of Shakespeare – by which I mean stagings of classical plays that are presented in a naturalistic style – are often evaluated in terms of plausibility, recognising 'plotted possibility as a bounded field or closed set' (Sack 2015: 30). As such, stagings are unhappily required to balance the expectations of an ephemeral performance occurrence with the false sense of stability regarding what the well-known play is. David Cote articulates the contradictory impulses that drive fandoms of the famous plays in his giddy review of Ruth Negga's 2020 portrayal of Hamlet. Cote defines theatre attendance as an accumulative practice of consumption when he explains that

> theatre lovers collect Lears, Medeas and Blanches DuBois the way others accumulate random matchbooks or Apple earbuds. The Great Roles are routinely assayed over the years, and one stuffs the memory of them in a miscellaneous drawer thinking that they might be useful one day. Critics keep lord knows how many Hamlets in that drawer: some live, some on film or via NT Live. I've just acquired a new melancholy Dane that is so fresh, aching and aflame with life, I want to savour it before squirreling it away. (Cote 2020)

Cote's example illustrates the challenges that face performance scholars and audiences alike. He defines Lears, Medeas and Blanches in performance as individual, discrete objects, while simultaneously gathering them up as part of a larger definition of singular literary 'Great Roles'. The objectification of these roles, and by extension the plays themselves, contradicts any suggestion that in performance studies we ought to view Shakespeare as a medium or a platform through which other messages are disseminated.

Famous plays are objects that maintain an onstage presence and resist the subjection that meta-critical performance would demand of them.

Worthen's (2014) theorisation of Shakespeare as a performance medium is well suited to an avant-garde performance practice that draws attention to the text only to deconstruct it, but the alternative position that M. J. Kidnie adopts is fundamentally appropriative, imagining performance as a sequence of rewrites of an 'original' text, suggesting that 'textual-theatrical instances are *productive* of the work' (2009: 64), eliding the problem of how the play itself is manifest. Stagings of Shakespeare challenge performance theory because they conceptually undermine Shakespeare's universality by standing on equal footing with print culture, and the authority of performance allows most contemporary stagings to claim a reiterative fealty to the script and promise authenticity while presenting the play in a fresh historical or aesthetic context. Cote's suggestion of collectibles, however, invites us to think about the power of the plays as celebrity objects and explore the materialist value of the text as it shapes its performance.[2] An object-oriented perspective enables a more critical approach to those productions that appear somewhere between original practices and the avant-garde and considers the ways in which the celebrity object exists in a dialogic adaptive relationship with the ideological forces that engage with it.

In spite of a significant celebrity network that is organised around the interplay of texts and their Great Roles as celebrity objects, theatre reviewers continue to perpetuate an unrealistic expectation of surprise, and a demand that a performance obscure its text to represent events, thoughts and feelings as if they were happening for the first time. This is the reality of performing famous texts and creates a problem for the classically trained Stanislavskian actor who seeks to model Coomer's invisible craft by inhabiting a Great Role that is already laden with expectations. Rory Kinnear acknowledged this anxiety as he worried about how to navigate 'a certain degree of the train track that lies ahead' (Croall 2018: 108) when he played Hamlet in 2010. Paul Taylor's criticism of Benedict Cumberbatch's 2015 Hamlet further exemplifies the contradictory expectations placed on an actor when he notes that 'we don't sense that he [Cumberbatch] is laying himself bare, as is the case with the greatest exponents of the role such as Mark Rylance and Simon Russell Beale' (Croall 2018: 123). Even if such a comparison feels a little unfair to Cumberbatch, the critique is typical of theatre reviewers who have seen countless Hamlets, and who walk into the theatre with an acute sense of what they believe Shakespearean theatre is (or should be). The misplaced optimism that Taylor exhibits in his anticipation of Cumberbatch reinventing this particular wheel simultaneously recognises the value of Cumberbatch's fame, and in essence, privileges it over Hamlet's. Taylor assumes that Cumberbatch, as a great actor taking his place in a continuum of leading men, will validate his fame by single-handedly transforming *Hamlet* into a new experience for his audience. Moreover, Taylor's critique unwittingly proves Cote's point – his complaint evinces the affective power of *Hamlet*'s celebrity as it demonstrates the way the play's fame has already shaped the criteria by which Taylor will consume Cumberbatch's performance.

Performance Studies and the Celebrity Text

Postmodernism, and the subsequent changes that have occurred in theatre studies since the late twentieth century, has manifested itself in the emergence of a performance theory that defines theatre primarily as an event, giving precedence to unscripted or deconstructed performances that make art out of the stage's own artificiality. This popular critical conception of performance as an event has dominated scholarship since Hans-Thies Lehmann's 1999 theorisation of post-dramatic theatre. By defining performance as a singular, unrepeatable event, because of performance's ephemerality, performance theory implies that *Hamlet* can only exist once in the moment that it happens – it is potentiality, it occurs, it becomes history. But the script retains traces of these material events, of its prior assemblages, and these attachments manifest themselves as part of the object's celebrity impacting the past, present and future of its staging. Scripts, then, become objects that 'tantalise and hold us in suspense, alluding to a fullness that is elsewhere, to a future that, apparently, is on its way' (Bennett 2010: 32). Daniel Sack attributes this richness to the performing body, but if we apply it to the classical theatre, a play becomes more than 'an instrument of performance' (Worthen 2014: 97) because it retains its affective power, manifest in the imagined authority of the Great Role.

As long as it separates the textual object from its labour of realisation, then, performance theory is of limited use to much contemporary Shakespearean performance. William West notes how 'a performance-centred approach seems required to choose between the relative (but also frustrated) immediacy of a current production, or to rely on archived documents of various kinds to reconstruct performance practices that have already disappeared' (West 2006: 31), implicitly acknowledging the extent to which the script is erased from theoretical visibility once one identifies staging as an event. Critics invite us to dismiss the text in favour of its context, and yet, in spite of a recognition that, in the twenty-first century, theatre is 'a compound of media' (Lavender 2016: 9), performance theory's tendency to facilitate a mistrust of scripted language that would erase the materiality of the text entirely creates challenges for those of us who study well-known texts as they move from one staging to the next. While Lehmann elsewhere boldly declares Shakespeare's theatre to be one with 'no restrictive unity of style, no atmosphere without ambiguity' (2004: 104), he returns dogmatically to the script in order to validate such ambiguity. Elsewhere, Lehmann claims that 'Shakespeare's characters and plots prove compelling precisely *because* essential aspects have an unclear or contradictory motivation' (2006: 238), illustrating a simultaneous desire to shake off the presence of the script even as he recognises its centrality to new performance. Famous plays, Lehmann implies, sustain an elusive energy that requires us to filter them through our own subjective positioning, but to adopt the stance that the script is no more than a medium elides its inevitable presence as it shapes both production and reception.

As Andrew James Hartley notes, to unequivocally position performance as an event results in an 'overly dogmatic and intellectually suspect' erasure of a play's value (2006: 91), and too often critics end up discussing something other than Shakespeare. Original practices aside, many Shakespeare stagings eschew historicism, instead utilising the popular belief in Shakespeare's universality to play with a production's aesthetic and attributing this freedom to the timeless genius of Shakespeare, rather than acknowledging the potent materiality of the text. David Cote once more illustrates this point when he critiques Jude Law's 'yoga Hamlet', defining the audience's anticipation in terms of the play itself:

> When will you know that you've seen a truly great *Hamlet*? For one thing, you won't be glad when Ophelia drowns in the brook. You will shed a tear for the fratricidal Claudius as he vainly prays for forgiveness. You will not check your watch during the Act V funeral, impatient for the duel. You will find yourself alternately loving and loathing the title character, as magnificent a portrait of human cogitation and self-revelation as ever put on paper. (Cote 2009)

Even though he somewhat derisively describes how 'the lean movie star pads about the stage barefoot in stretchy pants and a clingy T-shirt, often squatting and lunging with the sinewy ease of a Bikram vet (downward-facing Dane, perhaps?)' (Cote 2009), Cote is enthusiastic about Law's Hamlet as it offered the satisfaction of a new aesthetic, and the opportunity to dwell in his favourite moments of the play. For Cote, fidelity to representation is not bound up in fidelity to historicist staging, which is why he can gently mock the production's style, but not let it be the defining factor in his evaluation – Cote welcomes the appropriative impulse that drives stagings of this famous play. As Komporaliy notes, 'there is a close connection between the processes of stage adaptation, instances of new writing, elements of devising and the theatrical and literary canon' (2017: 7–8). The propensity towards appropriation that characterises stagings of classical plays, however, is part of their appeal, and for audience members such as Cote it creates a continuity that undermines the idea of performance as discrete, separate entities.

To return to a performance theory that posits staging as an event, then, inadvertently reinforces a historicist theoretical framework because it can only recognise the text as an archival performance document, rejecting the 'determinative or clearly causal' relationship between text and performance in favour of new iterations and unrepeatable events (Hartley 2006: 82). Although I would not subscribe wholesale to the assumption that the trajectory from script to performance is 'clearly causal', as Hartley does, I would like to cautiously walk back the methodological reliance on context as the defining feature of performance and more carefully unpack West's suggestion that 'performance is less an event than the management of a rhythm or repetitions – a practice of filling an ordinary gesture, word, or phrase with meaning through iteration, spacing, and change' (2006: 35). That these repetitions can be fruitfully destabilised implicitly acknowledges the degree to which a classical text is imaginatively constructed because of the recognition it has achieved through a long history of diverse and celebrated productions.

The 'oddly timeless and consistent' (Hartley 2006: 78) visibility that Shakespearean drama maintains on stage is a direct result of its celebrity. I wish to draw from the ideas of Jane Bennett to interrogate how we might approach the famous play, known variously through its narrative, its language, its images and occasionally other elements (such as music), as a variable celebrity object that is endowed with an almost limitless capacity for meaning that does not so much yield its secrets as make visible the artistic labour that occurs as we interact with it in performance. Performance, particularly as it pertains to actors, must navigate this celebrity, and by thinking about the performance text as one singular object, it is possible to see how celebrity text lays out its certain degree of train track as a speculative, entelechial construction that moves forward (as opposed to the backwards-facing memory machine of Marvin Carlson [Carlson 2001]). Vibrant materialism enables the performance event to be absorbed within the scripted object, and suggests staging as an attempt to materialise what the text could be. When we think, therefore, about how performance materialities activate unpredictable elements (such as the competing fame of directors, performances and spaces), we must also recognise the object-power of the script. Such intersecting materialities generate new networks of meaning that are defined by these subjective relations. The celebrity play makes demands of an actor that routinely confound the desire for invisibility of craft.

From a semiotic standpoint, the stage is a place where 'human being and thinghood overlap' and slide in and out of one another (Bennett 2010: 4), and as such, both performer and stage properties become affective objects to be read by the audience. Even though it is not as materially present as props or actors, I wish to establish a space for the famous play as equally agential an object as the performing body. Recognising the similarities of text and the performing body (particularly the celebrity body) poises performance at a place of absolute presentness, in which the past is made visible and the future is made possible, and we, as performers, practitioners, spectators and objects, exist as part of this transition between what has been, what is and what could be. A new materialist approach allows us to 'throw out, or at least question, the opposition between subject and object and the idea of the artwork as a fixed endpoint (of making) or a fixed beginning point (of interpretation)' (Jones 2015: 32). That is to say that these Great Roles, these celebrity objects, are definable only insofar as we acknowledge them through relations to other material objects. Shakespeare performance, then, is an entelechial process that continues to evolve, but resists any identifiable resting point at which the play becomes revealed as essentially and entirely Shakespearean. As we gather up and collect these Great Roles (either through acts of theatrical creation or participatory spectatorship during a staging), the objects themselves remain unchanged by our interactions, retaining a vitality that attracts us with their celebrity and invites us to attach other material objects that give them the shape they find in performance.

Object Celebrity and Vibrant Matter

Celebrity, or 'it' according to Joseph Roach, is at its very essence thing-power (Roach 2007). Although celebrity studies 'remains ever tethered to a live body' (Holl 2013: 6),[3] celebrity indicates 'a vitality intrinsic to materiality' (Bennett 2010: 3). Celebrity is, fundamentally, a subjective phenomenon that has the capacity for thing-power, only unleashing its vitality when put into relational perspective. That is to say, 'it' is always there, vibrant and present, but its capacity to work on us, its capricious agency, is unleashed when understood in context with other matter – that is, celebrity objects are 'never entirely exhausted by their semiotics' (Bennett 2010: 5). As such, they are not fully containable nor autonomous, as the humanistic-driven scholarly studies of celebrity would have us imagine. A popular character such as Hamlet is a perfect example of the object–human collapse that celebrity affords. For the last four hundred years, the role of Hamlet, which has sustained a quasi-embodied existence straddling page and stage, has been in possession of a celebrity that is both culturally ubiquitous, yet most clearly visible when attached to a performing body. As Sean Redmond notes, 'celebrity representations carry the range of politicised values and means that are attached to their image when in circulation' (2018: 36), because celebrity is presumed to perform something unique and essential about the famous person and, like performance, celebrity puts forward an agreed-upon lie that both recognises and disavows the medium that facilitates it (Mills 2010: 192). Object celebrity makes explicit a thing's affective power as communities continually reposition themselves in relation to it, as it remains seemingly unchanged, accessible yet alien, refusing to give up its secrets. Think, for example, of the US Constitution. Although it exists in the Barthesian realm of text, subject to intellectual play, the material thing itself – paper, ink, words and signatures – is a quasi-mythical object, validated by the names inscribed upon it and wielded by pundits on CNN and Fox News alike as a locked cabinet of solutions to political and civic issues. From medieval reliquaries to Stonehenge to the *Mona Lisa*, celebrity objects are recognised for an immanent vitality, and are put into a reinscriptive process that continually strives to contain their energy by defining it in contrast (or as complement) to other objects, and that changes as cultural material values evolve and mutate.

Celebrity depends on both the combination of intimacy and distance and its ability to take shape only in relation to other objects. This proposition works well for the Shakespeare text as it is manifest in a variety of media, offering different experiences across (and beyond) transmedia. Douglas M. Lanier's proposition (2011) that Shakespeare is 'post-textual' recognises the shifts that occur as the medium of Shakespeare collapses and conflates, understanding Shakespearean celebrity as infinitely mutable, depending on how we position ourselves in relation to it. What Lanier is implicitly acknowledging here is the celebrity of a text such as *Hamlet* that is present in its material presence – the black clothes or Yorick's skull portray Hamlet as effectively as the 'To be or not to be' soliloquy does. *Hamlet*, then can be present in stagings, in adaptations and in slight, convoluted allusions that draw from its celebrity to denote something (usually gravitas) – it is an 'immanent vitality flowing across bodies, objects, and space' (Bennett 2010: 75). Stagings of Shakespeare highlight the expectations placed on celebrity objects, because, as Cote repeatedly ponders, a great play is at once familiar by its cultural ubiquity and mysteriously refreshed by the production materialities that manifest it anew. Cote's pleasure in 2020 at the 'new melancholy Dane that is so fresh, aflame, and aching with life', for example, actually speaks more to Hamlet's celebrity that it does to Ruth Negga's performance (Cote 2020). As a textual object, a play offers a similar combination of knowledge and mystique, and in many ways is a more 'pure' celebrity object than a human subject because as a mere 'thing', a product of humanity, it stops just shy of having agency of its own until it is put into relationship with other objects, a process that we recognise as performance.

To understand *Hamlet*'s celebrity is to recognise the play as one of Lanier's 'post-textual' Shakespeare objects that both absorbs and transcends the language that signifies it, engaging with adjacent materialist networks and becoming recognisable through image and association, in much the same way than, for example, Marilyn Monroe is signified by a dress, or Brad Pitt's fame is as indelibly affiliated with the actresses he has married as it is with the roles he has played. Mills observes that human celebrities are 'able to carry their star persona across texts' (2010: 192), and new materialism suggests ways in which this is true for a post-textual Shakespearean celebrity object as it traverses genre, media and text, all the while remaining identifiable as Shakespeare. Moreover, celebrity maintains its own networks of meaning, which, as both Kim and Blackwell observe in this volume, can be either complementary or critical (and occasionally both) of the ideological structures of knowledge that underpin any Shakespeare play.

In the theatre, during its performance, the vibrancy of the celebrity play is rendered visible and, rather than watch a repetition or an iteration of the text, we participate in a process of actualisation that occurs when material objects are put into a contextualising network. The realisation of a text that performance promises becomes apparent during a staging of the play but, by virtue of theatre's ephemerality, is not necessarily completed, because no interpretation, iteration or repetition can stabilise the ontological insecurity of the vibrant play. During a Shakespearean production, we participate in a partial realisation, a coming-into-being that performance practitioners more commonly define as embodiment and limit to the corporeal presence of the actor. In her work tracing celebrity back to the early modern stage, Holl suggests that celebrity is dependent on the semiotics of theatre, 'in which the momentary spectacle of live performance produces a tension-laden environment that gives rise to heightened affectivity, simulating the bonds of intimacy' (2013: 18). On the stage, material objects and visual culture are inextricable from one another and conflate human and non-human objects in Holl's simulated bonds of intimacy that cannot be construed as the 'real' thing. Moreover, in spite of their careful placement by a set designer or a stage manager, visual objects – a chair, a gun, an actor's body part – become performative on their own terms, and their capacity to 'make things happen, to produce effects' (Bennett 2010: 5) as they engage with one another habitually exceeds the intentionality of the human subjects that set them. A Great Role is no exception to this premise. Holl's emphasis on intimacy manifests itself in a definition of celebrity that can be equally applied to the Shakespeare text: a sign, a recombinant amalgam of an individual's enacted roles (broadly defined) and publicised personal life conflated with cultural fixation, all projected on to the bodies of living individuals (Holl 2013: 12). That such signification is also projected on to the classical play is not an extreme claim to consider and renders explicit the play's instability. Moreover, to claim the celebrity play as vibrant matter highlights its dependence on the political ecologies that not only create it, but speculate on it and consume it as audience members. Thus, stagings of famous plays become an ongoing process of material negotiation between actor, text and audience that, as Cote suggests, does not necessarily end when the staged event concludes, but instead attaches new material connotations to the play-object, further enhancing its celebrity.

A conative Shakespeare identity that 'is distributed across a mosaic' (Bennett 2010: 38) results in matter that engages with other archontic materialities, such as set design, props and bodies, which sustain cultural memory and put forward a material semiosis that can (and often does) exist interchangeably with human agency. As Cote demonstrates, because of what we might consider as a widespread affective Shakespeare fandom, the very act of attending a famous play's production is an implicit acknowledgement of this distribution of agency by the audience. Moreover, if we view a playtext as a vibrant object, loaded with potentiality rather than ghosted, then the question of performance as the realisation of a text can never be resolved. This interminability challenges the idea of performance as event, and instead looks to a larger process of actualisation and accounts for the impenetrability of Great Roles. Unlike Sack's performance-based potentiality, which is rooted in the intentionality of the performing body, a text-based potentiality recognises the 'federation of actants' that contribute to the experience of staging and watching a celebrity play (Bennett 2010: 28).

Applying a combination of affective celebrity and vibrant materialism to the classical text (in this case, the Shakespeare play) highlights the limitations of framing a performance as an event, preferring instead to regard the production of a play as part of a larger accumulative materialist progression that accommodates, but does not always adhere to, human intentionality. If we view a Shakespeare play's fame as archontic, something that accrues meaning, developing its own archive, then, in theory, performance becomes interminable (DeKosnik 2016). The theatrical production is absorbed in a longer process of materialisation that can never fully conclude because the celebrity text, defined by its relationship to mechanisms of fame and culture, is constantly repositioning itself and generating new meaning. As a play becomes better known, a celebrity in its own right, its performance is speculatively consumed in advance and stagings offer glimpses of what Shakespeare could be when the text engages with other performance materialities. Sack's dismissive recognition that 'regardless which possibility the actor utilises in pursuit, the objective remains the same; the event is tamed' (2015: 45) not only presumes a homogeneity to the performing body, and a stability to the transience of language, but evinces a peculiarly conservative approach to the transhistorical and cultural permutations of literature. Futurity makes its presence felt when a text is a sufficiently known quantity to be remediated, reframed and detached from the bounded space of authorial intent. As the text accrues value, historical specificity falls away and authorial intent is diminished – historical connotations of word choice, acting styles, stage management practices are stripped of their usefulness. Under these circumstances, a script connotes and exists on its own terms – the best example being Pinter's famous pauses. Moreover, increased accessibility of translations, editions and annotations offer ongoing opportunities to renegotiate meaning, and outside materialities draw our attention to unpredictable elements. For example, the denial in 2017 by the Albee estate of permission for a cross-racial cast in an Oregon production of *Who's Afraid of Virginia Woolf?* illustrates the futility of intentionality as a means of circumventing speculation and controlling the meaning of a playscript. The publication of the estate's denial, only noteworthy because of the play's fame, worked against their intentions by inviting a speculative reconsideration of the racial politics not only of the play under discussion, but of Albee's work in a more general sense. The overall result, then, is that Pinter's pauses are no longer authorial directions, but markers of a Pinter play's stylistic identity, straddling both print and performance – they become as laden with celebrity meaning as the Marilyn Monroe dress or Judy Garland's slippers.

If we accept the script as Bennett's vibrant matter, it becomes an entelechially infused object that exists as part of the larger federation of actants when it is staged. Its progression towards actualisation is made visible through performance and yet, as a famous play whose future iterations are both assured (by its cultural value) and unknown (because its affective power shifts as cultural values change), it can never be fully realised. Rebecca Schneider correctly notes that 'performance . . . becomes materialisation' (2015: 12), but when this materialisation is integrated with a play's ongoing celebrity, meaning becomes fruitfully dependent on the shifting semiotic grounds that its contemporary performances offer, whether they be rooted in the avant-garde or original practices. By retracing our steps back to the text, then, we might resist the complacency that tells us that 'agency is also bound up with the idea of a trajectory' (Bennett 2010: 32) and recognise that the vibrancy inherent in the classical text is negotiated by both actor and audience with unexpected results. A play's object-celebrity generates a capacity for its own autonomy and potentiality in performance that conflates both the literary and performed text as part of the theatrical existence.

The vibrant materiality of the classical play, then, acts upon the audience member by eliciting an affective navigation between what they experience and what they have anticipated. In performance, agency is 'distributed across a mosaic' (Bennett 2010: 38) and elicits a meta-critical engagement with the play's materialities that is generally only made explicit in postmodern performance. Keith Hamilton Cobb's *American Moor*, for example, interrogates Shakespeare's place as an archontic object in an attempt to separate it from the networks of institutional racism that habitually exclude actors of colour in the United States. In particular, Hamilton Cobb's choice to intersperse meditations on institutionalised racism in American classical theatre with performed chunks of *Othello* is designed to highlight the artificiality of Shakespearean language as much as it draws attention to Hamilton Cobb's dexterity, but few people would recognise his play as particularly experimental in its form. The classical script, variably constructed as it is across time, space and media, contains these multitudes of ongoing negotiation that *American Moor* dramatises, and consistently confounds our desire to see the text through fresh eyes, even in stagings that do not openly call attention to the text. Recognising the play's celebrity allows for ways to conceptualise stagings on their own terms, rejecting notions of textual fidelity in favour of participatory and interactive play, even when they appear in less obviously appropriative performative texts such as the yoga *Hamlet*. A theory of the celebrity text, then, allows us to think more theoretically about performances such as Phyllida Lloyd's 2017 *Julius Caesar* or Watermill's 2001 *Rose Rage*, as well as recognising the dialogic performative relationship that a play such as Taylor Mac's 2019 *Gary* has with *Titus Andronicus*.

When a Shakespeare play acquires a celebrity of its own, the willing suspension of disbelief becomes considerably more difficult to achieve as performance conditions us – both as practitioners and critics – to assume an anthropomorphic stance and assume that the role will always yield to accommodate the body that intends to control it, even when the role is familiar to the point of being a trope. Staging *Hamlet* elicits paratextual expectations that are defined partly by the play – think, for example, of Hamlet's madness, his acerbic humour, or the technical requirements of the soliloquies – but also by its status as a Great Role. *Hamlet*, described by Oskar Eustis (2017) as 'the greatest dramatic work in the history of literature', is unarguably the definitive role of an actor's career. Susannah Clapp (2015) echoes Roach's understanding of celebrity when she explains that for Hamlet, 'what matters is not the order of the speeches, or some adventurous departure – not even the range of his performance. Another, more elusive quality is crucial'. While Clapp (2015) cannot quite define what this thing is, she articulates it in terms of fame; it is, she suggests, 'the difference between a thinker and an administrator, and perhaps between a classical actor and a star'. Only a fellow celebrity, she implies, can fully explain Hamlet.

Performances of *Hamlet*, therefore, are arguably as defined by its status as 'one of the glories of world literature' (Croall 2018: 1) as they are by the text itself. Put simply, when it comes to Hamlet, its celebrity is frequently conflated with heroism, by virtue of its identity as a Great Role, and compounded by the renown of those who play him. In spite of Hamlet's ineffectual grandstanding during *The Mousetrap* or at Ophelia's funeral, his misogyny, and a level of self-obsession that can, for example, only value Horatio's life for its capacity to tell his story, Hamlet's affiliation with Clapp's elusive star quality makes it the domain of leading male (and occasionally female) actors, who subject Hamlet to the tropes of masculinity that are often attached to leading men in both popular entertainment and commercial theatre culture. Hamlet's celebrity, rather than his personality, make him magnetic, and this makes demands on producers who are then perhaps required to choose between a classical actor and a 'star', and also works on actors who want to prove themselves worthy of the role. These political ecologies are essential for objects to contribute as active things. *American Moor*'s discussion of the limited classical roles available to actors of colour shows the extent to which all of these processes are shaped by external ideological, cultural and economic factors.

Celebrity Intersections in Sam Gold's *Hamlet*

In 2017 the Public Theatre presented a mildly controversial production of *Hamlet*, directed by Sam Gold and featuring movie star Oscar Isaac. The production had previously been scheduled as part of Theatre for a New Audience's (TFANA) 2017 season, but the 'pretty aggressive adaptation/ cut of the play' was deemed unsuitable 'because Theatre for a New Audience does not produce Shakespeare adaptations' (Barone 2016). TFANA's attempt to isolate the text away from the adaptive collaboration of Gold's direction returns us to the paradox of the inescapable yet invisible script. It is perplexing, to say the least, that an artistic director of a classical theatre company would insist on the sanctity of text, but TFANA's sour observation that the replacement play, *Measure for Measure*, 'would make half the money than "Hamlet" would have' made acknowledges the extent to which the celebrity of the text matters (Barone 2016). Gold conceptualised the play as a domestic contemporary tragedy, with a cast of nine and a small, flexible, red playing space in the Anspacher Theatre upstairs at the Public's Astor Place building, with audience on three sides, and no constructed set, only props. These practical choices not only shied away from the paratextual myth of Hamlet's nobility, but promised a subtle rejection of authenticity, ostensibly teasing its ability to redistribute the matter of the play and find something new. This meta-critical production framework, when combined with the paratextual production drama, established a degree of uncertainty as to the fidelity of the production and drew attention to the script.

The uneasily juxtaposed acting styles at play within the production suggested the diverse ways in which the celebrity text exerted its agency on different actors. Isaac, a lead actor in the newest *Star Wars* movies, is a charismatic, established movie star, following the pattern of handsome, young, well-credentialled actors taking on the role of Hamlet. Public Theatre artistic director Oskar Eustis's accompanying programme note makes clear the assumption that Isaac has earned his right to play the Danish Prince. Eustis tells the story of watching 'the brilliant young Oscar' at his first audition, then lists Isaac's considerable Shakespearean accomplishments for the Public Theatre before reminding the audience that 'he has since gone on to extraordinary stardom and recognition'; he acknowledges that even though Isaac's performance in *Show Me a Hero* is 'one of the greatest television achievements of the millennium', 'his roots have always been in the theatre' (Eustis 2017). Eustis's note demonstrates the celebrity paradox facing actors who as 'stars must be able to play a range of characters in order to show their skill . . . while at the same time each performance must hold to the sense of the star in order for the associations of that star to imbue the performance with meaning and pleasure' (Mills 2010: 192). This paratextual material is only unusual in how it makes explicit the rationale that so often drives the casting of Hamlet. Nonetheless, Eustis's rationale is indicative of *Hamlet*'s celebrity as part of a larger ecology of Shakespeare that is 'lively, affective, and signaling' (Bennett 2010: 117), absorbing human exceptionalism as part of a larger materialist assemblage. Framed as an aspirational role, then, Hamlet demanded a particular performance from Isaac that was psychologically realistic, the 'method' acting that movie stardom celebrates, to reify Isaac's skills and validate Eustis's praise (Eustis himself, as a celebrity director, brings his own affective network into play). As a result, Isaac's Hamlet was required to continually negotiate the enforced absence of the fourth wall in his performance. As Gold's *Hamlet* manifests itself as an unstable Shakespeare object, both intimate and strange, it makes visible Isaac's work towards inhabiting a Hamlet that is predicated on twentieth-century psychological interpretation and haunted by the spectre of Great Actors. Isaac's performance, framed as it was by Eustis's fanfare, ostensibly resisted the play's 'thing-power', but the search for new insights only led him to other objects, particularly as he sought to illustrate Hamlet's madness. Isaac walked around in his underwear, hurled lasagne around the stage, and sat in a reserved seat in the audience, speaking to patrons as though they were part of the performance. Sitting in the front row of the audience for the beginning of *The Mousetrap*, Isaac spoke his comments to audience members, waiting delightedly for their uncomfortable responses before moving to sit with Ophelia and watch the play. Isaac's use of audience members as props speaks to the interchangeability of object and human in the theatrical space, drawing attention to the presence of the script even as he maintained his character.

The casting of Keegan-Michael Key, of *Key & Peele* fame, however, more overtly recognised the ways in which the materialities at play shaped his performance, arguably to greater payoff. Comedy is a genre that thrives on the detachment of its performers, thereby activating its own set of (occasionally disruptive) expectations upon the theatrical assemblage. Key's casting, however, recognised the celebrity power of the text as it worked on him and continually drew attention to performance's transparency in a manner that ultimately endowed his performance with great emotional affect. Perhaps unsurprisingly, in spite of a career equally as prestigious and popular as that of Isaac, Key's casting lacked the equivalent fanfare. The reasons for this are varied. Key is a television actor and a comedian, which stands in stark opposition to Isaac's reputation as a 'serious' actor in film which, as Eustis's note explained, generated 'extraordinary stardom and recognition' (Eustis 2017). Key is also a biracial actor and subject to the 'parameters and limitations imposed by racial bias' that Keith Hamilton Cobb explored in his play *American Moor* (qtd in Yargo 2019); he also lacks the 'Internet's boyfriend' heart-throb status that Isaac enjoys. Unexpectedly for a comedian, Key was not cast as the gravedigger, but instead he doubled as both Horatio and the Player King. As well as contributing to the materialist value of his celebrity, Key's profile as a comedic celebrity in his own right was empowered by the detached critical eye that comedy demands. Comedy is a style of performance 'at odds with the dominant realist tone of classical Hollywood' (Mills 2010: 194) and is a style that 'plays with modes of representation and performance, offering audiences pleasure in such disruption and experimentation' (Mills 2010: 194) because it facilitates a more participatory experience. A clown invites recognition of the extrafictional status of staged classical theatre, treating the objects on stage – including the audience and script – as his own ludic props. *Hamlet*, therefore, worked on Key differently than it did Isaac, encouraging a more self-consciously visible process that, as Ben Brantley (2017) notes, enabled the audience to 'pass the four-hour production with some of the best storytellers [it has] ever met'.

As a comedian, Key's deliberate positioning outside the drama empowered him to explicitly confront the textual materiality of performance – 'when you cannot abject your abjection . . . you laugh' (Limon 2000: 74) – and the laughter he generated reflected the corporeality of the text as the basis of his performance. At the opening of the play, Key greeted the audience members as they found their seats, gleefully informing us all of the four-hour run time and ad-libbing jokes about *Hamlet* and the audience's response to his announcement. Because of the small company, the actors were required to be on stage for the duration of the play, and as Brantley (2017) noted, they engaged the audience: 'many of their observations are pitched directly to us, as if the audience were their grievance committee', which further heightened the stand-up element of Key's overall performance. As the Player King, Key further drew attention to the artificiality of performance by deliberately overacting in *The Mousetrap*. The contrast between acting styles was made further evident when Isaac delivered the 'speak the speech' instructions with particular emphasis at Key. Hamlet's warning, to 'o'erstep not the modesty of nature' (III.ii.17–18), sets up a paradigm of invisible performance, and his emphasis on the modesty of nature is particularly applied to the clown, whose excess threatens to undo the imitation of humanity that Hamlet craves. For Hamlet – and for Isaac – successful performance rests on the actor's ability to mitigate the text's artificiality, to 'beget a temperance that may give it smoothness' (III.ii.6–7), but for a clown, success is defined by the visibility of the text, and the warning falls flat.

Key made a mockery of overblown acting styles during his protracted and comical death in *The Mousetrap*, which led Isaac's Hamlet to sit with his head in his hands – a moment in which these two diverse acting styles potently overlapped. By allowing a performance that both drew attention to and was affected by his own particular celebrity, Key participated in a rich materialist history of clowning in relation to Shakespeare. In the Player King's transition from a nuanced performance of Hecuba to the slapstick demise of Gonzago, Key's deliberate choices to disrupt the text provided much-needed comic relief in the lengthy production. The Player King's choices were treated with an affectionate indulgence by Isaac that threatened to destabilise his own commitment to his role as he smiled wearily at *The Mousetrap*, and for a split second – as I wonder if the actor was fighting back a giggle – the performance was destabilised. Arguably, in addition to newness, these are also the moments that fans of the celebrity text live for. Rather than alienate his audience, however, Key's affective acting style was crucial to the pathos of the production and reinforced Gold's vision of the play as a domestic tragedy. Doubling of roles inevitably leads to the conflation of a performer's attributes across the parts they play, and the collapse of the Player King and Horatio, as the only characters that Hamlet seems genuinely to profess enthusiasm for, intersected Key's vibrant performance with Isaac's. At the close of the play, the absurdity of the Player King's death was powerfully mirrored in Horatio's gently humorous offer to demonstrate himself as 'more an antique Roman than a Dane' and commit suicide with his friend. The offer, matched with an exaggerated mock drinking from Hamlet's poisoned cup, disrupted the melodrama of the moment, turning the gesture into a comic act specifically designed to make his dying friend smile. Ironically, Key's recognition of the artificiality of the text he was performing resulted in one of the most unexpectedly moving moments of the production and offered (for this audience member anyway) the type of revelation that Cote so consistently craves, and that brings us back to favourite plays time and again.

Coda: Never-ending Performance

This chapter has relied primarily on my own recollection of Gold's *Hamlet*, as well as Ben Brantley's *New York Times* review of the play, and at present the production is not available in digital form. The material traces left by Brantley, other critics, fans and even this chapter are now a part of *Hamlet*'s performance archive, inviting memorial or speculative reconstruction that will, in turn, contribute to perpetuating the fame of Hamlet as a Great Role. Theatre is, at its core, an act of imaginative good faith and, as such, the theatrical staging can be expanded to accommodate all dimensions of the spectator experience – the paratextual expectation (or imagining), the onsite experience itself, and the memory (or speculation for those unable to attend the performance) leave materialist traces that contribute to an archontic celebrity of *Hamlet* that draws from its vibrant matter and tries to contain it. New materialism alerts us to the affective visibility of the Shakespearean text on stage, and what is dramatised is the ways this affective object works on its actors and audience as part of a longer process of dramatic growth. Through their engagement with the text as a vibrant celebrity object, both Isaac and Key inserted themselves into an ongoing materialist history of the play, both drawing from, and contributing to, its enduring fame.

Notes

1. Hans-Thies Lehmann defines dramatic theatre as 'anchored in bourgeois life' (2016: 300), and as a movement that is primarily located between the eighteenth and twentieth centuries. I, however, apply the term more broadly to refer to performed productions that are defined by their linearity and adherence to a script, and the postmodern deconstructed performance form that Lehmann terms 'post-dramatic'. Work by, for example, the RSC, the ASC, the National Theatre and many other mainstream companies falls into the 'dramatic' category; performances by such organisations as The Wooster Group, Forced Entertainment and Punchdrunk belong to the 'post-dramatic'.
2. There are, of course, other materialist values to consider. As Blackwell and Sawyer implicitly suggest, the networks of a celebrity play are often expressly utilised for economic profit and shaped through connections with other known quantities, such as actors, theatre companies and sites.
3. Even Blackwell's excellent work on Richard III's recent celebrity attaches him to the person, centralising embodiment as she recognises the two facets of Ricardian celebrity – 'first, the interconnected and self-sustaining distinctiveness of the theatrical Richard and second, that of the stars who

perform or adapt him' (Blackwell 2018: 144). As Loren Glass (2015) illustrates, studies of 'literary celebrity' almost exclusively centre around the author and not the work.

Bibliography

Barone, J. (2016), 'Director Pulls *Hamlet* from Theater for a New Audience', *New York Times*, 13 July, <https://www.nytimes.com/2016/07/14/theater/director-pulls-hamlet-from-theater-for-a-new-audience.html> [accessed 18 August 2020].

Bennett, J. (2010), *Vibrant Matter: A Political Ecology of Things*, Durham, NC: Duke University Press.

Blackwell, A. (2018), *Shakespearean Celebrity in the Digital Age: Fan Cultures and Remediation*, New York: Palgrave Macmillan.

Brantley, B. (2017), 'Review: The Greatest of Danes, as Oscar Isaac Takes On *Hamlet*', *New York Times*, 13 July, <https://www.nytimes.com/2017/07/13/theater/hamlet-review-oscar-isaac-public-theater.html> [accessed 18 August 2020].

Carlson, M. (2001), *The Haunted Stage: Theatre as Memory Machine*, Ann Arbor: University of Michigan Press.

Clapp, S. (2015), 'Genius, Coward . . . or Madman? Why Hamlet Gives Actors the Ultimate Test', *Observer*, 5 August, <https://www.theguardian.com/culture/2015/aug/09/hamlet-ultimate-actors-test-benedict-cumberbatch> [accessed 18 August 2020].

Cote, D. (2009), '*Hamlet*: Jude Law as the Melancholy Dane', *Time Out*, 4 October, <https://www.timeout.com/newyork/theatre/hamlet-5> [accessed 1 April 2020].

Cote, D. (2020), 'As Hamlet, Ruth Negga is an Emo Dreamboat with a Vengeance', *Observer*, 2 October, <https://observer.com/2020/02/ruth-negga-hamlet-review/> [accessed 18 August 2020].

Croall, J. (2018), *Performing Hamlet: Actors in the Modern Age*, London: Bloomsbury.

DeKosnik, A. (2016), *Rogue Archives: Digital Cultural Memory and Media Fandom*, Cambridge, MA: MIT Press.

Eustis, O. (2017), *Hamlet*, programme notes.

Gardner, L. (2018), 'What Makes an Actor Great?', *The Stage*, 24 October, <https://www.thestage.co.uk/features/2018/what-makes-a-great-actor-lyn-gardner/> [accessed 18 August 2020].

Glass, L. (2015), 'Brand Names: A Brief History of Literary Celebrity', in D. P. Marshall and S. Redmond (eds), *A Companion to Celebrity*, New York: Wiley Blackwell, pp. 55–73.

Hamilton Cobb, K. (2020), *American Moor*, London: Methuen Drama.

Hartley, A. J. (2006), 'Page and Stage Again: Rethinking Renaissance Character Phenomenologically', in S. Werner (ed.), *New Directions in Renaissance Drama and Performance Studies*, New York: Palgrave, pp. 77–93.

Holl, J. (2013), 'Stars Indeed: The Celebrity Culture of Shakespeare's London', unpublished dissertation, CUNY Graduate Center, New York.

Jones, A. (2015), 'Material Traces: Performativity, Artistic "Work", and New Concepts of Agency', *TDR: The Drama Review*, 59:4, 18–35.

Kidnie, M. J. (2009), *Shakespeare and the Problem of Adaptation*, New York: Routledge.

Komporaliy, J. (2017), *Radical Revival as Adaptation*, New York: Palgrave Macmillan.

Lanier, D. M. (2011), 'Post-Textual Shakespeare', *Shakespeare Survey*, 64, 145–62.

Lanier, D. M. (2017), 'Afterword', in C. Desmet, N. Loper and J. Casey (eds), *Shakespeare/Not Shakespeare*, New York: Palgrave Macmillan, pp. 293–306.

Lavender, A. (2016), *Performance in the Twenty-First Century: Theatres of Engagement*, Abingdon: Routledge.

Lehmann, H. (2004), 'Shakespeare's Grin: Remarks on World Theatre of Forced Entertainment', in J. Helmer and F. Malzacher (eds), *Not Even a Game Anymore: The Theatre of Forced Entertainment*, Berlin: Alexander Verlag, pp. 103–17.

Lehmann, H. (2006), *Postdramatic Theatre*, trans. K. Jürs-Munby, London: Routledge.

Lehmann, H. (2016), *Tragedy and Dramatic Theatre*, London: Routledge.

Limon, J. (2000), *Stand Up Comedy in Theory, or, Abjection in America*, Durham, NC: Duke University Press.

Mills, B. (2010), 'Being Rob Brydon: Performing the Self in Comedy', *Celebrity Studies*, 1:2, 189–201.

Redmond, S. (2018), *Celebrity*, Abingdon: Routledge.

Roach, J. (2007), *It*, Ann Arbor: University of Michigan Press.

Sack, D. (2015), *After Live: Possibility, Potentiality, and the Future of Performance*, Ann Arbor: University of Michigan Press.

Schneider, R. (2015), 'New Materialisms and Performance Studies', *TDR: The Drama Review*, 59:4, 7–17.

Shakespeare, W. (2008), *The Norton Shakespeare*, ed. Stephen Greenblatt et al., New York: W. W. Norton.

West, W. N. (2006), 'Replaying Early Modern Performances', in S. Werner (ed.), *New Directions in Renaissance Drama and Performance Studies*, New York: Palgrave, pp. 30–50.

Worthen, W. B. (2014), *Shakespeare Performance Studies*, Cambridge: Cambridge University Press.

Yargo, J. (2109), '"All this life made this play": An Interview with Keith Hamilton Cobb', *LA Review of Books*, 19 January, <https://lareviewofbooks.org/article/all-this-life-made-this-play-an-interview-with-keith-hamilton-cobb/> [accessed 18 August 2020].

11

'The Promised End': Shakespeare and Extinction

Michael Lutz

This chapter supposes, first of all, that Shakespeare's *King Lear* and its infamous panorama of disaster is not – or not only – a bleak representation of nihilism, destruction and despair. Rather, I take the play as an invitation to speculate about futures radically different from and, in some cases, admittedly hostile to present modes of social life. But by bringing *Lear* into conversation with speculative realist philosophy – particularly Ray Brassier's theorisation of extinction – I aim to recontextualise the critical tradition of Shakespeare's futurity in a moment when economic, political and ecological disasters loom ever larger. If, in following Brassier, we recognise extinction as a cosmological fact according to contemporary science, an inevitable annihilation where matter itself is destined to dissipate into elementary particles, how might Shakespeare's work help us theorise and accept a future not of tradition, heritage and continuity, but rather one of difference, loss and discontinuity? I outline how in the process of adaptation, Shakespeare's *Lear* becomes 'disaggregated' across a variety of media and genres, from avant-garde film to contemporary novels (Desmet 2017: 1). In the theory of adaptation put forth by Christy Desmet for her study of 'Alien Shakespeares', to recognise Shakespeare or his texts as potentially 'disaggregated' means to see them not as self-identical entities or unitary concepts, but as conglomerations of particular systems, processes, or signs of meaning making that can be decomposed, 'carved up and recombined' in novel ways (Desmet 2017: 6).

To understand Shakespeare and his plays as 'disaggregated' is to see them in the 'variable' capacities with which this collection is concerned. This variability can be understood as an extension of Jane Bennett's theory of vibrant materiality, where non-human objects – such as the textual and cultural materials that constitute 'Shakespeare' – are 'vivid entities not entirely reducible to the contexts in which (human) subjects set them, never entirely exhausted by their semiotics' (2010: 5). Desmet and Bennett's rearticulations of speculative philosophy and object-oriented ontology draw attention to the reciprocating loops of stimulus and response by which cultural production operates: Desmet writes elsewhere that Shakespearean appropriation might be better understood as a mode of 'reception' built on 'contingent moments of recognition and insight', when a text's appropriation of another signals for itself and for its audience the 'acceptance of responsibility for the bond that binds disparate narratives conceptually and emotionally in the face of manifest differences' (Desmet 2014: 55). Thus, by always expanding towards an apocalyptic horizon, *Lear* and its adaptations develop a grammar for imagining futures that, by representing the obliteration of the present (and the present's Shakespeare), might also suggest opportunities for radically different futures, and radically different Shakespeares.

Beginning with Jean-Luc Godard's *King Lear* (1987), I situate modernity's conception of humanity's end in the film's post-Chernobyl wasteland. This is a scientific eschatology, however, and I compare it to the theologically apocalyptic meanings historically attributed to Shakespeare's play. After noting the evacuation of such religious themes in Godard – and their replacement with the modern technological idol of cinema – I look to Emily St John Mandel's 2014 novel *Station Eleven*. The novel's preoccupation with Shakespeare and his enduring fame, through even the global collapse brought on by an influenza pandemic, might seem to offer only an affirmation of the old bromide of Shakespeare's timelessness. But I propose that its reliance on Shakespeare might read differently, suggesting Shakespeare's endurance through disruption is to be better understood as his disruption through endurance. I conclude by turning to a video game that is more definitively concerned with Shakespeare after human extinction, 2017's *Nier: Automata*, which contains an unusually bleak – and disconcertingly hilarious – adaptation that imagines just what Shakespeare might mean after we're gone.

Though the following sections of this chapter are intended to be read in order, and though they reference each other in a gradual development of the central concerns outlined in this introduction while looking at a series of texts in chronological sequence, I do not intend any one of the 'versions' of Shakespeare and extinction they imagine to be embraced with finality by the reader. Rather, by insisting that each of the following sections is a different possible 'ending' to the investigation of what Shakespeare means in relation to human extinction, I want to emphasise the variety of valid possibilities that are opened to us as scholars, teachers and thinkers when we take speculation and Shakespeare seriously.

Ending One

Early in Jean-Luc Godard's *King Lear*, the narrator and protagonist, William Shakespeare Jr, the Fifth, announces that 'suddenly, it was the time of Chernobyl', referring to the catastrophic nuclear disaster that occurred during the film's shooting, after which 'everything disappeared'. But this ending is also a beginning, as Shakespeare tells us: 'And then after a while everything came back. Electricity, houses, cars, everything except culture and . . . me.' Insofar as Godard's *Lear* has a plot in the traditional sense, this is it: Shakespeare Jr has been tasked to travel the world and recover the lost works of his 'ancestor', the original Shakespeare. 'We're in a time now when movies and more generally art have been lost, do not exist', he says later, 'and they have to somehow be reinvented.' Of course, historically speaking, not everything was 'lost' with Chernobyl – but what seems important for Godard was that it could have been. What worth is art, or cinema, or Shakespeare, in a world where mutually assured destruction and global catastrophe are very real possibilities?

Timothy Murray argues that Godard's experimental film engages in cinema's 'new baroque era caught between clashing systems of analog and digital representation' (2008: 98), paralleling the technological and social innovations/disruptions of early modern visual art and culture that precipitated what we historically term the Baroque period. But to press this association a little further means to see in Godard not just a transhistorical resonance of media upheaval – for Murray, the fact that Godard engages with Shakespeare's *King Lear*, written and performed at the dawn of the Baroque period, seems mostly like a happy accident. This chapter, however, supposes that even though its status as an adaptation of Shakespeare's *Lear* in the traditional sense is fraught, Godard is performing a kind of speculative Shakespearean criticism.

At the end of Shakespeare's play, Lear enters howling and carrying in his arms the dead Cordelia. 'Is this the promised end?' asks Kent, to which Edgar replies: 'Or image of that horror' (V.iii.261–2).[1] It takes such an astounding catachresis to capture the magnitude of despair they feel: Kent wonders if they are witnessing the biblical Judgment Day, and even if they aren't, Edgar replies, it is certainly an 'image' of such a thing, a representation or anticipation of it. And *Lear* has long been understood as a kind of apocalyptic play, though the apocalypse it concerns is largely understood to be, in some way, the Christian one. William Elton's extended study, *King Lear and the Gods*, provides a useful summary of critics taking what he calls the 'optimistic Christian' position of this 'promised end' and finds them all lacking: 'the devastating fifth act shatters, more violently than an earlier apostasy might have done, the foundations of faith itself' (1966: 337). The sting is lessened somewhat by Elton's insistence that the faith shattered is (within the world of the play, at least) only a pagan one and hence reserves some hope for Christian futurity. Joseph Wittreich, less interested in situating the play within a specific Christian narrative topology, instead notes its imbrication within prophetic and apocalyptic discursive modes that include Tudor and Stuart views of the Christian revelation, but are not wholly ensconced by them, since the play also evokes traditions of Merlinic prophecy and apocalypse. For Wittreich, apocalypse thus emerges as a persistent historical metaphor, 'a record of man's [sic] spiritual and psychic history' (1984: 96) through the trials and tribulations of life, projected outward on to the world, and culminating in its best cases with a kind of progressive evolution of the human spirit and the possibility of a better tomorrow, no matter the horrors of today.

Godard's apocalypse is not so cheery, as the disaster of Chernobyl synecdochally invokes two depressingly plausible ends of modernity: nuclear war and human-caused environmental catastrophe. These are not endings of righteous judgment, and after them no better tomorrow seems conceivable. Instead, those who come next are imagined to be consigned to lives of misery in our rubble. Indeed, in their most extreme forms, both weapons of mass destruction and environmental collapse gesture towards possibilities of the most total ending of all: human extinction. What can art possibly do in the face of this potential for a new 'Last Judgment' outside the bounds of Christian or pagan eschatologies? Godard's *Lear* posits an answer to this question. A little over midway through the film, in his search for his ancestor's art, Shakespeare Jr meets with the cinema guru Professor Pluggy (played by Godard himself) in Pluggy's editing bay, where the professor is working on an experimental new form of montage.

Pluggy, though glimpsed earlier in the film, here remains unseen. An immobile figure (Pluggy's servant, Edgar) stands in the corner, shrouded in darkness, while on a set of dual monitors beside him a series of strange images – some representational, some abstract, some by Henry Fuseli, some by Tex Avery – blend together in succession. This is all intercut with shots of a diorama, a cardboard box full of small plastic dinosaurs illuminated in fits and starts by an incandescent bulb being swung, apparently by Pluggy, above it.

'What's it all for, Professor? Please?' Junior asks. The shot lingers on the diorama, and Pluggy responds in his strange, gravelly voice: 'The Last Judgment'. Junior, with notebook and pen in hand, scribbles as Pluggy continues his lecture: 'And you, my dear Mr. Shakespeare, you see, all those reckless words for the simple things on earth. That's only life, and how it works.'

'Thank you indeed for this definition of life', Junior responds, quite earnestly, but he has apparently missed the point. 'No', Pluggy insists, 'not life. Only an image of life.'

'An image?' asks Junior. 'What's that again?'

A pause, and the lecture resumes:

> The image is a pure creation of the soul. It cannot be born of a comparison, but of a reconciliation of two realities, that are more or less far apart. The more the connections between these two realities are decent and true, the stronger they get to be, the more it will have emotive power.

Shots of Junior, Edgar next to his montage set-up and the diorama are now intercut with shots of a strobing light illuminating something like a cinema, complete with the hints of silhouetted people looking at the screen where the flashing light is being projected – but this might also just be footage from an improperly loaded camera. Pluggy goes on:

> Analogy is a medium of creation, it is a resemblance of connections. The power or virtue of the created image depends on the nature of these connections. What is great is not the image, but the emotion that it provokes. If the latter is great, then one esteems the image at its measure. The emotion thus provoked is true because it is born outside of all imitation, all evocation, and all resemblance.

These scenes have, for the most part, been interpreted as Godard's own ruminations on cinema, the power of the image and the technique of montage – and certainly the self-reflexive quality of the film supports such readings. But I quote them at length for what they tell us about how we might understand Godard's film's relation not just to Shakespeare's play, but to the apocalypse it images/imagines. Of particular interest to me is the negativity of Pluggy/Godard's thesis, the notion that the emotive power of an image does not reside in the representation itself but in its ability to evoke what it is not.

This is the significance of Pluggy's strange diorama: the toy dinosaurs remind us that humans are not the first species to face extinction on this planet. The wavering light over these plastic reproductions of prehistoric life recalls those actual creatures' end, when 66 million years ago an asteroid or comet 10–15 metres in diameter struck what we call today the Yucatán peninsula, kicking up so much debris into the air that it blocked out the sun, resulting in worldwide climate disruption and the extinction of some 75 per cent of extant species. Godard here reinvents Shakespeare's art in light (so to speak) of the realities of species extinction, answering Kent and Edgar's call and response from *King Lear* V.iii: every promised end is only ever an image of the horror of such extinction, since the thing itself would extinguish all capacity for human thought and reflection. The image is all we will ever have; as Pluggy says, it is an analogy, a mechanism of resemblance that produces a 'reconciliation of two realities . . . more or less far apart', and whose merit is judged by 'the emotion it creates', by the way imagistic synthesis can surpass the particulars of what is seen to allow access to a feeling 'born outside of all imitation, all evocation, and all resemblance'.

What Godard's entire project suggests, then, and what the reams of criticism on the play's apocalyptic tenor support, is that Shakespeare's *Lear* has historically functioned in and of itself as a kind of 'image of that horror': as an instrument of comparing one's present situation with the realities of future death, whether at the individual level, or even the world's end in either a religious or (as Godard refits it) scientific-secular register. The play's ability to incite attendant feelings of desolation are, of course, well attested, and readings of it tend to imply or validate metaphysical frameworks where the suffering, carnage and death visited upon the characters are redeemed through a kind of deferred rebirth or, in the case of Nahum Tate's notorious adaptation, justified by discarding the queasiest elements of Shakespeare's plot. Indeed, Tate's adaptation, by preserving the happy ending of the traditional King Leir legend with Lear and Cordelia's survival, might suggest how strongly Shakespeare's first audiences echoed Kent's question about the 'promised end' – the death of Lear and Cordelia is simply not how this story was supposed to go. Nevertheless, so it has.

Looking at the state of the world today – after the bloody conquest of the Americas and the Atlantic slave trade, the Holocaust, the bombings of Hiroshima and Nagasaki, and in the midst of a global far-right resurgence during an endless war carried out by an oligarchic superpower, all in the shadow of looming climate catastrophe, none of which, one hopes, was *supposed* to happen – we too might feel something like what Kent feels.

Is this how it ends? The myth of Western modernity said otherwise: allegedly, we were working towards a better tomorrow, and the future was going to have fewer problems and more happiness. Yet here we are! And in this context, to say that Shakespeare's play is nihilistic (that is, the suffering of the characters therein has no greater purpose) would be either uncontroversial or glib. It would simply invert the error of Elton's 'Christian optimists' by tethering the play to a view of history that writes off the reality and experience of suffering and the idea of a cataclysmic end in service of some greater notion about what or how the world 'is'. Godard avoids this error, however, instead recognising in the Cold War the importance of Shakespeare's play as an image for considering the suffering and unexpected disaster rife in a world with a palpable, material end in sight. Godard is a Shakespeare user in the sense theorised by Fazel and Geddes, part of 'a continuously expanding archive that accommodates the far-reaching permutations of a network of linguistic, aesthetic, and cultural associations' (2017: 3), subject to the fluctuations of a culture's needs and desires. Godard uses *King Lear* to raise the question of the role of art in the face of the real possibility of human extinction, and he recognises that in order to even ask this question, the original text must in some sense be 'reinvented'.

Many people throughout history have recognised that they were destined to die, but today we are in the unique position of knowing that we all might die *at once*, or in such close succession to one another that, in the global chronology, it might as well be all at once. And as modern science would have it, this is not necessarily so much accident as it is inevitable fact: even if we avoid the wrath of climate change or nuclear war, current projections by physicists have mapped out the general arc of the physical universe such that it is reasonable to assume, in the words of philosopher Christopher Norris, 'that human beings and all other sentient (including extra-terrestrial) life-forms will be subject to total extinction with the heat-death and final dissolution of the universe' (2013: 41). Norris is summarising the position of the 'neo-nihilist' philosopher Ray Brassier, who considers extinction as 'the thought of the absence of thought' (2007: 229–30). For Brassier, the new 'Last Judgment' is not the sorting of the good and the wicked by an omniscient creator at the end of all things, but rather how to grapple with a radically non-human world that will extinguish us for no other reason than that it seems built to do so.

Godard does not speculate this far into the future – but he does speculate. Indeed, as I have been arguing, he rebuilds Shakespeare and *Lear* into an instrument for such apocalyptic speculation (reflection, contemplation, theorisation), making it a cousin to the sort of 'organon of extinction' Brassier advocates for in his philosophy (2007: 239). In a radical rereading of Freud, Brassier conflates philosophy's 'will to know' with a 'will to nothingness', understood as a version of the Freudian death-drive. Returning to Freud's original hypothesis that there is 'an urge inherent in organic life to restore an earlier state of things', that is, that the aim of organic life is to return to the 'initial state' of inorganic, non-living matter (Freud qtd in Brassier 2007: 235), Brassier argues that philosophy's 'will to know' – the will to rationally master the world and life within it by increasing and perfecting human knowledge – in fact seeks much the same end. By aspiring to resolve the traumatic antagonism between a non-human world and human life, Brassier argues that philosophy in fact gestures towards the conditions of its own abolition in the return to inorganic matter, or in other words, the reality, inevitability and universality of death:

> Just as the reality of the inorganic is not merely a function of the existence of the organic, so the reality of death is not merely a function of life's past, or of its future. Death, understood as the principle of decontraction driving the contractions of organic life is not a past or future state towards which life tends, but rather the originary *purposelessness* which compels all purposefulness, whether organic or psychological. (Brassier 2007: 236)

The above applies not only to individual death, for by centring death as the precondition of what we understand as life, Brassier calls for the philosophical reckoning of death at the level of the species, which is to say, extinction. Since our extinction can be thought about but not experienced – for to experience our extinction necessarily entails the loss of the sensory and cognitive apparatuses through which we process experience – the event becomes 'transcendental yet not ideal', a hard limit to human meaning as it is phenomenologically anchored, and 'in this regard, it is precisely the extinction of meaning that clears the way for the intelligibility of extinction' (Brassier 2007: 238).

Godard, recognising the potential for the extinction of humanity and hence the extinction of artistic meaning in the shadow of Chernobyl, chastises Shakespeare Jr, who thanks Pluggy for a 'definition of life' that the mad professor insists is not a definition but an 'image'. An image, as Pluggy/Godard says, is true not because of what it is but because of the feeling or sensation it mediates, and so the instrument is useful not because it offers a solution to problems of meaning, death and extinction, but because it provides a sociocultural space in which we can communally grapple with these problems' associated affects/effects. While we may contextualise *Lear* as a drama of early modern religious apocalypse, there is nothing in it that bars us from understanding it as a 'modern' one: the gods that Gloucester says torture humans in the way small boys torture flies are nowhere to be seen, figures of rhetoric only, and every misfortune that befalls the characters in the play – on the whole seeming to exceed any one discernible or just cause – can be traced back to nothing more than the fact that the characters exist in a world where human striving, whether good or bad, leads to death.

Ending Two

With Brassier's points in mind, and with the understanding of *Lear* so far developed, there is another ending to consider. While Godard's film offers cinema as the new medium through which the possibility of extinction and dissolution of meaning might be contemplated, it shies away from the more pressing concerns of our contemporary apocalypses. Godard's ruminations preserve the social comforts of Cold War postmodernism – towns, restaurants, beachside walks, film-editing bays – since it is only 'culture' (and by association, Shakespeare) that fails to return to the world in the wake of the nuclear age's technological nihilism. But twenty-first-century apocalyptic fiction is much more concerned with the material loss of 'modernity' itself. Emily St John Mandel's 2014 novel *Station Eleven* begins at the end of the world, which from the reader's perspective is introduced as a performance of *King Lear* in Toronto, on the night of the outbreak of a deadly strain of flu that will kill most of the world's population. The novel shuttles back and forth in time, from the days and years preceding 'the collapse' to the characters who live years after it, tracing the strange connections of family, friendship and coincidence that bridge the divide of the apocalypse.

Arthur Leander, an ageing Hollywood star making a go at stage acting, suffers a heart attack while playing Lear on the night of the outbreak; one of the children playing Lear's daughters in the production's inserted flashback scene, a girl named Kirsten, many years later travels through the remains of the Canadian/American Midwest with a band of musicians and actors called the Traveling Symphony. They perform 'classical, jazz, orchestral arrangements of pre-collapse pop songs – and Shakespeare' (Mandel 2014: 37). Indeed, 'audiences seemed to prefer Shakespeare', and as one of the leaders of the Symphony avers, 'People want what was best about the world' (2014: 38). There are some prickly assumptions embedded in these ideas, however, and it would be well to unpack them. Philip Smith has astutely pointed out how this notion of Shakespeare's universality, and the novel's apparent suggestion that his works contain 'the seeds of civilization', replicate an imperialist fantasy of taming native savagery through the importation of Anglophone culture (2016: 289–303).

This is indeed one possible reading of the novel and may even be the most common: it is easy to see how the book suggests that Shakespeare, in a sense, is a kind of basic substrate of 'civilisation', a bedrock to which we can be pared down but from which any number of new societies may spring forth. But there's more to it than that if we are going to take the reality – or at least the reality of the possibility – of a 'collapse' or a 'post-apocalypse' seriously. To assume that, after a disaster, things 'revert' to a more 'primitive' state of affairs in fact upholds a teleological and linear progression of 'civilisation', itself an artefact of imperialist thinking. True, the novel hints that the collapse of 'civilisation' might make Shakespeare more relevant; as one character puts it, 'Shakespeare had lived in a plague-ridden society with no electricity and so did the Traveling Symphony' (Mandel 2014: 288). But importantly, what this character sees as regression is what the novel presents as the future, or as a second character rejoins the first: 'the difference was that they'd seen electricity, they'd seen everything; they'd watched a civilization collapse, and Shakespeare hadn't' (2014: 288). This seems a direct reply to the assertion at the end of *Lear*, spoken variably by Edgar or Albany: 'The oldest hath borne most; we that are young / Shall never see so much, nor live so long' (V.iii.324–5). Shakespeare paints a future that, like Godard's vision of the world post-Chernobyl, is effectively over before it has come to be, lost in the wreckage of its past.

Is *Station Eleven* a representative of the 'fantasy of a harmed future', theorist Rebekah Sheldon's term for a recent trend in popular books and films that orbits the topic of dystopian, apocalyptic or outright foreclosed futurities? As she explains, the fantasy indicates 'our intense awareness of continuing mutations and movements, of material futurity', and, simply put, a concomitant denial of that mutable futurity (Sheldon 2016: 49). That is, Sheldon argues, these contemporary dystopias are born of our current sense that whatever the future holds, it is not for *us*. The fantasy of the harmed future is myopic: it privileges the present moment, and shudders at the inevitable loss of the things we take for granted, asserting in its melancholy doomsday premonitions that '*these forms, these relationships*, are the only ones we have' (Sheldon 2016: 50). For Western audiences, Shakespeare's *Lear* might be a primordial secular text of such fantasies, ending as it does with the implosion of ancient Britain's monarchy and the not terribly convincing plea, to 'the gored state sustain' (V.iii.319). In Shakespeare, the future is bleeding out. Though we as scholars might see the play as anticipating the dissolution of feudal monarchy, the rise of the bourgeois individual, the emergence of the capitalist state, or any number of other things, we must also recognise that the text itself insists that it looks into its own future and sees nothing.

Our privilege is that we need not take nothing as necessarily bad. It might in fact be liberating, in the sense theorised by Marika Rose and Anthony Paul Smith, who write in the context of teaching in the neoliberal university. In the face of a system that offers fantasies of institutional prestige and job security for increasingly few, while continuing to expand and exploit the precarity of many, Rose and Smith advocate that 'we give up on the desire to secure a future for our intellectual work', instead opting to 'give ourselves over to a joy in the work for its own sake', not knowing when or how we will be received by job and tenure committees or posterity (Rose and Smith 2019: 5). In such instances, they argue, we may 'see that we do this work for nothing' (2019: 5). They do not mean, of course, that we should labour for free, for no remuneration or material benefit; rather, 'nothing' here is intended as it has been developed in mystical religious traditions, 'where even at the heart of the meaning of nothingness there is a further undoing of meaning' (Rose and Smith 2019: 5). In such apophatic or negative theology, God or the creative principle is understood only through what it is not – not like a human, not like a dog, not like a book, not like a stone, not like the sky, for God would be greater than all these – until we are left with, simply, 'God is nothing'. But this nothingness, being God, also supersedes and indeed provides the grounding for everything that it is not – it becomes the strange realm of extinction, in Brassier's theory, the abundant nothingness of inorganic matter out of which all that is and is possible emerges. Why do we work? For nothing and towards nothing; we do not and cannot know the future.

But perhaps we can glimpse it. In the final pages of *Station Eleven*, Kirsten is offered a sign of the future: from the top of an airline control tower she sees the distant lights of a settlement that has reactivated its power grid. Thematically, to imagine this 'resurgence' of modernity as entwined with Shakespeare's continuance is tempting. And yet there is some ambiguity to recover here, should we embrace the nothing that *Lear* faces and interpret it as the mystical nothing described by Rose and Smith, or even the possibility of the obliteratively different futures that Sheldon calls for. Should the return of electricity be a 'return' to modernity, or to civilisation? To read the novel thus is to accept the idea that what the characters have lived in since the collapse – travelling from agrarian settlement to agrarian settlement, playing in exchange for supplies and board – was not some form of civilisation, though clearly it is. There are communities and travellers, cult leaders and librarians, all living and working and, of course, dying in a world that quite clearly follows not simply mid-century modernism but late-century postmodernism as well.

In the future of *Station Eleven*, most settlements visited by the Traveling Symphony are nestled in the remains of the commercial main streets of pre-collapse towns and interstate exchanges, with the Symphony practising in the parking lots of former Wal-Marts, and families taking up residence in almost compulsively named franchises: hotels such as the Motor Lodge, and restaurants such as IHOP, Wendy's and McDonald's. Portions of the novel even trace the development of the so-called 'Museum of Civilization', a settlement in and surrounding a regional airport in Michigan, where the Symphony ends up by the end of the story, and from which Kirsten views the distant electric lights. Mandel imagines the future coagulating around spaces that French anthropologist Marc Augé calls 'non-places', which are special spaces in contemporary capitalism 'formed in relation to certain ends (transport, transit, commerce, leisure)' (2009: 94). These spaces are unique to the present, Augé argues, for they are intended not to establish bonds of community or bear the weight of historical emplacement. They are rather designed for fleeting, characterless contact between isolated and often migratory individuals; and yet in Mandel's novel, the shells of postmodernity's endlessly replicable non-places become the beds of new communities, forced back into history as signs of a time that was and is no more. Along with Kirsten's vision atop the Museum of Civilization, this might indeed read as nostalgia for late capitalism – and certainly elements of the book invite such suspicions[2] – but the novel's insistence on situating itself in capitalism's ruins should remind us that any future is going to bear traces of this traumatic present. Shakespeare himself, being so culturally saturated, might in fact function as another version of the novel's gallery of 'non-places' that, like the big box stores and chain restaurants, have suddenly found themselves host to a new set of inhabitants ready to put them to new uses.

The Traveling Symphony has never been to the distant settlement Kirsten sees at the end of the novel. The troupe has gone very far afield by this point in the narrative, pulled from their normal itinerary into strange territory, and it's not clear if Shakespeare has any currency outside their regular route. It's plausible to think that Shakespeare survived aside from his use in the Traveling Symphony – but it would, perhaps, not be the same Shakespeare as the one we have come to know through these characters. And besides, just as people have managed without electricity for quite a while by now, must we assume the perfect coincidence of Shakespeare and futurity, or our fantasies of it?

Ending Three

What of a future where 'Shakespeare' as we understand him has changed so much it might qualify as a truly 'alien Shakespeare' – disaggregated, in Desmet's terms, nearly to the point of unrecognisability? Like Brassier's contemplations of extinction, this seems to be a limit that can be thought but not experienced. It is the sort of thing, in other words, that calls for *speculation*: derived from the Latin *specula*, meaning 'watchtower',[3] the word suggests that even the most outlandish act of speculation must acknowledge its situatedness, and indeed evokes where *Station Eleven* left us, with Kirsten atop an airport control tower looking at a distant and unfamiliar place. So, having established how *Lear* speculates and how its adaptations refurbish and modify the lens it provides, this chapter concludes by peering just outside its own parameters, away from films and printed texts to video games, and away from *King Lear* and its variations towards another play entirely.

Romeos and Juliets is the name of a brief interlude in the 2017 action game *Nier: Automata*. Set in the ludicrously distant future of AD 11495, the game has players inhabit the roles of two androids named 2B and 9S, a pair of special combat models who descend to Earth from an orbital military space station to aid the remaining androids in the fight against an army of 'Machines', a faction of robots created by a species of alien invaders in the distant past. For both androids and Machines, death means something different than it does for humans: android and Machine minds are periodically backed up to a central server, so when one perishes in combat their personalities and memories are downloaded into a replacement body that rejoins the fray. The invading aliens have gone into hiding while the remains of humanity have similarly fled to a bunker on the moon, resulting in a centuries-long proxy war between the effectively immortal androids and Machines.

In the first third of the game, 2B and 9S are tasked with clearing out an abandoned human amusement park that is now home to a mixture of hostile and non-hostile Machines. Disconcertingly, as 9S notes, the Machines here appear to be developing emotions and personalities, even as 2B insists this isn't possible. Nevertheless, many of the Machines – which generally look like walking industrial trash bins – appear in elaborate carnival costumes and wearing clown make-up, mechanically repeating 'What fun!' and 'Let's be happy together!' even as some of them open fire on 2B and 9S. After clearing out the enemies from the park, the pair meet Pascal, a Machine who is tired of fighting and has established a secret village where he and other pacifist Machines can live. If the player chooses to return to the amusement park, they will find it still occupied by similarly friendly Machines. Upon receiving a 'stamp' from a Machine at the front of the park, the player is challenged to explore all the attractions (or what remains of them) to collect a full stamp set.

Most stamps are found by speaking to Machines scattered around the map. However, if the player enters the massive, Disney-like fairytale castle in the park's centre, they find themselves in an auditorium just as the curtain rises. A lone Machine named 'Juliet 1' runs out into the spotlight, pronouncing, 'O Romeo, Romeo, wherefore art thou, Romeo?' She is then joined by another Machine, 'Romeo 1', who responds: 'Ah, Juliet, Juliet, wherefore art thou, Juliet?' At this point Juliet 2 enters: 'O Romeo, Romeo, which one of thou art Romeo?' The answer is provided by a new character, Romeo 2: 'Ah Juliet, Juliet, I am not wholly sure!' In a sudden turn of events, Juliet 3 enters to proclaim, 'O Romeo, Romeo, then let us cull thy numbers!' Romeo 3 now enters, more than happy to oblige: 'Ah Juliet, Juliet, then I shall take thy life!' The Machines then set to destroying one another on stage, complete with bizarre trash talk (Juliet 1: 'Die, Romeo! Thou stupid asshole!'). When only Juliet 3 remains standing, she soliloquises: 'My Romeos are no more. I have slain them each and all. I must join them anon.' She then explodes.

With the end of this production of *Romeos and Juliets* announced, the player can speak with the scattered Machines who observed the play. 'I haven't been this deeply moved by anything before!' says one, and most of the audience has similarly glowing reviews. But you cannot please everybody, and the one negative response, from a Machine standing off to the side of the crowd, is simply 'This play doesn't make any sense at all.' And while neither 2B nor 9S have any voiced thoughts on the drama, it is likely that the player feels closer to the unimpressed Machine than the play's adoring fans. Though Shakespeare is never mentioned, it's clear that we are to understand this short scene as part of the evolution exhibited by the Machines thus far, as they turn from their designated roles as alien weapons and – as is the case of the amusement park more generally – set about building new lives in and with the remains of human culture.

This fusion of human and non-human seems incredibly silly when considered merely as an adaptation of the original *Romeo and Juliet*. And while the scene is clearly meant to be comedic relief, within the total context of the game it takes on more pressing dimensions. As 2B and 9S eventually learn, sometime in the distant history of the interminable war the Machines rose up and exterminated their alien creators. Nevertheless, forced by their programming to 'defeat the enemy', the Machine network continued to battle Earth's androids; the increasingly strange and peaceful behaviours that the Machines exhibit during the game are in fact the symptoms of the Machine network's gradual splintering and adaptation of human culture in search of a mode of life not focused on warfare. Furthermore, and most distressingly, 2B and 9S learn that humanity has also gone extinct. The bunker on the moon holds not survivors, but rather some historical archives and a copy of the human genome. The command structure of the android military is dedicated to safeguarding the secret of humanity's extinction, wiping the memories of any units that learn the truth, all to fulfil their own initial programming: the total defeat of the alien Machine army.

These revelations and their consequences are presented piecemeal throughout *Nier: Automata*'s various possible 'endings' – in one the Machines, after deciding that humanity's ruins hold little potential for their future, launch their collective consciousness into space in search of a new home. Furthermore, this context impacts how *Romeos and Juliets* may be understood. What at first seemed like the most threadbare grasp of human aesthetic achievement is revealed to be essentially the only thing that remains of it: androids such as 2B and 9S, while they look almost identical to humans, have no culture or art aside from endless warfare in service of what turns out to be a fraudulent ideal (the motto of the android military is 'For the Glory of Mankind'). *Romeos and Juliets*' light treatment of death not only carries forward the idea of self-destructive tragedy from Shakespeare's play, but suggests how that theme might be reinterpreted by beings who, up until relatively recently, understood themselves as interchangeable, purpose-built cannon fodder, who fought and died in one body only to fight and die the next day in another.

Nier: Automata does not offer what might be called an 'authentic' alien Shakespeare – meaning a version of Shakespeare truly produced by non-human intelligence.[4] It was written and designed by a human team of developers; nevertheless, of the examples studied in this chapter, it most seriously speculates about what happens to the thing we call 'Shakespeare' after we are gone. While many video game adaptations of Shakespeare offer the opportunity to intervene in a play's familiar plot (Harrison and Lutz 2017; Flaherty forthcoming), *Nier: Automata* positions the player as a spectator and consumer of (an unnamed) Shakespeare. And by putting the player at a future scene of Shakespearean reception, the game inverts a dynamic that Gina Bloom has recently ascribed to the early modern theatre with the idea of 'vicarious play' (2018: 178).

Studying in parallel the history of the early modern theatre and the history of games, Bloom argues that early English commercial plays used staged scenes of game playing – from cards, to backgammon, to chess – to solicit the audience's involvement in the play's action. Since most people in the audience were familiar with these games, Bloom says, to see them played in the novel environment of the theatre could 'trigger spectators' cognitive and emotional involvement not in spite but *because* of [the play's] withholding of information about and physical participation in the game in progress' (2018: 6). That is, precisely because the audience knew how the game on stage should or could be played but could not themselves intervene, they became more invested in seeing how the dramatic action that surrounded the game played out. *Nier: Automata* flips the script, placing a non-interactive stage play within an interactive video game. The effect, however, is not terribly different from what Bloom describes. We know how *Romeo and Juliet* is supposed to go, but because we are incapable of influencing the play, and our player-avatars of 2B and 9S don't allow us to respond to it in any significant way, we as players become acutely aware of how this adaptation pushes us away from a *Romeo and Juliet* we know and towards unfamiliar ways of thinking about and relating to Shakespeare and his drama.

Unlike the performers of the Traveling Symphony, or even Professor Pluggy's authoritative speeches, *Nier: Automata* provides no figures to explain how we should feel about Shakespeare's continuance: the uses the alien Machines put him to, while to some extent intelligible and sympathetic, are quite simply not ours. Crucially, though, this does not make them incorrect. Indeed, the game uses the interlude to query the player's familiarity with 'human culture', providing a point of contact through which a non-human perspective might be imagined. By asking what non-humans do – or might do – with Shakespeare, *Nier: Automata* dares to speculate about what becomes of Shakespeare when humanity is long gone. And while we cannot and will not know what that eventual end looks like, the image the game provides is not entirely unpromising.

Notes

1. R. A. Foakes's 1997 Arden edition, which I cite throughout, places a question mark at the end of Edgar's line – indicating that he is as uncertain about what he sees as Kent. However, the textual history is not final on this point: in the play's First Quarto printing, both lines end in periods, while the First Folio ends Kent's line with a question mark and Edgar's with a full stop. This is maintained through at least F2, F3 and F4. I have thus omitted Foakes's question mark, as it seems to me contrary to an intended sense of Edgar's certainty: what he sees, and indeed what we see, might not be the promised end itself, but it is certainly in some sense an 'image' of it.
2. The inside cover of the US paperback edition contains elements from the publisher's marketing campaign, which presents the question 'What would you miss most?' followed by a variety of possible answers: 'No more ballgames played under floodlights' or 'The perfect cup of tea' or 'No more porch lights with moths fluttering on summer nights' and so on. The campaign's focus on small moments and creature comforts underscores the novel's conception of the collapse of modernity as deeply material, suggesting that part of the book's appeal is the way it allows the reader to experience nostalgia for a present moment that seems increasingly unsustainable.
3. Special thanks to Lowell Duckert, who pointed out this etymology in the 'Speculative Shakespeares' seminar during the 2018 Shakespeare Association of America conference, for which an early version of this chapter was written.
4. Experimental playwright Annie Dorsen's play *A Piece of Work*, an algorithmically generated play based on the text of *Hamlet* and performed by voice synthesisers, might be a close real-world approximation (Cartelli 2016).

Bibliography

Augé, M. (2009 [1992]), *Non-Places: An Introduction to Supermodernity*, trans. John Howe, New York: Verso.

Bennett, J. (2010), *Vibrant Matter: A Political Ecology of Things*, Durham, NC: Duke University Press.

Bloom, G. (2018), *Gaming the Stage: Playable Media and the Rise of English Commercial Theatre*, Ann Arbor: University of Michigan Press.

Brassier, R. (2007), *Nihil Unbound: Enlightenment and Extinction*, New York: Palgrave Macmillan.

Cartelli, T. (2016), 'Essentializing Shakespeare in the Shakespeare Aftermath: Dmitry Krymov's *Midsummer Night's Dream (As You Like It)*, Matías Piñeiro's *Viola*, and Annie *Dorsen's Piece of Work: A Machine-Made Hamlet*', *Shakespeare Quarterly*, 67, 431–56.

Desmet, C. (2014), 'Recognizing Shakespeare, Rethinking Fidelity: A Rhetoric and Ethics of Appropriation', in A. Huang and E. Rivlin (eds), *Shakespeare and the Ethics of Appropriation*, New York: Palgrave Macmillan, pp. 41–58.

Desmet, C. (2017), 'Alien Shakespeares 2.0', *Actes des congrès de la Société française Shakespeare*, 35, DOI: 10.4000/shakespeare.3877 [accessed 18 August 2020].

Elton, W. (1966), *King Lear and the Gods*, Lexington: University Press of Kentucky.

Fazel, V. M., and L. Geddes (2017), 'Introduction', in V. M. Fazel and L. Geddes (eds), *The Shakespeare User: Critical and Creative Appropriations in a Networked Culture*, New York: Palgrave Macmillan, pp. 1–22.

Flaherty, J. (2021), 'Shakespeare's Gamer Girls: Playable Female Characters', *Borrowers and Lenders: The Journal of Shakespeare and Appropriation*.

Harrison, M., and M. Lutz (2017), 'South of Elsinore: Actions that a Man Might Play', in V. M. Fazel and L. Geddes (eds), *The Shakespeare User: Critical and Creative Appropriations in a Networked Culture*, New York: Palgrave Macmillan, pp. 23–40.

Mandel, E. St John (2014), *Station Eleven*, New York: Vintage.

Murray, T. (2008), *Digital Baroque: New Media Art and Cinematic Folds*, Minneapolis: University of Minnesota Press.

Norris, C. (2013), 'Speculative Realism: Interim Report with Just a Few Caveats', *Speculations*, IV, 38–47.

Rose, M., and A. P. Smith (2019), 'Hexing the Discipline: Against the Reproduction of Continental Philosophy of Religion', *Palgrave Communications*, 5:2, <https://www.nature.com/articles/s41599-018-0207-4> [accessed 18 August 2020]

Shakespeare, W. (1997), *King Lear*, ed. R. A. Foakes, The Arden Shakespeare.

Sheldon, R. (2016), *The Child to Come: Life After the Human Catastrophe*, Minneapolis: University of Minnesota Press.

Smith, P. (2016), 'Shakespeare, Survival, and the Seeds of Civilization in Emily St. John Mandel's *Station Eleven*', *Extrapolation*, 57:3, 289–303.

Wittreich, J. (1984), *'Image of that Horror': History, Prophecy, and the Apocalypse in King Lear*, San Marino, CA: Huntington Library Press.

Index

actant, 13, 22–8, 62, 75–6, 194–6, 219–21
actantial ability *see* agency
actor-network theory, 26, 72, 111, 194
actualisation, 218–21
agency
 of actions, 31–3
 of algorithms, 62, 69
 of appropriation, 5–17
 of celebrity, 216–23
 in colonialist contexts, 85–9, 93–4, 101
 in critical race studies, 170, 184
 in *Elsinore*, 109–21
 of objects, 6, 22–8, 153–4, 196, 203–8
 Ofelia, 14, 38–9, 43–9, 54–5
 Othello, 15
 political, 24
algorithm, 9, 60–75
alien phenomenology, 61, 111
Alien Shakespeare, 61, 194, 230, 242
All is True, 142–3, 145
American Moor, 221, 222
anachronism, 143
anthropocene, 12, 17
anthropocentrism, 24, 88, 103
anthropomorphism, 2, 22–4, 204, 222

appropriation
 in critical race studies, 169–85
 in *Othello*, 21–4
 of the play, 201–3, 212–15, 221, 231
 theory, 2–17
 of time, 195
 in *Upstart Crow*, 128–42
 in *Westworld*, 86–8, 93
 see also agency: of appropriation
Ariel, 85–6, 93–100
assemblage, 10–15, 22–8
 in *Macbeth*, 193, 199, 205
 in *Othello*, 33–5
 of performance, 213, 224
 in Q1 *Hamlet*, 43
 'racialising assemblage', 151–62, 172–7, 184–5
 technology, 65, 75–6
Auerbach, David, 73
authority, 62, 93, 121, 142
 affective, 11
 cultural, 2–3, 17, 137
 patriarchal, 97–8
 of performance, 212–13
autonomy, 1–2, 12, 32, 74, 93–4, 115, 221
autopoiesis, 43

Baltimore, 59–60
Bannon, Steve, 63–4

INDEX

Barthes, Roland, 3–4, 138, 157, 217
Behar, Katherine, 40, 47, 48, 50
Bennett, Jane, 9–10, 12–13, 14, 22–5, 27, 32–3, 48, 75–6, 153, 155, 169, 172, 184, 215, 218, 219, 221, 224, 230–1
biopic, 16, 137–8, 142–4
Bitcoin, 59–77; *see also* cryptocurrency
Blackadder, 138–9, 141
blockchain technology, 59–72
Bogost, Ian, 9, 61, 109, 111, 112–13, 170–1, 193–4, 196
Braidotti, Rosi, 42, 45, 102
Branagh, Kenneth, 142–3, 152
Bristol, Michael, 3
Brook, Peter, 211
Burt, Richard, 129, 131, 134

Caliban, 86, 91–101
capital
   class, 129, 133, 137, 144–5
   cultural, 5–6, 15–16, 59–61, 68, 128, 134, 178
   moral, 140
   social, 3, 134, 144–6
capitalism, 13, 47, 240–1; *see also* capital; Marxism
Cartelli, Thomas, 5–6
celebrity, 3, 14–17, 128, 133–6
   mythology, 143–4
   network, 212
   objects, 16, 211–27
   paradox, 224
   see also Hamlet: celebrity of
chaos theory, 195; *see also* time: theatrical
Colbert, Soyica Diggs, 158
colonialism, 47, 100, 177
   post-colonial theory, 15, 24, 86–8, 91–103, 154
   proto-colonialism, 85–8, 90–1, 99–102, 176
   settler colonialism *see* Western colonialism (below)
   Western colonialism, 85–93, 103n
Cote, David, 211–12, 214–15, 218
critical race studies *see* critical race theory
critical race theory, 96, 154, 169–74
   in posthumanism, 186n
criticism, 3, 15, 112, 129, 232–5
   computational, 71
   literary, 71
   performance, 2, 212
   theatre, 6
cryptocurrency, 12, 15, 59, 63–9; *see also* Bitcoin
cult of authorship, 2
Cumberbatch, Benedict, 161, 212–13
cyborg, 38–56; *see also* robot

Deleuze and Guattari, 7, 25–6
Desdemona
   in *Iago* (2009), 31–4
   racial ontology, 168, 181–2
   significance of handkerchief, 22, 26–8
Desmet, Christy, 71, 77–8
   Alien Shakespeares, 2, 9, 61, 62, 67, 68–9, 173, 194, 230–1
   Fidelity, 9, 13, 231
Desmet, Christy and Robert Sawyer, 77
Desmet, Christy, Natalie Loper and Jim Casey, 7–8
disability studies, 155
disaggregation, 15, 64–7, 74, 128, 137, 194, 198, 230, 242
disempowerment, 109–11, 116–19; *see also* feminism; gender; patriarchy
Drakakis, John, 60
Dyer, Richard, 92

Elsinore (2019), 15, 108–21
Elton, Ben, 137–42, 145, 146

fandom, 13, 211, 219
feminism, 24, 34, 40, 47, 154
    feminist criticism, 124n, 134
    see also ontology: object-oriented: feminism
Flat Stanley, 37, 55
fridging, 88, 103n
    Simone, Gail, 103n

Gamergate, 108–9, 121
gatekeeping, 6, 62, 89
gender, 15–16, 97–8, 116–21, 130–4, 151–8
    femininity, 43, 52, 98, 116–19, 153–8: white womanhood, 96–100, 156; *see also* performance: of femininity; racism
    identity, 93, 117, 140–1
    masculinity, 146, 156, 222: Black, 96–7; toxic, 50; white, 92; *see also* patriarchy; racism
    representation, 15, 109, 117–18, 125n
Gil-Harris, Jonathan, 256
global Shakespeare studies, 13–16, 21
Godard, Jean-Luc, 232–7
González, Jennifer, 44–5, 50

Habib, Imtiaz, 170, 171
Halberstam, Jack, 129
Hall, Kim F., 23, 171
Hamilton Cobb, Keith, 221, 222, 225; *see also American Moor*
Hamlet, 1–2, 7, 48, 51, 53–4, 67, 97, 128, 167, 178–83
    character network theory of, 72
    first quarto (Q1), 15, 37–56
    folio, 56
    performances of, 211–14, 221–7
    second quarto, 56
    video game adaptation of, 108–21; *see also Elsinore*
Hamlet, 1–3, 217–27
    celebrity of, 17, 213–24
    in *Elsinore*, 110–21
    Ofelia, relationship to, 38–56
    portrayals of, 178–9, 210–14
Harman, Graham, 6, 11–12, 14, 63, 65, 75, 77, 78, 90
Hartman, Saidrya, 169–70
Hayles, N. Katherine, 65–6, 195–6, 201
Henry IV, 88–9
Henry V, 135, 152, 195, 200, 202
Henry VI, 68, 151–2, 156–8
hermeneutics, 70, 131
Hocking, Clint, 113
The Hollow Crown: The Wars of the Roses, 16, 151–62
hooks, bell, 97
Hughes, Langston, 183–4
humanism, 3–16, 73–4, 85–6, 100–2, 130, 216–18
    in *Hamlet*, 2, 226
    neo-humanism, 23
    posthumanism, 7, 15–16, 45, 62–5, 74, 93–7, 103, 186n
    in Shakespearean studies, 23–4
humanities, 9, 12, 15–17, 24, 70–8
    digital humanities, 59–63, 70–1, 76–7
humanity, 48–9, 52, 55, 66, 87, 92–5, 167–9, 181–2, 231, 245
    Black humanity, 170–6, 183
Hutcheon, Linda, 113

Iago (2009), 22, 31–4
Iago, 27–34, 174, 180–2
identity, 23, 70, 96, 116, 132–8, 141, 219–22
    Ofelia's, 15, 50
    Ophelia's, 117–20
    in posthumanism, 16, 64–6
    of race, 154–5, 186n

imperialism, 89, 93, 176; *see also* colonialism
Isaac, Oscar, 223–7

Joan of Arc, 151, 156–7

Kaliyattam, 22, 27–30
Key, Keegan-Michael, 167–85, 224–7
Key & Peele see Key, Keegan-Michael; Peele, Jordan
Kidnie, Mary Jane, 4, 5, 212
King Henry, 157–8
King Lear, 12–17, 62, 88–9, 230–8, 242

Lady Macbeth, 67, 173, 202–8
Lanier, Douglas M., 2, 3, 7
  post textual, 217, 218
LaTour, Bruno, 23, 26, 194
Law, Jude, 214
Lehmann, Hans Thies, 213, 214
Lester, Adrian, 210–11
liminal space, 34, 38, 112, 121, 169–70, 195
ludology, 109–13, 121
ludonarrative *see* ludology

Macbeth, 13, 16, 67, 69, 173, 192–208
Macbeth, 173, 195–208
Malvolio (of *Twelfth Night*), 177–8
Margaret of Anjou, 151–62
Marlowe, Christopher, 135–6
Marxism, 24, 60
materialism, 12, 50–1, 67, 155–8, 188n, 196
  archontic materialities, 219
  materialist assemblage, 11, 224
  materialist progression, 220
  materiality of objects, 4, 41
  materiality of text, 3, 7–10, 210–14, 225

new materialism, 8–9, 13–15, 25, 75, 216–18, 227
vibrant materialism, 22, 25–6, 215, 220–1, 230; *see also* matter: vibrant
vital materialism, 23–5, 34, 153, 216; *see also* matter: vital
matter, 1–5, 17, 26, 55, 151–6, 223, 230
  agentic, 157, 161; *see also* assemblage
  inorganic, 42, 237–40
  ontology of, 10
  paratextual, 43
  polychronic, 159
  race as, 162
  vibrant, 10–12, 22–4, 32, 75, 216–21, 227; *see also* materialism: vibrant materialism
  vital, 25, 34; *see also* materialism: vital materialism
Memni, Albert, 91–2
Miranda, 86, 93, 97–101
misanthropy, 129, 133
misogyny, 119, 222; *see also* sexism
Mitchell, David, 128, 133, 144–5
  as Mark Corrigan in *Peep Show*, 131–2
  as Shakespeare in *Upstart Crow*, 128–30, 134–6
Morton, Timothy, 88–9, 192–3, 194, 208
Murray, Timothy, 232

Negga, Ruth, 211, 218
Nier: Automata, 17, 231, 242–5
nihilism, 129, 132, 230, 236
  technological nihilism, 238
North, Ryan, 118–19; *see also To Be or Not to Be*

object, 21–34, 60–75, 92–102,
    108–21, 230–1
  affective object, 1, 16
  agential object, 87–8
  assemblage of objects, 25
  celebrity object, 16, 210–17;
    see also celebrity: objects
  disciplinary object, 14
  human object, 14–17, 168–85
  hyperobject, 192–208
  media objects, 6, 14
  object relations, 172
  objects as prostheses, 151–62, 179
  Ofelia's objects, 37–55
  organic objects, 46
  Shakespeare as an object, 2–17,
    71, 76–8, 86–91, 103, 131–43,
    174–81
  variable object, 1, 10–13, 21, 60,
    128–30, 133–4, 142–5, 196
  see also agency: of objects; object-
    oriented ontology
object permanence, 46, 49, 54
objectification, 17, 94, 211
  of LGBTQIA people, 24, 140
  of People of Colour, 24, 91–3,
    97–102, 154, 162, 170–7, 188n
  of women, 15, 24, 38–54,
    57n, 116
Okonedo, Sophie, 16, 152–8, 162
Olivier, Laurence, 178–9
Omkara, 22, 29–31
ontology
  alien, 109
  in critical race studies, 16, 168–84
  flat, 196
  of matter, 10
  object-oriented: in *Elsinore*,
    109–12, 120; extinction, 231;
    feminism, 15, 40, 47–52, 104n,
    154; global Shakespeare studies,
    10, 13, 22–5; Ofelia, 47–8;
    posthumanism, 75; in relation
    to quantum theory, 193; in
    The Tempest, 85–6, 91–3; in
    Westworld, 88–91, 94–103;
    see also ontology: in critical race
    studies
  tiny, 111–16, 193–4, 201, 205
OOO *see* ontology: object-oriented
Ophelia, 2, 10, 15, 42, 56, 214,
  222, 224
  in *Elsinore*, 109–21
  Ofelia, 14–15, 37–56
orthography, 197–9, 201
Othello, 15, 34, 142
  objects in, 21–7
  performances of, 30–2
  race in, 96–7, 159, 167–85, 221
Othello, 34, 97, 168–85
  interactions with handkerchief,
    26–7
  portrayals of, 28–9, 33
the Other, 155, 180

palimpsests *see* matter: polychronic
Parker-Starbuck, Jennifer, 38–9, 40,
  44, 46, 51
Paster, Gail Kern, 51, 52
patriarchy, 47, 96–8
Peele, Jordan, 167–85
Peep Show, 132
performance, 4, 16–17, 64–6, 133–6,
  139, 210–27, 236
  as appropriation, 13
  of class capital, 133, 140–5
  criticism, 2
  of femininity, 116; *see also* gender:
    femininity
  as a hyperobject, 192–208
  of Ofelia, 39–56
  of *Othello*, 34, 167, 172–5
  of race, 151–61, 184
  of *The Tempest*, 91
  theory, 5–8, 213–15
Pinter, Harold, 220

INDEX

postmodernism, 213, 238, 241
Prigogine, Ilya, 195
Prospero, 67, 85–103
prosthesis, 38–47, 53–6, 151–62, 179
Public Theatre, 223

quantum theory, 192–208; *see also* time: quantum

race, 15–16, 34, 93–100, 135
   in casting, 141–2, 152–62
   the colour line, 168, 175
   colour-blindness, 152–4, 157, 161–2
   in *Elsinore*, 116–19
   identity, 120, 153–5
   Indigenous Peoples, 23, 92
   lived experience, 92, 170–3
   People of Colour, 23–4, 152–62, 221–3
   racialisation, 169, 176
   racism, 27, 92–7, 120, 141, 157, 162: racist structures, 92, 134, 153, 221; white savior, 98–9, 104n; white supremacy, 5, 16, 89, 97–8, 155
   representation, 108–9, 112, 117, 121, 140, 152
   represented through objects, 169–85
   see also critical race theory
rhizome, 2, 6–7
Richard III, 161
Richard III, 161
robots, 86–8, 93, 242; *see also* cyborg
Romeo and Juliet, 17, 76, 88, 90, 134, 195, 243–5
Rose, Marika and Anthony Paul Smith, 240

Sack, Daniel, 213
Sarkeesian, Anita, 108, 122n
science fiction, 86, 93

semiotics, 13, 153, 201, 217–18, 231
sexism, 16, 108, 121; *see also* misogyny
Shaft (1971), 168, 175, 185
Shakespeare in Love, 137–8
Sheldon, Rebekah, 239
Sherlock Holmes, 132–3
Smith, Ian, 154–5, 159
social justice, 25, 86, 103
Sofer, Andrew, 40, 41, 43, 151, 196
Spillers, Hortense, 173–4
Star Trek: The Next Generation, 87, 103n
Star Wars, 87–8
Station Eleven, 14, 17, 231, 238–42

technology, 6, 13, 17, 59–60, 70
   digital technology, 46
   subject technology, 38, 54
   see also blockchain technology
That Mitchell and Webb Look, 132
The Tempest, 15, 85–103
Theatre for a New Audience, 223
Things
   scriptive things, 153–8, 161
   thing-power, 8–11, 15, 25, 48–9, 216, 224
   thinghood, 169–70, 216
   thingification, 40, 47–8, 85–7, 92–102, 171; *see also* colonialism
time, 192–208
   fictional, 195
   historical, 64
   quantum, 200–3, 208; *see also* quantum theory
   theatrical, 17, 195–6; *see also* chaos theory
To Be or Not To Be, 118–19
translation, 21, 174, 201, 220

Troilus and Cressida, 59, 69
Twelfth Night, 140–1, 177–8, 208

Upstart Crow, 16, 127–46

The Wars of the Roses, 16

Weheliye, Alexander, 172
Westworld, 15, 86–103
Who's Afraid of Virginia Woolf?, 200
Wilderson, Frank B., 169–70
Wittreich, Joseph, 233
Worthen, W. B., 4, 5

EU representative:
Easy Access System Europe
Mustamäe tee 50, 10621 Tallinn, Estonia
Gpsr.requests@easproject.com

www.ingramcontent.com/pod-product-compliance
Lightning Source LLC
Chambersburg PA
CBHW051608230426
43668CB00013B/2026